RE
BUSI
AND THE LEGAL
ENVIRONMENT
OF BUSINESS

Pg 52 for 4/2/91
Pg 161

Pg 155

READINGS IN BUSINESS LAW AND THE LEGAL ENVIRONMENT OF BUSINESS

Douglas Whitman, Editor

University of Kansas

McGRAW-HILL, INC.

New York St. Louis San Francisco Auckland Bogotá
Caracas Hamburg Lisbon London Madrid Mexico Milan Montreal
New Delhi Paris San Juan São Paulo Singapore Sydney Tokyo Toronto

This book was set in Times Roman by the College Composition Unit
in cooperation with Waldman Graphics, Inc.
The editor was Ken MacLeod;
the production supervisor was Denise L. Puryear.
The cover was designed by Karen K. Quigley.
Project supervision was done by The Total Book.
R. R. Donnelley & Sons Company was printer and binder.

**READINGS IN BUSINESS LAW AND THE LEGAL
ENVIRONMENT OF BUSINESS**

1 2 3 4 5 6 7 8 9 0 DOC DOC 9 5 4 3 2 1 0

ISBN 0-07-069994-1

Library of Congress Cataloging-in-Publication Data

Readings in business law and the legal environment of business /
   Douglas Whitman, editor
      p.   cm.
    ISBN 0-07-069994-1
    1. Business law—United States.   2. Business law—United States—
Cases.   I. Whitman, Douglas.
KF888.R39   1991
346.73´07—dc20
[347.3067]   90-6172

CONTENTS

LIST OF
CONTRIBUTORS

E. ELIZABETH ARNOLD
University of San Diego

JOHN W. BAGBY
Pennsylvania State University

JON D. BIBLE
Southwest Texas State University

MARIA BOSS
California State University at Los Angeles

ANITA CAVA
University of Miami

RENEE D. CULVERHOUSE
Auburn University at Montgomery

DEBRA DOBRAY
Southern Methodist University

TRACY DOBSON
Michgan State University

PAUL E. FIORELLI
Xavier University

SUSAN E. GRADY
University of Massachusetts

NANCY R. HAUSERMAN
University of Iowa

JAMES P. HILL
Central Michigan University

CAROLYN HOTCHKISS
Babson College

DENNIS R. KUHN
Villanova University

VIRGINIA G. MAURER
University of Florida

CAROL J. MILLER
Southwest Missouri State University

CHARLES C. SHEPHERD, JR.
George Washington University

DAVID SILVERSTEIN
Suffolk University

PAULETTE L. STENZEL
Michigan State University

PREFACE

This book contains articles written by well-known business law professors who teach in business schools throughout the United States. The authors wrote their chapters expressly for this book. I selected each person for his or her expertise and national reputation in a particular field. All the authors regularly write and speak on the subject matter covered in their respective chapters. The material represents their thoughtful reflections about matters with which they are intimately familiar and deeply concerned.

Often professors teaching the introductory business law course face the problem of how to bring current developments and supplemental issues into their classrooms. They ponder which of the important current events are worthy of extra attention. The law changes constantly; every day some legislature enacts an important new statute, a judge decides a precedent-changing case, or a governmental agency announces a shift in its policy. At the same time, the worldwide nature of business changes daily in response to changing market conditions.

Not only must the business community keep up-to-date with changes in the law and business, its members need to develop an awareness of the historical forces that have brought about important changes in the law. A grasp of what various interest groups and legislators wish to accomplish by enacting a statute helps business people see the direction the government wants society to follow. Knowing the goals of the law makes it easier to structure one's behavior to comply with governmental regulations of the private market.

To fill the void in many texts, some instructors use supplemental class handouts. This book eliminates the need to copy recent articles and cases. It also focuses on the major issues of concern to business, thus eliminating hours spent in the library searching for useful, current information to supplement a legal environment or traditional text.

This book was designed as a supplemental text to help students relate the law they are studying to "real world" management decisions and situations they'll encounter in the working world. Each chapter covers a topic frequently dealt with in the introductory legal environment or business law course. However, the readings go beyond the coverage typically found in the average business law text. Often professors fail to spend sufficient time on any given topic to give their students an appreciation for the complexity of the material covered in class. This book gives readers the chance to delve into selected material. Each chapter covers a matter of vital concern to business managers who need to know in what manner the law restricts their freedom of action.

Each reading begins with a problem of interest to persons in business. The next section deals with historical and other background information. The authors generally follow up with a discussion of either a case or statute of historical significance or one that announces an important new rule. Following the case or statutory discussion they then discuss how the information in the chapter influences business decisionmaking. Every reading also includes useful references and questions and answers.

It has long been the feeling of the editor of this book that students fail to grasp the *relevance* to their career goals of the various rules of law covered in the typical business law course. The cumulative effect of the material in this book should help future business managers to see the relationship between law and business.

Professors who teach either from a traditional, full-line text or a legal environment text in their introductory course will find the material in this book both helpful and interesting. The many provocative points will stimulate class discussions that advance students in their long-term career goals.

This book is the product of years of thought and effort by me and the authors. I wish to thank all of them for their efforts, patience, promptness, and outstanding material.

Douglas Whitman

READINGS IN BUSINESS LAW AND THE LEGAL ENVIRONMENT OF BUSINESS

INTRODUCTION: THE INTERRELATIONSHIP OF LAW AND BUSINESS

Douglas Whitman
University of Kansas

PART 1: INTRODUCTION TO LAW AND BUSINESS

This book focuses on selected topics of current importance to business managers. The first part introduces the reader to the general topic of law, business, and ethics.

The abuse of drugs has become a major social problem in the United States today. Employers need to concern themselves with this issue because many employees use drugs *on* and off the job. It is estimated that over 23 percent of the workers have used controlled substances at work. The use of drugs on the job creates a host of problems for employers, such as lower productivity, high absenteeism, and personal injuries. The first chapter entitled "Workplace Drug Testing: Its Legal and Managerial Aspects," by Jon D. Bible of Southwest Texas State University, focuses on the question of whether a company may require its employees to take a drug test.

As with so many other managerial decisions today, testing employees raises a number of constitutional issues: search and seizure, due process, and equal protection. Firing an employee for taking drugs on the job may result in a suit by the former employee for breach of a covenant of good faith and fair dealing and invasion of privacy.

The law in this area is evolving, although there have been several recent important Supreme Court cases that the author discusses. Professor Bible suggests a number of rules for private employers to follow if they choose to test employees for drugs.

Not only must today's business manager be concerned with complying with the law, but he or she also needs to reflect on the ethics of important decisions.

1

Sometimes the law permits behavior that one could argue a company, for ethical reasons, ought not to engage in. The Nestle Corporation became engaged in a celebrated battle over the sale of infant formula in third-world nations. Many people alleged that such a product could not be used safely in the conditions that prevail in those countries. Furthermore, they questioned the fairness of trying to sell such a product to very poor people. In the end, the Nestle Corporation was forced to make some concessions in light of the massive public relations campaign launched against it for its actions in these countries.

The Nestle case illustrates the point that a company may choose to engage in perfectly legal behavior, only to find that a different course of action would have made better sense. This suggests that a manager should consider both the legal and the ethical ramifications of his or her actions before committing the company to a particular course.

Professor Anita Cava of the University of Miami applies several ethical theories to the question of trade secrets in her chapter entitled "Business Ethics and Trade Secrets: Judging the Judges of Commercial Morality." At the outset, Professor Cava discusses in depth the major ethical theories of analysis: the teleological approach (consequence-based), the deontological approach (duty-based), and John Rawls's theory of rights. She then applies these theories to the sale of manuals of tubular lock key codes by Victor Fanberg.

The Cava article's discussion of the various ethical theories serves as an excellent background for further consideration in the chapters that follow.

Part 2: THE FOUNDATIONS OF LEGAL SYSTEMS AND BUSINESS

Part 2 of this book deals with the foundation of the legal system: constitutional law and the regulation of international business.

One question that arises in a host of situations is: Does the U.S. Constitution guarantee corporations—as opposed to individuals—a right to free speech? For example, from time to time interested parties have suggested that the right of employers to speak to union employees, or the right of corporations to express their opinions in advertising, can be circumscribed. For many years it was not clear that the Constitution's provisions on freedom of speech even extended to commercial speech.

For many years the U.S. Supreme Court took the position that the Constitution did *not* protect commercial expression. This meant that persons and businesses who wished to discuss a commercial proposition were not guaranteed a right to express those views. All this began to change in a seminal case discussed in a chapter by Professor Susan Grady of the University of Massachusetts entitled "Commercial Speech: *Virginia State Board of Pharmacy v. Virginia Citizens Consumer Council, Inc.*" The Supreme Court did observe, however, that commercial speech may be regulated. Thus, a business wishing to engage in commercial speech is subject to some regulations.

Not only does the Constitution serve as a foundation for our legal system, but various provisions of international law also serve as the cornerstone of our system of laws. The foundation of the international business transaction is the contract between the parties. The contract defines the relationship between the parties and allocates the risks between them. Obviously, if the courts worldwide would not enforce contracts freely negotiated between persons, such contracts would be of little value. The case *Scherk v. Alberto-Culver Co.* is discussed in the chapter entitled "International Law: *Scherk v. Alberto-Culver Co.*," by Carolyn Hotchkiss of Babson College. *Scherk* stands as a landmark for freedom of contract.

To resolve the issue of which law and legal system governs disputes arising under a contract, parties to a contract generally include choice-of-forum and choice-of-law clauses. Quite often the choice-of-forum clause requires the parties to arbitrate any dispute arising from the contract. In *Scherk*, the U.S. Supreme Court upheld the enforceability of an arbitration clause. Managers need to realize that if they sign a contract with such a provision, the U.S. courts will force the parties to arbitrate a dispute.

PART 3: THE AMERICAN LEGAL SYSTEM

Part 3 deals with the court system, methods of alternative dispute resolution (ADR), the legislative system, and administrative agencies. Before a person examines rules of law it is useful to consider the process by which those rules of law are enforced. Quite often the manner in which the rule is enforced will influence the outcome of a dispute.

One question of great concern to business managers is the extent to which the government has the power to force them to engage in or refrain from certain activities. This question was settled early in U.S. history in the case *Gibbons v. Ogdon,* discussed in the chapter entitled "The Constitutionality of Regulating Business: Judicial Review of the Interstate Commerce Clause Since *Gibbons v. Ogdon,*" by Carol Miller of Southwest Missouri State University. Professor Miller notes that the *Gibbons* case gives the federal government extensive power to regulate the activities of business. She examines the application of the *Gibbons* precedent to cases decided by the courts over the last century and a half. The federal government's extensive power to regulate is of great concern to managers because it is now clear that the federal government has virtually unlimited power to force business to comply with any federal law. Thus, the courts have virtually unlimited power to force business to comply with federal laws.

Businesses may bypass the court system, and many businesses are choosing to do so by including arbitration clauses in their contracts (the enforceability of which is discussed in Professor Hotchkiss's chapter.) In a chapter entitled "Alternate Dispute Resolution," by Professor Debra Dobray of Southern Methodist University, the various types of ADR procedures that can be utilized by businesses today are discussed. Managers need to recognize that unlike in the past, courts today are increasingly willing to enforce such alternatives to resolving a dispute in court.

A very significant matter for managers to consider is how judges go about deciding a case. Many people believe that judges learn the law and then blindly apply it to the facts of a particular case. This suggests that a person merely needs to learn the law, and then he or she can predict the outcome of any factual dispute. Many writers differ with this thinking—for example, Judge Jerome Frank.

The manner in which judges and juries decide cases is discussed in the context of the *Texaco v. Pennzoil* suit in a chapter by Charles Shepherd of George Washington University, entitled "*Texaco v. Pennzoil* and the Unhelpfulness of Black-Letter Contract Rules." Professor Shepherd, in his thought-provoking chapter, suggests that people studying the law should concern themselves more with the constructs used for situational decision making than with black-letter rules. These maxims explain better why judges and jurors rule in a particular manner than one would expect according to the actual rules of law. Black-letter rules, in his opinion, are mere building blocks used by litigants in constructing an argument in a largely political contest. The rules of law are of little value except in application; thus, a person needs to see how the rules of law are applied in a particular situation. He suggests several criteria that ought to be considered by persons in predicting the outcome of a contracts case: the voluntary nature of the parties' actions, whether the parties acted in good faith, the reasonableness of the parties' behavior, and the concept of comparative fault.

Managers need to understand not only how the court system operates and how judges decide cases, but also the manner in which the legislative and executive branches of government operate. In an illuminating chapter by Professor James Hill of Central Michigan University, entitled "Business and the Legislative Imperative: Gramm-Rudman-Hollings and the Budgetary Process," the point is made that business managers need to be aware of the process followed in enacting an act in order to understand the true dynamics of a court decision. To make this point, Professor Hill discusses a very controversial act, the Gramm-Rudman-Hollings (balanced-budget) Act—a law enacted to deal with the ever-increasing federal deficit—and the landmark case *Bowsher v. Synar*. He notes that the aftereffect of the *Bowsher* case has been to shift the making of spending policies from Congress to the executive branch. The long-term effect of this may be to create some very significant budgetary problems for Congress, and thus for business, in the future.

The final chapter in this section, by Professor Renee Culverhouse of Auburn University at Montgomery, deals with the issue of administrative agencies. Her chapter is entitled "Administrative Law: *United Technologies Corp. v. U.S. EPA*." This chapter discusses why it is important for an agency to have a proposed rule classified as interpretive rather than legislative. Interested parties are not entitled to notice and an opportunity to comment if an agency issues an interpretive rule. This is very important to business because if a rule is an interpretive one, businesses lose the opportunity to challenge the regulation before it goes into effect. In light of the fact that governmental agencies can adopt interpretive rules that have a great impact on business, businesses need to keep in touch with what governmental agencies are doing— probably through their trade associations or through a representative in Washington.

PART 4: THE COMMON LAW FOUNDATIONS OF CAPITALISM

Part 4 addresses the bodies of common law that form a foundation for the capitalistic system.

A very significant foundation of the capitalist system is the contract—an agreement voluntarily arrived at between the parties. If the courts refused to recognize the enforceability of contracts, it would be very difficult for the free-enterprise system to operate.

In her chapter entitled "The Contract Law Duty to Read," Professor E. Elizabeth Arnold of the University of San Diego discusses the question, Under what circumstances will the courts release a party from a contract that the person failed to read? It is well settled that a party has agreed to the terms of a contract that he or she signs. In spite of this fact, people often raise the failure to read a contract as a defense in a contract suit. Professor Arnold discusses the various court and legislative solutions to the problems that arise when a person fails to read a contract before signing it. Managers need to realize that the law generally binds the parties to contracts even if they fail to read them prior to signing. In light of the tendency to protect consumers, however, businesses should alert consumers to important terms in the contract.

Tort law is also a significant basis of the capitalistic system. One issue in tort law that has generated a great deal of litigation in recent years concerns the tort of wrongful discharge. Although many employees in the United States are protected by collective bargaining agreements negotiated by a union, millions of other workers have no job protection. They work at-will. The at-will employment doctrine holds that in the absence of an express contract to the contrary, an employee may be fired for no cause or for any cause whatsoever without a legal wrong being committed by the employer.

In recent years there has been a trend in the law to limit the absolute right of an employer to fire an employee. This matter is discussed in a chapter entitled "Wrongful Discharge and the *Foley* Case," by Professor Maria Boss of California State University at Los Angeles. This chapter focuses on the *Foley* case because of the enormous influence of the California Supreme Court on the decisions of courts in other states. In this chapter Professor Boss discusses several theories on which an employee could argue that he or she was wrongfully discharged. The *Foley* case has such great impact because the California Supreme Court held that tort damages are not recoverable for breach of the implied covenant of good faith and fair dealing. It will thus be difficult, at least for litigants in California, to collect tort damages when the employee has been wrongfully discharged.

PART 5: LEGAL ASPECTS OF THE FIRM
AND THE REGULATION OF ITS POWER

Part 5 of the book deals with the business firm and certain laws regulating businesses.

The trading of stocks and bonds is essential for the financing of the modern corporation. Early in this century we learned that some regulation of the securities market was essential. Congress passed laws governing the trading of securities in the early 1930s.

The price of securities is influenced by information. For this reason, the government penalizes persons who keep valuable information secret and then trade on the stocks affected by this information. Professor John Bagby of Pennsylvania State University, in his chapter entitled "Corporate Property Rights in Information: Misappropriation by Insiders after *Carpenter v. United States*," discusses a facet of the issue of the disclosure of information: the misappropriation theory.

Under the misappropriation theory, an insider is any person with access to confidential, nonpublic information that would affect a reasonable investor's decisions to buy, sell, or hold securities. In effect, this rule protects confidential information and requires that it be disclosed before a person attempts to take advantage of the information. The *Carpenter* case discussed in this chapter specifically deals with R. Foster Winans' disclosure to some acquaintances of information that would be printed the next day in the *Wall Street Journal*'s "Heard on the Street" column. The Court's ruling in the *Carpenter* case suggests that companies should adopt rules prohibiting employees from disclosing confidential information.

In addition to securities law, federal antitrust laws significantly regulate the power of business. In the late 1800s Congress became concerned with the problems associated with the concentration of power in the hands of a few businesses such as the Standard Oil Company. Operating through trusts, some businesses gained monopoly power over entire industries. Congress passed the Sherman Antitrust Act in 1890 to deal with the problem of monopolies and unreasonable restraints of trade. Businesses must be careful to avoid monopolizing an industry or unreasonably restraining trade.

One of the most significant cases in the history of the antitrust laws is the *Standard Oil* case discussed in a chapter entitled "*Standard Oil Company of New Jersey v. United States*," by Professor Virginia Maurer of the University of Florida. In this chapter, Professor Maurer explores the historical events that lead up to the adoption of the Sherman Antitrust Act. In this case, the U.S Supreme Court adopted the rule of reason. Under the rule of reason, only unreasonable restraints of trade, unreasonable attempts to monopolize, and unreasonable monopolies are illegal.

Business managers must also realize that they are subject to the criminal laws in the United States. Businesses can be the victim of crimes. They can also commit crimes. Crimes perpetrated by businesspeople are often referred to as white-collar crimes, which is the topic examined in a chapter entitled "White-Collar Crime: Fundamental Causes and Possible Solutions" by Paul Fiorelli of Xavier University. In this article Professor Fiorelli discusses why employees commit crimes. He then examines the Sentencing Reform Act of 1987, which has sentencing guidelines and a challenge to these sentencing guidelines in *Mistretta v. United States.*

PART 6: REGULATION OF BUSINESS ACTIVITY

The final part of this book deals with various areas of government regulation.

One area in which we have seen a great deal of legislation passed both at the federal and at the state levels of government is consumer protection. For many years consumers were unable to obtain relief when they had been unfairly dealt with by business. Today, a tremendous number of laws regulate virtually every imaginable consumer transaction.

One of the most irritating situations in which consumers often find themselves is when they sign an agreement that turns out to be grossly unfair. As noted in an earlier chapter by Professor Arnold, a person is generally bound by a contract when he or she signs it. The courts and legislatures have adopted exceptions to this rule, however—the foremost exception being the doctrine of unconscionability. Professor Tracy Dobson of Michigan State University discusses this doctrine in her chapter entitled "Unconscionability: Contract Abrogation by the Courts Protects the Consumer." In this chapter, Professor Dobson discusses the movement of the law from the doctrine of *caveat emptor* to today's protective environment. She then examines a famous case dealing with this issue: *Williams v. Walker-Thomas Furniture Co.* Managers need to be aware that judges will set grossly unfair contracts aside based on the doctrine of unconscionability.

Consumers are not the only ones who have been upset with their dealings with business. Employees have become increasingly more assertive each decade. One of the great changes in the law has been to attempt to equalize the bargaining power of labor and management through the recognition of collective-bargaining agreements voluntarily entered into between labor and management. Such agreements, from a managerial standpoint, tie the hands of management and limit the options available to a company—a point discussed by Professor David Silverstein of Suffolk University in his chapter entitled "Managing Labor Relations in a Changing Legal and Social Environment: The Lesson of *Flood v. Kuhn.*" Professor Silverstein feels that managers who fail to appreciate the dynamic and evolutionary nature of the U.S. legal system and the interaction among legislation, judicial decisions, and collective bargaining will miss the opportunity to influence the law. Such managers fail to seize the opportunity to influence the law during its developmental stages and to adapt to new social priorities. Instead, they tenaciously cling to the status quo. To illustrate this point, Professor Silverstein discusses the case *Flood v. Kuhn*. In the *Flood* case, the U.S Supreme Court upheld the antitrust exemption for baseball and baseball's reserve clause. Although baseball management won the case, they lost the final round because they failed to take into account the reaction of the players to management's victory in the *Flood* case. A management more sensitive and responsive to the needs of its work force and aware of the potential for government or union intervention could have responded in a more creative, flexible manner.

Indeed, U.S. law takes a different approach to labor relations than some countries in Europe, such as Germany. German law allows workers to participate in making decisions affecting the management of a company. Instead, the U.S. Congress passed laws to allow management and labor to negotiate with respect to the concerns of labor. The government works to ensure that the process followed is fair.

Professor Dennis Kuhn of Villanova University, in his chapter entitled "Protecting Employees' Right to Collectively Bargain: *NLRB v. Gissel Packing Co.*," discusses the U.S. approach to resolving labor disputes. In particular, Professor Kuhn examines the conduct of a representation election in the context of the case *NLRB v. Gissel Packing Co.* In that case, management engaged in unfair labor practices and so tainted the atmosphere in its company that the Court felt it would be impossible to conduct a fair representation election. The Court upheld the National Labor Relations Board (NLRB) ruling that the employer must bargain with the employees even though the union lost the election. In addition to enacting legislation that gives employees the right to join unions and engage in collective bargaining, in more recent years Congress has passed additional legislation to protect certain groups of persons who have been the objects of unfair treatment by employers.

A fairly recent refinement of the law in this area has given rise to decisions protecting workers from sexual harassment on the job, a point discussed by Professor Nancy Hauserman of the University of Iowa in her chapter entitled "Sexual Harassment: *Meritor Savings Bank v. Vinson*." In that case, the U.S. Supreme Court for the first time announced that Title VII of the 1964 Civil Rights Act protects workers from sexual harassment. It found that employees have a right to work in a place free of hostility and abuse. The Equal Employment Opportunity Commission (EEOC) has suggested some factors relevant in deciding whether an employer created a hostile working environment. Professor Hauserman feels that employers should generate written policies directed at prohibiting sexual harassment. This policy should be widely distributed. Appropriate sanctions for violations should also be adopted.

Finally, matters of great concern to persons in the United States and throughout the world are the activities of companies that pollute the environment. The topic of pollution of the environment with toxic substances is discussed in a chapter entitled "The Crucial, Yet Difficult, Partnership Between Science and Law in Litigation and Regulation Related to Toxic Substances," by Paulette Stenzel of Michigan State University. In this chapter Professor Stenzel discusses how the courts use scientific data to determine toxicity and acceptable exposure levels and why that data is often uncertain.

CONCLUSION

The chapters in this book discuss many of the important rules of law of interest to businesspeople. In particular, they emphasize the connection between the rules of law and actual business behavior. Quite often, the business community fails to see the importance of knowing the law. They focus, instead, on what many of them perceive as their primary goal: helping their companies prosper. The law, therefore, strikes some people as *irrelevant*.

Many people fail to recognize the role that law plays in helping or hindering business from attaining its goal of maximization of profits. The chapters in this book show readers in specific instances how law and business interrelate and thus helps readers understand how a knowledge of law relates to their career goals and can help them achieve those goals.

PART ONE

INTRODUCTION TO LAW AND BUSINESS

1

WORKPLACE DRUG TESTING:
Its Legal and Managerial Aspects

Jon D. Bible
Southwest Texas State University

INTRODUCTION

Whether or not employers may resort to compulsory urinalysis to detect illicit workplace drug use has been one of the most controversial legal issues of the 1980s. Testing advocates stress the problems that drug-impaired workers may cause, including safety risks, faulty products, and the heightened risk of resulting litigation, and they emphasize the effectiveness of testing in identifying employees who use drugs. Opponents grant the need for a drug-free work setting but insist that urinalysis is an unreliable and unduly intrusive way to obtain one.

The number of urine testing programs has mushroomed in recent years, and this has produced a spate of legal attacks. Public employment cases involve claims that testing violates the Fourth Amendment ban on unreasonable searches, the Fifth Amendment privilege against forced self-incrimination, the Fourteenth Amendment guarantee of due process and equal protection of the law, and the constitutional right of privacy. Private sector cases raise wrongful discharge, breach of contract, and invasion of privacy claims. This chapter addresses these arguments. It discusses why employers engage in drug testing, how tests operate, and some concerns about drug testing. It also describes those employers who must be cognizant of constitutional constraints when they test. It then reviews case law, including recent landmark rulings of the U.S. Supreme Court. Finally, it explores some of the managerial considerations involved in urine testing.

CONSIDERATIONS UNDERLYING EMPLOYEE DRUG TESTING

On-the-job drug abuse is a serious problem in U.S. industry. In its March 17, 1986, edition, *Time* estimated that 23 percent of the workforce has used controlled substances at work. The same article underscored the staggering costs of substance abuse, noting that industry lost $60 billion in productivity in 1983. The strongest argument for drug testing is that it can reduce these figures dramatically by assisting employers in singling out workers and applicants who take drugs. This aids immeasurably in protecting the integrity and security of an employer's business, to say nothing of the opportunity it affords to salvage broken lives.

Apart from whether it is economically wise to try to detect drug users, employers have compelling legal reasons to do so. Indeed, one of their most pressing concerns in this litigious age—and a main reason for the mounting enthusiasm for drug testing—is the legal implications of job-related drug use. Under the legal doctrine of *respondeat superior,* employers may be liable for torts committed by workers during the scope of their employment. Drug use increases the chances of such torts that can lead to costly and time-consuming litigation. The negligent hiring and negligent retention doctrines, which make employers liable for not exercising sufficient care in hiring and retailing employees, may also be the basis for lawsuits against an employer.

Employees taking drugs are more likely to produce shoddy goods and services, and suits seeking reimbursement for resulting harm to third parties are a main source of business litigation. Far more threatening to employers are suits for injuries stemming from defective products, accidents, and safety hazards attributable to employees impaired by drugs. These suits raise the specter of devastating compensatory and punitive damage awards. Cases involving such awards, in turn, have profound insurance implications: They prompt insurers to increase premiums drastically, making it difficult if not impossible to obtain suitable coverage.

Lawsuits to redress injuries caused by impaired employees may arise outside of, as well as at, the job site. In *Otis Engineering Co. v. Clark,* 668 S.W.2d 307 (Tex. 1983), a supervisor found a machine operator intoxicated and sent him home. Upon arriving at the parking lot, the employee said he could get home on his own. While driving, however, he was involved in an accident, which killed himself and the occupants of the other car. The court held that the victims' families could sue the *company* for wrongful death, even though the employee was off duty when the accident occurred. According to the court, a jury should decide whether the supervisor was negligent in not restraining the employee—forcibly, if necessary—from leaving alone.

Such cases arguably impose a duty on employers to try to identify drug users, and to deal responsibly with known users, that extends far from the workplace. The Occupational Safety and Health Act and related safety laws, moreover, require employers to provide a safe workplace. Given these realities, it is easy to see why employers want to test employees for drugs. The less diligent they arc in trying to detect impaired workers, and the more tolerant they are in retaining such workers, the more likely it is that an accident will occur and that they will end up on the wrong side of a lawsuit.

THE MECHANICS OF—AND SOME CONCERNS ABOUT— URINALYSIS

The most popular test is the enzyme multiplied immunoassay test (EMIT), which comes in inexpensive, portable kits and can be given by nontechnical personnel. It uses a process called competitive displacement and binding in which urine is added to a substance containing an "antibody" and an "indicator." If, for example, marijuana is the drug sought, it has an element known as a THC metabolite, which will displace the indicator and bind itself to the antibody. Displacement occurs because the metabolite's competitive displacement and binding properties are stronger than the indicator's. After being separated from the antibody, the indicator is measured to determine the concentration of the metabolite in the sample.

The flaw is that the displacement and binding properties of unidentified compounds in the urine being tested may be stronger than those of the elements in the drug sought. With marijuana, compounds with these properties may interact with the indicator and antibody as the THC metabolite does, causing these compounds to be mistaken for the metabolite. Compounds that interact in this way are said to "cross-react" with the metabolite. Cross-reactive displacement yields a "false positive"—a mistaken conclusion that marijuana is in the sample.

Cross-reactions occur for many reasons. Ingredients in nonprescription medicine such as Dristan and Midol can produce false positives. Urine also contains polar acids, whose displacement and binding properties vary with the body chemistry of the person tested, and they may cross-react. A pigment in dark-skinned people may separate into chemical fragments similar to those in the drug sought. Given the individualized nature of urine composition, the probability that an unidentified compound will cross-react in an EMIT test cannot be accurately predicted. Cross-reaction is the main reason that this test is not deemed conclusive in confirming the presence of illicit substances in the person being tested.

Another test is the gas chromatography/mass spectrometer (GC/MS). It measures drug molecules by separating urine into individual ions. Unknown compounds that may cross-react in an EMIT test may also cause inaccurate results in GC/MS tests. Of the available tests, however, the GC/MS is considered the most reliable; thus, it is often used to confirm results in other tests. Because it requires a laboratory with special equipment and technicians, it is expensive, costing up to $100 per sample.

In addition to the deficiencies inherent in urine tests, critics of testing cite external problems. Carryover from a preceding sample may yield a positive reaction, and problems may also occur as a sample is passed among handlers or as a result of improper test administration. These problems are of special concern in on-site tests using untrained personnel. Another limitation is that tests can prove only past marijuana use, not present intoxication. For example, the THC metabolite that tests for marijuana may remain in the body for weeks. Because biochemical tests seek to determine whether this metabolite is in a urine sample, they cannot affirm that a subject was impaired by the drug when tested. This problem is compounded by the fact that one may test positive by passively inhaling marijuana smoke. Finally, test results may be skewed by factors affecting the rate at which people process and excrete drugs, such as body weight, menstrual cycle, or stress. Differences in excretion rates may cause the number of metabolites in the urine of a person who smoked marijuana just before being tested to be the same as that of one who smoked much earlier. Thus, a person with X metabolites in his or her system may be impaired by marijuana, whereas someone else with that number may not be impaired, and a test cannot distinguish between these people.

SCOPE OF THE CONSTITUTION

If a test is challenged on federal constitutional grounds, the threshold question is whether or not the employer who gave the test is subject to the U.S. Constitution. The first eight amendments of the Bill of Rights apply to federal employers. The Fourteenth Amendment due process clause, which prohibits "state action" denying people life, liberty, or property without due process of law, "incorporates" the Bill of Rights and applies it to state employers. Local governments, such as cities, are also within the ambit of the amendment.

Private parties may also engage in "state action." Such action may exist if a government assists a private party in violating a constitutional right, or if that party exercises power usually reserved to the government. The extent of governmental involvement in private conduct may so blur the line between the private party and the government that the conduct is considered state action. State control of private acts may make the acts the state's responsibility. Finally, a private party that implements a governmentally prescribed drug testing plan may be deemed a state actor.

The tendency of the courts in recent years has been to narrow the state action concept, but this should not make private employers involved with a governmental entity too confident about their status vis-à-vis the Constitution. An employer who becomes so enmeshed with a government that the latter controls its workers, for example, would still likely be deemed an arm of the government, and the same is true if private employees perform their tasks on government property or under its supervision. As noted, the Constitution may also be triggered by tests conducted under federal authority.

EMPLOYEE URINE TESTING AND THE CONSTITUTION

The Fourth Amendment

The most frequently litigated issue raised by urinalysis involves its status under the Fourth Amendment to the Constitution, which provides:

The right of the people to be secure in their persons, houses, papers, and effects, against unreasonable searches and seizures, shall not be violated, and no warrants shall issue, but upon probable cause, supported by oath or affirmation, and particularly describing the place to be searched, and the person or things to be seized.

Whether a governmental investigation is a "search" is the initial issue in an analysis under this amendment. If it is, then it must be determined whether the investigation required a warrant and was conducted in a "reasonable" way.

In 1989 the U.S. Supreme Court considered the "search" implications of workplace drug testing in *Skinner v. Railway Labor Executives' Ass'n.*, 109 S. Ct. 1402, and *National Treasury Employees Union v. Von Raab*, 109 S. Ct. 1384. In doing so, the Court did not write on a clean slate, as scores of state and lower federal court precedents existed. These precedents agreed on many issues relating to drug testing but disagreed in some critical respects. To appreciate the impact of the Supreme Court decisions, it is important to understand something of what the lower court cases had said.

The cases agreed that a urinalysis involves a "search" because it invades reasonable privacy expectations. Courts compared compulsory testing to a government taking of blood, which entails a search, *Schmerber v. California*, 384 U.S. 757 (1966), and noted that tests invade privacy and dignity and allow both the discovery of personal medical data unrelated to drug use and the observation of off-duty activity. They also agreed that the exigencies of testing demand prompt action, making it impractical to require a warrant for a test. Third, they found that because workers cannot be forced to accept illegal conditions of employment, an unconstitutional test will not be upheld simply because employees "consented" to it, although advance consent may lessen privacy expectations regarding it. Fourth, urinalyses must be conducted in a "reasonable" fashion. This is determined by balancing a test's intrusion on privacy against its promotion of valid government interests, considering the manner, place, and justification of the intrusion.

The cases differed sharply over when a test is justified and reasonably conducted. The split centered on these issues: (1) How significant is the job—for example, whether it affects the public welfare—in terms of privacy interests and the justification for testing? (2) Does it matter if there is a history of drug use in the industry or evidence of a current problem? (3) May tests be given randomly or only when there is reason to suspect that a certain worker is impaired by drugs, and if the latter, how much suspicion is needed? (4) How important are the accuracy of a test and test conditions? A sampling of federal appeals court cases illustrates the differences in approaches to these issues.

Likening urinalysis to an administrative premises inspection, which requires little suspicion of wrongdoing, some courts held that individualized suspicion of impairment is not needed to test if the industry has a history of intense state regulation and privacy rights are protected. In *Shoemaker v. Handel*, 795 F.2d 1136 (3d Cir. 1986), for example, New Jersey was allowed to randomly test horse racing jockeys. The court stressed the need to preserve public confidence in racing, a sport in which wagering is heavy and corruption is a threat;

the state's heavy regulation of racing since 1939; the reduction of the jockeys' privacy expectations through their advance knowledge of the testing plan; and the plan's safeguards, which protected privacy and limited the testers' discretion. Finding the police industry the most heavily regulated in New Jersey, the court in *Policeman's Benevolent Ass'n. Local 318 v. Township of Washington,* 850 F.2d 133 (3d Cir. 1988), used the same theory in allowing random testing of police.

Other cases upheld random testing plans deemed "reasonable" upon an assessment of the facts. In *Transportation Workers Local 234 v. SEPTA,* 4 IER Cases 1 (3d Cir. 1988), for example, the court held that a plan to test transportation workers randomly was reasonable in light of the state interest in ensuring public safety, documented cases of accidents involving workers impaired by and applicants testing positive for drugs, the fact that the plan applied only to jobs affecting the public welfare, and the safeguards in the plan, including confidentiality and verification of results, chain-of-custody procedures, and a careful selection process. *Rushton v. Nebraska Public Power District,* 844 F.2d 562 (8th Cir. 1988), upheld a nuclear power plant testing plan, stressing that it does not require the act of urination to be witnessed, that results are used solely to assess job fitness, and that the industry affects public safety. *McDonell v. Hunter,* 809 F.2d 1302 (8th Cir. 1987), held that individualized suspicion is not needed if employees in sensitive jobs—prison guards, in that case—are tested uniformly, for example, in routine physical exams or by systematic random selection, but that other tests require a suspicion of drug use within 24 hours.

Many courts, however, required particularized suspicion to test. In *Copeland v. Philadelphia Police Department,* 840 F.2d 1139 (3d Cir. 1988), a city was allowed to test a police officer accused by his former girlfriend of using drugs only if there was a "reasonable suspicion" that the officer had done so. Relevant factors included the nature of the tip, the informant's reliability, and the degree of corroboration. The court found enough suspicion in Copeland's having been off his beat with a drug seller and not reporting this in his patrol log, coupled with the girlfriend's claim. *Lovvorn v. City of Chattanooga,* 846 F.2d 1539 (6th Cir. 1988), also imposed this standard in voiding a random testing plan for city fire fighters. Although it acknowledged the interest in drug-free fire fighters, the court noted that urine samples would be given under observation, and it stressed the privacy interest at stake. It then said that the permissibility of random testing depends not on whether an industry is heavily regulated, but on the nature of the industry and the harm that would likely result to society if mandatory tests were forbidden. Finding the likelihood of enormous societal losses because of an impaired fire fighter to be relatively low, the court held that for a test of fire fighters to be reasonable, there must be either evidence of a departmental drug problem or suspicion of an individual.

When *Skinner* and *Von Raab* appeared, therefore, the main question regarding urinalysis and the Fourth Amendment was whether tests require individualized suspicion of drug impairment. There, the Court answered in the negative. The facts of those cases seem to have played such a large role in their outcome, however, that it would be too much to say that across-the-board random testing is now clearly permissible.

Skinner involved federal rules requiring railroads to test workers' blood and urine in the event of an accident involving death, serious injury, or property damage. Specimens are obtained at a medical facility and sent to a laboratory for analysis. Employees are notified of the results and given a chance to respond before a final report is prepared. The rules also allow testing after certain rules violations or accidents if a supervisor reasonably suspects either impairment or that an employee's acts were a contributing factor. If results will be used to discipline, the employee must be allowed to provide blood for independent analysis. The rules also seek to prevent specimen tainting through chain-of-custody problems and require samples to be reliably analyzed.

A 7–2 majority of the Supreme Court held that tests given in reliance on federal authority involve enough government action to trigger the Fourth Amendment, that the tests involve "searches," that neither a warrant nor "probable cause" is required to conduct them, and that their reasonableness depends on all the circumstances. But it declined to hold, as had the Ninth Circuit, that particularized suspicion is needed to ensure that tests will detect current impairment. Where the privacy interests implicated by a search are minimal and important government interests would be harmed by an individualized suspicion requirement, the Court said, a search may be reasonable despite its absence. Conceding that requiring the performance of an excretory function traditionally deemed private is not a minimal privacy concern, the Court noted that the rules do not require urine to be given under observation and call for it to be analyzed in a laboratory; thus, the testing process is like that used in a regular physical examination. Finally, the Court found that the workers' privacy expectations were lessened by their being in an industry regulated pervasively to ensure safety.

The Court also stressed that on-the-job intoxication is a major problem in the railroad industry and that workers, who discharge duties fraught with such risks that even a momentary attention lapse may be disastrous, can cause great loss before signs of impairment will be noticeable. History also shows that even the threat of discharge for working while impaired is not an effective deterrent unless violators know they will likely be detected; by ensuring that employees in sensitive jobs know they will be tested after a triggering event, the timing of which cannot be predicted, the rule increases the deterrent effect of its penalties. And given the chaos at accident sites, it would be hard to find evidence creating a suspicion of impairment in a given employee. An individualized suspicion rule would thus bar testing in many cases, which could hamper efforts to pinpoint the cause of an accident.

In *Von Raab,* a 5–4 Court upheld testing rules of the Customs Service, which enforces customs laws and seizes contraband. Tests are a condition in jobs involving drug interdiction and in which classified material is handled. The district court described the testing process as follows:

After an employee qualifies for a position covered by the Customs testing program, the Service advises him by letter that his final selection is contingent upon successful completion of drug screening. An independent contractor contacts the employee to fix the time and place for collecting the sample. On reporting for the test, the employee must produce photographic identification and remove any outer garments, such as a coat or jacket, and personal belongings. The employee may produce the sample behind a partition, or in the privacy of a bathroom stall if he so chooses. To ensure against adulteration of the specimen, or substitution of a sample from another person, a monitor of the same sex as the employee remains close at hand to listen for the normal sounds of urination. Dye is added to the toilet water to prevent the employee from using the water to adulterate the sample.

Upon receiving the specimen, the monitor inspects it to ensure its proper temperature and color, places a tamper-proof custody seal over the container, and affixes an identification label indicating the date and the individual's specimen number. The employee signs a chain-of-custody form, which is initialed by the monitor, and the urine sample is placed in a plastic bag, sealed, and submitted to a laboratory.

The laboratory tests the sample for the presence of marijuana, cocaine, opiates, amphetamines, and phencyclidine. Two tests are used. An initial screening test uses the [EMIT]. Any specimen that is identified as positive on this initial test must then be confirmed using gas chromatography/mass spectrometry (GC/MS). Confirmed positive results are reported to a "Medical Review Officer," [a] licensed physician... who has knowledge of substance abuse disorders and has appropriate medical training to interpret and evaluate the individual's positive test result together with his or her medical history and any other relevant biomedical information.... After verifying the positive result, the Medical Review Officer transmits it to the agency.

Customs employees who test positive for drugs and who can offer no satisfactory explanation are subject to dismissal from the Service. Test results may not, however, be turned over to any other agency, including criminal prosecutors, without the employee's written consent.

As in *Skinner*, the Court held that the tests involve a search and must be reasonable. It also ruled out warrants, noting that requiring one for each work-related intrusion would make it difficult for offices to function. It then turned to the issue of individualized suspicion. Analogizing this search to building code inspections, which seek not to enforce the criminal law but to prevent conditions hazardous to the public, and to suspicionless searches of airline passengers, the Court said that sometimes the government's need to discover such latent conditions justifies suspicionless searches. Searches of Customs workers are in this category: Their safety is continually threatened by drug traffickers, and this, coupled with their access to contraband and their susceptibility to bribes, necessitates their unimpeachable integrity.

Also relevant in a "reasonableness" inquiry, the Court said, is the degree of interference with liberty caused by a test. Conceding that the intrusion on privacy involved in collecting urine could be substantial, the Court nonetheless said that the operational realities of the workplace may justify work-related intrusions by supervisors that might be unreasonable in other contexts. Certain public jobs, moreover, may diminish privacy expectations vis-à-vis searches.

The Customs workers' diminished privacy expectations and the fact that the testing plan contains safeguards to minimize its intrusion on privacy made the plan reasonable.

The challenge to the plan involved two other claims: It is unjustified because there is no perceived drug problem among Customs workers; and because drug users can avoid detection through abstinence or adulterating samples, it is not sufficiently productive to justify its invasion of privacy. In reply, the Court said that the "extraordinary" safety and national security interests at stake justified attempts to ferret out even casual drug users, and that the fact that most employees will test negative did not impugn the program. Where potential harm is substantial, the need to prevent it may justify reasonable searches designed to achieve that goal. To the other argument the Court responded that addicts may be unable to abstain or are unaware of the fade-away effect of some drugs. And because the time it takes for drugs to become undetectable in urine varies with the person, no employee's pattern of elimination for a particular drug can be predicted.

What is "the law" of drug testing after *Skinner* and *Von Raab?* Although it is too early to gauge the impact of these cases, these conclusions seem warranted: (1) Public and some private employment testing involves a "search." (2) Neither a warrant nor probable cause to suspect drug impairment is needed to test, but a test must be "reasonable," which is determined by weighing its intrusion on privacy against its promotion of valid interests, considering its justification, scope, and place. (3) If an industry affects the public welfare or has a history of intense state regulation or a drug problem, random testing is legal. The less a job affects the public or is regulated by the state, the more that evidence of a drug problem is needed for random testing; as the job's effect on the public, the amount of state regulation in that area, and the evidence of a drug problem decrease, so does the basis for suspicionless testing. (4) That tests cannot measure impairment and are not 100 percent accurate is no basis for automatically voiding them, although the more guarantees in a plan—for example, chain-of-custody safeguards, procedures to ensure the confidentiality of results, backup tests given if an initial test is positive, and the administering of tests under laboratory conditions—the more likely it will be upheld. (5) Although neither advance notice nor employee consent necessarily validates a test, they increase the likelihood of its passing muster. The extent to which a plan limits the testers' discretion is also important. (6) The more a plan protects employee privacy, the greater its chances of surviving. The circumstances under which samples are taken will be crucial.

The Fifth Amendment

The Fifth Amendment states that no person "shall be compelled in any criminal case to be a witness against himself." It has been argued that to use in legal proceedings evidence of drug use obtained through urinalysis forces employees to yield this privilege. Courts, however, have uniformly rejected this claim. For example, relying on *Schmerber v. California,* 384 U.S. 757 (1966), which refused such a challenge to the use of forcibly obtained blood in a DWI (driving while intoxicated) case, the Fifth Circuit held in *Von Raab* that the privilege protects only testimonial evidence, and that urine does not reveal donor knowledge. *Von Raab* left the door ajar for a claim that a rule requiring employees to fill out forms revealing certain medical facts (for example, medications taken) might violate the amendment, but given the attitude towards these claims shown by courts so far, it is hard to envision this argument succeeding.

The Fourteenth Amendment

The Fourteenth Amendment requires states to provide due process of law before denying people life, liberty, or property. Procedurally, deprivations must be preceded by notice of the alleged violation and a hearing; substantive due process bars unreasonable deprivations. Workers disciplined in connection with a urinalysis may have a due process claim if a property or liberty interest is thereby infringed.

Whether an employee has a property interest in his or her job depends on its nature. "At-will" employees, who serve at their employer's pleasure for an indefinite period, may be dismissed at any time; they have no expectation of continued employment and hence no property interest in their jobs. If, however, the law, company policy, a contract, or even verbal assurances create an expectation of job security, employees have a property interest of which they may not be deprived without notice and a hearing. Liberty interests are infringed by actions that illegally restrict the freedom or harm the reputation of an employee.

The cases say little about the due process implications of urinalysis, but standards can be gleaned from other sources, especially *Cleveland Board of Education v. Loudermill,* 107 S. Ct. 1487 (1985), which dealt with the firing of an Ohio civil service employee, with no hearing, for lying on his job application. Because Ohio law allowed the person to keep his job absent good cause for dismissal, the Court said he had a property interest in his job, and absent a need for summary removal from the workplace, he was entitled to a preremoval hearing. In *Fraternal Order of Police, Lodge No. 5 v. Tucker,* 4 IER Cases 168 (3d Cir. 1989), the court applied these standards in finding that the plaintiffs were denied due process because they were not given specifics about the charges against them, although they were told they were to be disciplined; thus, they had no meaningful chance to rebut the evidence of their on-duty drug use.

A urinalysis might also yield a substantive due process claim. A firing based on an unconfirmed positive result could do so, as may the unreliability of test conditions. In *Von Raab,* the Fifth Circuit rejected a due process attack on the Customs plan, apparently because of the careful handling and measurement techniques used. The Court in *Jones v. McKenzie* 833 F. 2d 335 (D.C. Cir. 1987) also expressed concern about the reliability of urinalysis. The Supreme Court's curt handling of the accuracy-based challenge in *Von Raab,* however, does not bode well for this argument in future cases.

The Fourteenth Amendment also entitles people to the equal protection of the law, meaning that governments may not differentiate among people similarly situated without valid reasons. In *Shoemaker v. Handel,* the jockeys complained that they, but not other track employees, were subjected to random urine tests. The court, however, held that in trying to solve its problems, a state may take a step at a time. Requiring only jockeys to be tested was justified, as they were the most visible participants in a sport in which there is an interest in the appearance of integrity. This suggests that although the best prospect for an equal protection challenge would exist if an employer applied a policy only to some workers, a court might even give short shrift to this kind of attack.

The Constitutional Right of Privacy

Drug testing cases have also invoked the constitutional right of privacy recognized in *Griswold v. Connecticut,* 381 U.S. 479 (1965). This right has two aspects: autonomy—freedom from unwanted government intrusions in decisions about one's life—and a right to protect certain personal facts from public disclosure. Although the cases say little about the privacy implications of urinalysis, *Schmerber v. California* and *Rochin v. California,* 342 U.S. 165 (1952), indicate that minor bodily intrusions will be tolerated and that a balancing approach which considers the nature of and need for a test, its reliability, and test conditions, and whether less intrusive options are available will be used to decide privacy claims. Random tests given to detect drug use stand a better chance of violating privacy rights than tests accompanying physical exams or based on reasonable suspicion.

The right of disclosural privacy is limited, and whether employers who divulge test results or insist that employees reveal personal data (for example, medicine being taken) violate it depends on whether the interest in disclosure outweighs the intrusion. In *Shoemaker,* the court found that the tests did not violate disclosural rights because results would not be disclosed, even to law enforcement authorities. The court stated that although privacy rights in medical data exist, governmental concerns may warrant access to such data if it is protected from unauthorized disclosure. Because the racing commission's concern for racing integrity justified its access to data revealed by the tests, the jockeys' privacy interest was limited to having that data protected from public disclosure, and the rule did this. If the commission ceased to comply with the rule, said the court, "the jockeys may return to court with a new lawsuit."

PRIVATE SECTOR DRUG TESTING

Cases involving private sector testing are on the rise. Because the Bill of Rights does not affect most private employers, these cases typically involve claims that drug testing invades state constitutional, statutory, or common law privacy rights. In states that recognize the concepts of "wrongful discharge" and "breach of the covenant of good faith and fair dealing," it is argued that dismissing an employee for failing or refusing a test is illegal under those theories as well as an invasion of privacy.

In *Luedtke v. Nabors Alaska Drilling, Inc.,* 768 P.2d 1123 (Alaska 1989), oil rig workers fired for refusing a urinalysis attacked their dismissal on the grounds noted hereinabove. The company replied that the Luedtkes were at-will employees subject to dismissal at any time and for any reason, and that even if they could be fired only for "just cause," such cause existed because the plaintiffs had violated company policy in refusing to be tested.

The court began by tracing the evolution of the privacy concept from its inception in the late 1800s through its incorporation in state constitutional, contract, and tort law, including "the emerging mixture of theories known as the public policy exception to the at-will" employment doctrine. A "Right of Privacy" in the Alaska constitution did not aid the plaintiffs, the court held, because it applied only to state officials. But the court also found Alaska to be among the states that recognize an "implied covenant of good faith and fair dealing" in at-will contracts. A public policy violation could breach this covenant, the court said, and protecting employee privacy is such a policy under state law. Finding that the Luedtkes were not hired for a specific term, the court also ruled that they were at-will employees.

The court then held that public policy creates "spheres of employee conduct into which employers may not intrude," and it asked whether employer monitoring, through urinalysis, of off-duty employee activities illegally invades this sphere. Applying the reasoning of Fourth Amendment cases, the court noted that in *Von Raab,* a Fifth Circuit concurrence had asked how intrusive urinalysis really is, because it involves a waste product which, if public toilets are used, is yielded under observation, and how different from routine background and security checks a testing plan is if it is based on a "generalized lack of trust and not on a developed suspicion of an individual." Its review led the court to conclude that it should assess the legality of urine testing by focusing primarily on the reason for, not the conduct of, the test.

According to the court, the limits of a privacy sphere are determined by balancing the interests in privacy and in others' safety. The Luedtkes could not claim that whether or not they use marijuana off duty is private information, because oil rig work is dangerous and marijuana impairs one's faculties; where the public policy favoring privacy in off-duty acts collides with safety concerns, the court held, the latter prevails. But the court also cautioned that because the employer's interest is in monitoring drug use that affects job performance, not in controlling societal drug use, tests must reasonably coincide with the employee's work time. Notice of the adoption of a testing program must also be given. Because both conditions were met with regard to the Luedtkes, their employer did not act illegally in imposing the testing rule and in firing them for refusing to abide by it.

In *Jennings v. Minco Technology Labs Inc.*, 765 S.W.2d 497 (Tex. App., Austin 1989), the company informed its employees that they may be required to submit to random drug testing at any time during their employment, for any or no reason. Jennings refused a test and then challenged her subsequent dismissal on privacy grounds. The trial court found that she had suffered no illegal invasion of privacy because she had the choice of consenting to the test or rejecting further employment under the newly required condition of employment. The state appeals court affirmed. That court also observed that the plan contained safeguards for accuracy, confidentiality, and modesty, and was administered only on the basis of employee consent.

Not all states recognize the "wrongful discharge" and "implied covenant of good faith" concepts, and their privacy law varies greatly. The analysis and outcome of cases such as *Luedtke* and *Jennings,* therefore, might be quite different elsewhere. These cases, however, offer a useful study of claims typically advanced in private sector cases; show how Fourth Amendment analyses may be used to resolve state law issues; reflect the sympathy toward drug testing often found in cases today, while imposing limits on testing to strike a workable balance between employer and employee interests; and stress the utility of obtaining employee consent and of seeking both to ensure testing accuracy and to protect employee privacy. Their approach will likely be followed in other cases.

MANAGERIAL IMPLICATIONS

At this point, one may ask: "What does all this mean to a company wanting to test its employees for drugs? Can—or should—it test, and if so, under what conditions?" Although no testing plan is fail-safe, employers should be on solid footing if they remember some basic principles:

1 Because employers can require applicants to pass a preemployment physical examination as a condition of employment, drug testing can be done at that time with the least risk of litigation. In order of increasing risk to the employer, other testing circumstances are: postaccident, "for cause" (for example, based on individualized suspicion of impairment), and random. If a job affects the public welfare or has a history of state regulation or a drug problem, and if a test is given under a policy tailored to minimize privacy intrusions, random tests will likely be upheld; otherwise, they are legally suspect.

2 Policies on employee drug use and drug testing should be written in detailed but concise language, published, and explained to workers. Courts are also more likely to be receptive if an employer tries to rehabilitate as well as discipline employees with a drug problem. Under the Drug-Free Workplace Act of 1988, government contractors who receive grants or hold or seek government contracts of $25,000 or more must meet these requirements.

3 Drug testing should be done uniformly pursuant to a written policy. Applicants should be told that a medical examination, including a drug test, is part of the application process, and that if employed they must work without impairment and may be required to take a test as a condition of employment. The latter information should be given to current employees as well.

4 Employee consent forms are not dispositive of the legality of a test, but they are helpful. Employees should be asked to sign an authorization form consenting to testing for controlled substances.

5 Information acquired in a test should be kept confidential. Even if another company asks about a rejected applicant, an employer risks being held liable for defamation if he or she reveals that the applicant failed a test. Within the company, this information should be revealed on a need-to-know basis.

6 Urine samples should be taken under conditions that maximize privacy and minimize the chance of sample switching or contamination. The location for collection should provide for controlled access. If collection is done in a restroom, bluing may be added to toilet water to prevent sample dilution; access to sinks may be limited or the water turned off; and after collection, the sample should be examined for unusual color (indicative of dilution or adulteration) or a temperature different from normal body temperature (indicative of urine substitution or dilution).

7 When a sample has been collected, reasonable steps must be taken to ensure that it is not tainted in storage or handling. Testing laboratories will usually assist in this area. Chain-of-custody procedures may include having the employee initial the sample jar and the seal on the jar lid; sealing jars in plastic bags closed with tamper-proof evidence tape; having samples accompanied by a record showing everyone who had custody; and keeping samples under lock and key during shipment, testing, and storage.

8 An EMIT should be used only as an initial screening device, with positive results confirmed in a GC/MS test. No employee should be dismissed or disciplined based on an unconfirmed test. Again, reference should be made to the Customs policy.

9 The federal Vocational Rehabilitation Act of 1973, which applies to employers who are government contractors or who receive government funds, considers many former and habitual drug users handicapped, and requires that an employer not consider that handicap when hiring, promoting, or firing unless the handicap makes the job unreasonably difficult or hazardous to the individual or to fellow workers. People who test positive for drug use may be within the ambit of this act.

For a model policy that addresses the foregoing points, refer to the Customs Service policy set out earlier in this chapter.

CONCLUSION

In view of the myriad of business-related problems caused by employees impaired by drugs, courts are generally sympathetic to employers wanting to conduct workplace drug testing. But courts have not given employers *carte blanche* to test under whatever conditions they please. In assessing the legality of a plan, courts will consider the extent to which the industry affects the public welfare, has been regulated by the state, and has a history of drug use among workers; how adequately the plan protects employee privacy and attempts to safeguard both the collection process and the urine samples obtained; whether employees were given advance notice of the tests and validly consented to them; whether there is reason to suspect impairment among particular employees; and whether efforts have been made to ensure test accuracy. When employers have made reasonable attempts to address these issues, their testing plans have generally been upheld.

REFERENCES

Bible, "Screening Workers for Drugs: The Constitutional Implications of Urine Testing in Public Employment," 24 *Am. Bus. L. J.* 309 (1986).
Geidt, "Drug and Alcohol Abuse in the Work Place: Balancing Employer and Employee Rights," 11 *Emp. Rel. L. J.* 181 (1985).
Hanson, "Drug Abuse Testing Programs Gaining Acceptance in Workplace," *Chemical & Engineering News,* June 2, 1986.
Leal, "Admissibility of Biochemical Urinalysis Testing Results for the Purpose of Detecting Marijuana Use," 20 *Wake Forest L. Rev.* 391 (1984).
Lehr and Middlebrooks, "Work-Place Privacy Issues and Employer Screening Policies," 11 *Emp. Rel. L. J.* 407 (1985).
Lykken, "The Validity of Tests: Caveat Emptor," 27 *Jurimetrics J.* 263 (1987).
Miller, "Mandatory Urinalysis Testing and the Privacy Rights of Subject Employees: Toward a General Rule of Legality under the Fourth Amendment," 48 *U. Pitt. L. Rev.* 201 (1986).
Rothstein, "Screening Workers for Drugs: A Legal and Ethical Framework," 11 *Emp. Rel. L. J.* 422 (1985).
"Survey of the Law on Employee Drug Testing," 42 *Miami L. Rev.* 553 (1988).
Zeese, "Marijuana Urinalysis Tests," 1 *Drug L. Rep.* 25 (1983).

DISCUSSION QUESTIONS

1 How does one explain the differences in the justices' votes in *Von Raab* and *Skinner*—7-2 in the former case and 5-4 in the latter? What does the voting pattern suggest about how the Court will resolve future drug testing cases?

2 Why should a company consider adopting a drug testing plan? How relevant to the success of a plan will the accuracy of a test and testing conditions likely to be in future litigation?

SUGGESTED ANSWERS

1 In *Skinner*, seven justices essentially held that if the tests are administered reasonably, random drug testing is permissible in an industry which directly affects the public safety and in which there is evidence of a drug problem among employees. In *Von Raab*, five justices agreed that even if there is no evidence of a past or present drug problem, reasonable random testing may be done if a job sufficiently implicates public interests.

Dissenting in *Von Raab*, Justices Scalia and Stevens stressed that they joined the majority in *Skinner*—Chief Justice Rehnquist and Justices White, Blackmun, O'Connor, and Kennedy—because of the proof of a drug problem in the railroad industry. In *Von Raab*, they found no evidence of a drug problem among Customs workers, and thus no basis for requiring these workers to submit to the privacy intrusion caused by random testing. Justices Brennan and Marshall argued that individualized suspicion of impairment should be required in both cases.

Justice Blackmun was the puzzle. Usually on the "liberal" side of issues, he voted with the majority, without comment, in both *Skinner* and *Von Raab*. Had he voted the other way in *Skinner*, there would still have been six justices holding that proof of a drug problem in an industry affecting the public warrants random testing. Had he voted the other way in *Von Raab*, however, a majority would have opposed random testing in that case.

It may thus be argued that whether or not random drug testing is allowed in future cases will depend primarily on three factors: the manner in which tests are conducted, the nature of the industry, and whether there is a history of drug use in that industry. If testing is done in a manner that minimizes its intrusiveness and ensures its accuracy, random testing may be permissible in an industry that directly affects the public welfare, even absent proof of a drug problem in that industry. At some point, however, the link between an industry and public interests will likely become sufficiently tenuous that a fifth justice—probably Blackmun—will conclude that the lack of proof of a drug problem in that industry is fatal to a random testing plan. In this instance, employee privacy interests will be held to outweigh the employer's interest in random testing.

In short, reasonable random testing will be allowed in an industry that affects the public even absent proof of a drug problem in that industry. If there is too tenuous a link between the industry and the public welfare, however, random testing will likely be allowed only if there is proof of a drug problem in that industry.

2 Employees taking drugs are more likely to be absent excessively from work and to be a disruptive influence while at work, to cause increases in health benefits and insurance premiums, and to produce poor services and goods. The latter may harm third parties, as may accidents caused by impaired workers, which may result in the employer's being held vicariously liable for damages under the doctrine of *respondeat superior*. Under the doctrines of negligent hiring and negligent retention, employers may also be directly liable for harm to third parties if they are found to have carelessly engaged or retained an impaired employee. Reasonable drug testing may help cut business losses resulting from such factors.

The mechanics of a urine test are vital. Almost every court case has focused on the conditions under which tests are given. In many cases, this issue has been dispositive in terms of the outcome of the case. Among other things, the cases establish that no employee should be disciplined based on unconfirmed test results; that care must be taken to minimize problems occurring during the storage or handling of urine samples; and that, to the extent possible, test results should be kept confidential. As noted previously, the Customs Service plan involved in *Von Raab,* which is set out in detail in this chapter, is a good model for a company testing plan.

2

BUSINESS ETHICS
AND TRADE SECRETS:
Judging the Judges of Commercial Morality

Anita Cava
University of Miami

INTRODUCTION

Trade secrets often provide the competitive edge necessary for success in the business world. An owner or claimant of secret business information obviously wants to keep it private. However, others may legitimately acquire the information, either by actually developing it or by learning it in a business relationship. Are employees, suppliers, or independent contractors forbidden forever from taking advantage of the information? Is there any limit to that cap on competition? And what about information that a company tries to keep proprietary, but which is discovered by detectives of one kind or another? Does the claimant lose all rights once the secret is no longer a secret?

These questions form the basis for the law of trade secrets, which mediates two strong business instincts: entrepreneurship versus private ownership. The Supreme Court has stated that trade secret law is intended to police "standards of commercial ethics,"[1] so trade secret cases provide a natural springboard for a discussion of ethics in business. To facilitate that discussion, this chapter is divided into four parts. The first explores theories upon which an analysis of ethics can be based, and the second presents the Ninth Circuit's decision in *Chicago Lock Co. v. Fanberg*, 676 F.2d 400 (9th Cir. 1982), in which the owner of a business idea does battle with a clever capitalist. A framework for judging the judges of commercial morality is offered in the third

The author wishes to thank Sandra Schuh, Ph.D., Adjunct Professor of Philosophy, University of Miami, who made helpful comments on an earlier draft of this chapter.
[1]*Kewanee Oil Co. v. Bicron Corp.*, 416 U. S. 470, 481 (1974).

section, followed by a discussion of the managerial implications of the business ethics issues raised in the *Chicago Lock Co.* case.

THEORIES OF ETHICAL ANALYSIS

What is business ethics? Before considering that question, it might be helpful to think about what it is not. Business ethics is not a "new," faddish phenomenon that dates from recent events on Wall Street. It is not a judgment simply based on what "I think is fair." Instead, business ethics is the study and application of theories offering frameworks for making the proper decision in any particular business situation. Using these theories, the decision maker can ask questions, examine alternatives, and suggest solutions that may be more insightful. This process of critical thinking can also be applied to legal resolutions of ethical conflicts in business and can generate discussion of the role of the law in arbitrating ethical dilemmas.

In order to analyze and defend the "ethical" choice in any situation, one must be familiar with the principles of the teleological (consequence-based) approach, the deontological (duty-based) technique, and even the strategy proposed by John Rawls to achieve justice. Each has a complex foundation in philosophy that is difficult to appreciate in a few short pages. However, even a simple explanation provides the basis for asking probing questions.

Considering the Consequences: Egoism and Utilitarianism

Consequence-based theories of ethics are familiar to most of us. For example, we are concentrating on consequences when we approach a decision by asking "What is best for me?" This familiar self-centered analysis has been explored by philosophers of very different persuasions and has been dubbed "egoism." An extreme example of ethical egoism is expressed by the nineteenth century German thinker Max Stirner (1806–1856), who wrote: "No one is my equal, but I regard him, equally with all other beings, as my property."[2] In Stirner's view, other people are objects in one's quest for the ultimate good: total independence.

Egoism notwithstanding, the major voice in the teleological school is that of utilitarianism. According to the utilitarians, the framework for choosing the proper course of action rests upon a calculation of the effects or the consequences of the decision. The goal is to choose the alternative that produces the "greatest good for the greatest number." In order to do so, however, one must be able to identify the "good" and the "number" in each transaction. In this regard, utilitarians differ.

Jeremy Bentham (1748–1832) argued that good is "pleasure" or the avoid-

[2] M. Stirner, *The Ego and His Own.* S. T. Byington (trans.), J. Carroll (ed.), rev. ed. (1971), quoted in Boyce and Jensen, *Moral Reasoning: A Psychological—Philosophical Integration*, University of Nebraska Press, p. 22, 1978.

ance of pain. An aspect of pleasure is happiness, and so the term *good* has a meaning more broad than physical sensations. Bentham adopted a scientific stance and proposed that pleasure and pain could be *quantified* using specific criteria, including intensity, duration, and extent, or the number of persons who are affected by it. One's obligation would be to consider options, predict consequences, and calculate the quantity of "good" produced by each alternative.

John Stuart Mill (1806–1873) suggested a different approach to the analysis. In his view, the *quality* of the pleasure or pain matters as much as the quantity, and the intrinsic value of happiness depends on an "impartial concern for the good of all persons."[3] Mill's notion of good appears to be broad and includes the concepts of harmony, integrity, and trust.

Utilitarians differ in other important ways. For some, the appropriate number of persons to take into account are those directly affected by the decision. Others argue that the consequences of any decision upon the community, the society, and even the universe must be weighed. To illustrate, imagine a stone being dropped into a pond, creating a splash and a series of ripples. Do you focus only on the splash or do you follow the ripples as far as you can see and beyond? Obviously, the calculation of the costs and benefits of the consequences differs depending on the point of view.

Decisions Based on Duty: The Kantian Approach

Another major school of thought in ethical analysis is deontology, a duty-based approach. According to duty-oriented thinkers, any decision must be made on the basis of obligations, not consequences. In effect, one must be able to recognize and articulate one's duty in any situation before considering any of the effects of one's choice. In order to do this, one must have a good sense of where one's duties lie and must also be able to resolve the dilemmas presented by conflicting duties. Immanuel Kant and W. D. Ross offer frameworks for doing just that.

Immanuel Kant (1724–1804) based his ethical philosophy upon the premise that, "[n]othing in the world—indeed nothing even beyond the world—can possibly be conceived which could be called good without qualification except a 'good will.'"[4] In Kant's view, the *good* will is a *rational* will, and a rational will is one that operates *consistently* and allows no contradictions. This principle of consistency generates the test by which one can recognize one's duty: the categorical imperative or "universal law."

According to the categorical imperative, one's duty in any situation becomes clear if one asks whether one's decisions could be universalized without a contradiction, or adopted by everyone in the same situation without making

[3] L. Garvin, *A Modern Introduction to Ethics,* p. 281.
[4] I. Kant, *Foundation of the Metaphysics of Morals* (1785), L. W. Beck (trans.), p. 9.

any exceptions. In addition, one must consider whether the decision at hand treats other people as ends in themselves, not as means to an end, and accords them respect for being rational human beings. Note that there are *no conditionals* to the law of consistency; rules of conduct based upon "ifs" (work hard if you want to be rich; act in moderation if you want to live long) or ones permitting special exceptions for certain situations are merely hypothetical imperatives, which hold no real moral authority.

Kant gives us the following example. A person is forced by circumstances to borrow money, but can do so only on the strength of a promise to repay it by a certain time—which he knows he will not be able to do. Does he make the false promise in the situation?[5]

Obviously, the answer is no. To make a false promise violates the universal law: One could not rationally will that everyone be free to make false promises; the decision cannot be universalized, and one cannot create special exceptions for oneself. Further, borrowing money under such circumstances treats the lender as a means to the end, and not with the dignity and respect that he or she merits. Kant takes the view to an extreme: He once was asked whether he would lie if a madman appeared at his door wielding a gun and wanting to know the whereabouts of Kant's close friend, who in fact was dining inside the house. Unable to justify lying even in that situation, Kant offered the possibility of remaining silent.[6]

What happens if one makes two legitimate but somewhat conflicting promises? Kant's approach is very rigid: One must identify one's primary promise, recognize the duty it creates, and behave such that no contradictions result. A modern philosopher, W. D. Ross (1877–1971), offered a version of deontology that defines duty by taking into account both pure obligations and the obligations to produce the best possible effects. The latter recognizes that certain relationships are more important than others, and certain consequences are more significant than others. In the case of conflicting duties, then, Ross permits us to assess certain consequences and prioritize our obligations accordingly.

Realizing Rights: Rawls's Veil of Ignorance

A third approach to ethical decision making has acquired stature in the last decade. John Rawls (1921–) is a rights-based theorist whose work is oriented toward exploring concepts of justice. However, his work lends itself to use in ethical analysis and has been widely adopted as a tool in business ethics education. In discussing justice and rights, Rawls posits a hypothetical mental test that can be used to determine what is "just." When asked to make a decision having ethical dimensions, you first step behind a "veil of ignorance." Once

---

[5] Ibid., p. 40.
[6] A. E. Teale, *Kantian Ethics,* pp. 173–75.

there, you are shielded from knowing not only your own status in the world, but also how the consequences of the decision will personally affect you. Then you approach the problem by contemplating the answer to a simple question: What appears rationally just, either in this case or as a general principle? The answer will be impartial, as you have removed your own personal circumstances from the outcome.

These three prongs of ethical analysis provide the springboard for exploring decision making in business situations. The process of asking the questions suggested by each theory tends to generate considerations one might not normally take into account. The same is true when evaluating judicial resolution of legal dilemmas based on genuine business ethics issues. Consider, for example, trade secret law and the particular case of *Chicago Lock Co. v. Fanberg*.

TRADE SECRET LAW: POLICING COMMERCIAL MORALITY

Successfully competing in the business world often depends on an original approach or an inspired solution to a problem. The idea, formula, process, or method may not fit the requirements for a patent, but may be valuable enough that one would wish to keep it secret. From this premise, the law of trade secrets offers a framework for identifying and protecting trade secrets.

Many jurisdictions follow the common law parameters articulated by the Restatement of Torts, Section 757. A trade secret can be claimed if it provides a genuine advantage in business, it was gained at the expense of the owner who intended to keep it confidential, and if the information is not generally known in the industry.

Certain comments to the Restatement suggest that courts might also consider other factors, including the extent to which others within the business know the secret, the extent to which the owner took security measures to protect it, and the ease or difficulty with which the information could *properly* be acquired or duplicated by others. The last refers to whether the secret can be "reverse engineered" or discovered by taking a product apart and putting it back together again. If this can be done through legitimate means, not by spying or stealing, then courts usually find the secret was not a secret after all. However, persons who learn the secret while in a "confidential" relationship, which is usually but not always created by contractual agreement, are forbidden from using the idea for their own advantage.

Several states have recently modified these common law standards by adopting the Uniform Trade Secrets Act, which offers a more specific definition of trade secrets and adds an element of "reasonableness" to the efforts taken to protect it. However, the basic framework remains the same.

The plaintiff in *Chicago Lock* manufactures "tubular" locks, which are designed to provide greater security than other types of locks. Sold under the registered trademark Ace, these tubular locks are frequently used on vending machines, bill-changing machines, and other maximum security devices. Their commercial appeal lies in the fact that the Chicago Lock Company makes it very difficult to reproduce the keys for the Tubular Ace lock. The company does not sell tubular key "blanks" to locksmiths; instead, Chicago Lock maintains a list of owners of the locks. If a key is lost, a duplicate may be obtained from the company only after providing proof of purchase or other identification of being the owner of record. In addition, keys are stamped with the legend "Do Not Duplicate."

In practice, a proficient locksmith can pick the lock, decipher the tumbler configuration, and grind a duplicate tubular key. The procedure is somewhat quicker than going through the company, but certainly more costly. Naturally, to ensure against having to pick the lock again in the future, the locksmith might record the key code along with the serial number of the customer's lock.

Enter the entrepreneur. Victor Fanberg, a locksmith and son of a locksmith, decided to compile and publish a list of tubular lock key codes. In 1975 he advertised this idea in a trade journal and asked individual locksmiths to send him serial number–key code correlations in their possession in exchange for a complete compilation. Many responded. About a year later, father and son Fanberg offered a two-volume manual of tubular lock combinations, including those of Ace locks, at the low, low price of $49.95. By 1979 at least 350 sets had been sold without regard to who was buying the information.

In other words, the key code configurations were on the street. Anyone with a tubular key grinding machine could fashion a key if the serial number of the lock were known. This was not much of an obstacle because certain models of Ace locks had the serial number on their face. Armed with the Fanberg's manuals, one could bypass the company's screening procedures entirely; it was both quick and cheap to make a key for legitimate or illegitimate purposes.

Chicago Lock Company sued the Fanbergs on a number of theories, including theft of trade secrets. The trial court found that the confidential key code data was a legitimate trade secret and that individual locksmiths owed a duty of nondisclosure to both their customers and to the company. Therefore, the Fanbergs' collection and publication of the codes had been accomplished through "improper means" and was impermissible. The court ordered the Fanbergs to stop selling the manuals. On appeal, the Ninth Circuit offered a different view of what constitutes "improper means."

Agreeing that the code combinations were protectable secrets, the court probed the limits of trade secret law. "It is well recognized that a trade secret does not offer protection against discovery by fair and honest means such as by independent invention, accidental disclosure, or by so-called reverse engineering, that is, starting with a known product and working backward to divine the process."[7]

Would the Fanbergs have violated this standard if they had bought and examined many locks on their own, publishing their results? Does their use of

---

[7] 676 F. 2d 400, 404 *quoting Sinclair v. Aquarius Electronics, Inc.*, 42 Cal. App. 3d 216, 226, 116 Cal. Rptr. 654, 661 (1974).

computer programs to generate some of the key code combinations constitute "improper means?" More important, did the Fanbergs or any of the other individual locksmiths who pooled their information owe any duty to the trade secret owner (Chicago Lock Company) to maintain the secret and refrain from disclosing it to others? In other words, did a confidential relationship of any sort exist between the actors in this scenario?

The Ninth Circuit answered "no" to each of these questions. It did note that the locksmiths might have violated a duty to their *customers* (the lock owners) not to disclose combinations, an argument not raised by plaintiffs in the case. The court reversed the trial judge's finding of unfair business practices on the specific grounds that the publication of trade secret information had been accomplished by taking the notion of "fair and honest means" one step further. Simply put, the court found that the Fanbergs had not stolen the information, but had simply collected it from others instead of deciphering it all by themselves.

EXAMINING ETHICS; JUDGING THE JUDGES

A discussion of the ethics of the Fanbergs' enterprise and the propriety of the court's decision in this case requires consideration of many variables. One might begin to explore these by asking the questions suggested by the philosophies mentioned previously. Obviously, there is no absolutely "right" answer, although some answers may appear to be more correct than others when critically analyzed. What follows, then, is a series of questions offered to stimulate critical thinking and recognition of the many ways in which one may approach a business ethics problem.

Is this court's decision supported by utilitarian analysis? Does disseminating the tubular lock configurations promote a "greater good for the greater number" than restricting the flow of that information? Who benefits from protecting the secret? Certainly, the company and its employees do, as well as those customers who rely on the security aspects of the lock but who have not had to replace a key. Any others? Who benefits from permitting the publication of the trade secrets? The entrepreneurial Fanbergs do, as well as other locksmiths asked to provide a duplicate key and some unknown number of other people with less legitimate intentions. Any others?

Is there a greater societal good that might be served by a general principle of protecting only those secrets that are genuinely secret? Might it not be in society's interest to more widely disseminate information not kept strictly secret? Although individual levels of profit might decrease, so might general cost levels. Competition would improve; general knowledge would too. What might be the downside risks?

Is there anything about this case that makes it subject to a different calculation? Does the creator of a secret simply risk discovery in today's technologically sophisticated environment? If so, then customers who rely upon certain characteristics of a particular product, such as the security offered by a particular lock, are also at risk. Where does the "greatest good" lie with respect to these concerns?

Turning to deontological analysis, where does "duty" lie in this case? Imagine you are the Fanbergs or even one of the individual locksmiths asked to transmit key code information in return for a manual. Do you owe a duty to the company or to the customers not to provide or publish the data? Would you be happy to permit all others in similar situations to share company information, thereby universalizing that choice? Does publishing the data treat others (locksmiths, customers, the company) as means to an end or as ends in themselves? Does it accord others the respect and dignity owed to people?

Next, imagine you are one of the Fanbergs, and step behind Rawls's veil of ignorance. Would you elect to publish the manuals knowing that you might wake up tomorrow as a corporate director of the Chicago Lock Company or someone who uses an Ace tubular lock to secure 20 vending machines? What other considerations might you take into account when put in such a neutral position? Do any of these support the Fanbergs' decision?

Finally, consider the overall meaning of "improper means" in this context. Does the court's opinion convince you that the law should approve the technique adopted by the entrepreneurs? Obviously, the court could have agreed with the trial judge and found that the conduct violated trade secret principles. Instead, the opinion reveals a strong bent toward protecting the entrepreneur and, by extension, demonstrates a certain distaste for offering legal protection to business information that is not strictly secret. What policy grounds support the trial court's opinion, and what arguments support the appellate court's view? Would a "court of ethics" reach a different result than that reached by the "court of law"?

MANAGERIAL IMPLICATIONS

From a managerial point of view, an obvious question might be raised: Why bother analyzing the ethics of the Fanberg's activity when the Ninth Circuit found nothing improper about it? The answer to the question is not so obvious and requires some reflection upon our legal process and its role in addressing issues of business ethics. Here the discussion is not specifically concerned with trade secrets, but is more generally applicable to the question of considering ethics in making business decisions.

The law is an imperfect system. *Chicago Lock* illustrates that judges have a great deal of discretion in evaluating the propriety of certain conduct; they may not necessarily reach a "correct" decision in every case. But this discretion also affords the law a tremendous amount of flexibility. Implicit in the *Chicago Lock* opinion is the reality that the appellate court could have resolved the dilemma exactly opposite to the way it did. Indeed, if presented with a similar case in the future, the Ninth Circuit might decide to reverse themselves. Alternatively, a court from another jurisdiction might openly disagree and decide not to follow the Ninth Circuit's lead.

By extension, then, a wise manager will not blindly rely upon an assessment of "it is legal, even if it appears to be unethical" as the bottom-line arbiter of difficult business decisions. Despite the apparent constraints of precedent, the law can change to accommodate shifting cultural values. Recently, especially in the areas of securities regulation and environmental protection, courts have demonstrated a willingness to serve as the enforcers of certain societal standards that business or businesspeople appear to have ignored.

Finally, consider that "winning" a case in court may be a very hollow victory. Imagine the cost of defending a lawsuit for over 5½ years, not only in terms of money but also in terms of energy, effort, and general aggravation. (Chicago Lock filed its complaint on December 2, 1976; a 4-day trial was held in January 1979; the trial court handed down a judgment in favor of Chicago Lock in November 1979, and the appellate court reversed that decision in May 1982.) Were the earnings of the manuals worth it? Remember that in our legal system, each party bears its own fees and costs unless otherwise provided by statute (such as where state or federal law protects civil rights) or by contract between the parties. Neither exception applied here.

A manager never wants to become "a case in the book." The promise of considering ethics in making decisions is that the ultimate choice will be more reasoned and will reflect better judgment. Two benefits might be seen to follow. The first is the pragmatic probability that decision making will be less subject to challenge, both within the organization and in a court of law. The second is that decisions tested by ethical principles are more likely to serve the organization, the community, and society in general for the long term.

CONCLUSION

To consider business ethics in making decisions is to engage in a process of critical thinking, which is always a productive endeavor. The framework offered by the ethical theories challenges the manager to explore alternatives and to marshall arguments in support of those alternatives. This is an important and perhaps even a crucial step to success in today's complex business environment—a world in which good decision making involves recognizing not only the immediate financial implications of a course of action, but also the less obvious long-term interests of business as well as society.

REFERENCES

Boyce, W. D., and L. C. Jensen, *Moral Reasoning: A Psychological and Philosophical Integration,* Univ. of Nebraska Press, 1978.

Conry, E., and D. Nelson, "Business Law and Moral Growth," 27 *Am. Bus. L. J.* 1 (1989).

DeGeorge, R., *Business Ethics,* 2d ed., MacMillan, New York, 1986.

Garvin, L., *A Modern Introduction to Ethics,* Houghton Mifflin, Boston, 1953.

Kant, I., *Foundations of the Metaphysics of Morals* (1785). L. W. Beck (trans.), MacMillan, New York, 1985.

Rawls, J., *A Theory of Justice,* Belknap Press of Harvard University Press, Cambridge, Mass. 1971.

Ross, W. D., *Foundations of Ethics,* Oxford, The Clarendon Press, 1939.

Stirner, M., *The Ego and His Own.* S. T. Byington (trans.), J. Carroll (ed.), rev. ed. (1971), quoted in Boyce and Jensen, *Moral Reasoning: A Psychological-Philosophical Integration,* University of Nebraska Press, 1978.

Teale, A. E., *Kantian Ethics* (1951).

Wiesner, D., and A. Cava, "Stealing Trade Secrets Ethically," 47 *Md. L. Rev.* 1076 (1988).

DISCUSSION QUESTIONS

1 Can the Ninth Circuit's decision be justified using the basic utilitarian analysis?

2 How would a Kantian have approached this dilemma confronting the Ninth Circuit? What questions would be asked, and how might they be answered?

3 Explain how a Rawlsian might decide the *Chicago Lock* case.

SUGGESTED ANSWERS

1 The basic utilitarian analysis requires determining what course of action yields the "greatest good for the greatest number of people." Although Bentham and Mill propose scientific standards for answering this question, one must acknowledge that the calculation often depends upon point of view. It may shift depending upon whether one takes the more immediate consequences of a decision into account, or whether one extends the calculation of consequences to include the long-term and wide-ranging effects.

With that caveat in mind, the "good" of permitting the publication of the lock configurations might be premised upon the notion of encouraging the entrepreneurial spirit and the idea that sharing knowledge is generally more beneficial to society than keeping information secret. Although this argument may have appeal in some situations, such as the cure for cancer, it has less weight here.

In this scenario, it appears that the Fanbergs' business enterprise benefits far fewer people than it harms. The business seems to be small, its economic support of the community appears to be negligible, and the overall contribution of this information to society is equally minuscule. On the other hand, the entire customer base of the company is harmed, as is the overall trust in that company to keep its promise of providing security. That breach of trust, according to utilitarian principles, might extend into a generalized breach of trust in business, with all the negative consequences that lack of respect and trust might generate.

2 Kantian deontology proposes a categorical imperative that determines one's duty in any situation. The primary test of the categorical imperative is whether the decision be universalized without contradiction. Another formulation asks whether the decision treats others with dignity and accords them respect for being rational beings; in other words, does it treat people as ends in themselves and not as means to an end? It appears that a deontologist would have little problem condemning the Fanbergs' entrepreneurial activity as unethical. The Fanbergs' conduct seems to fail each of the tests.

In the first place, business would find it almost impossible to function if it were universally accepted that people could solicit and publish information intended to be kept confidential. Remember, Kant forbids making any exceptions in crafting a universal law. Secondly, the Fanbergs' activity respects neither the lock manufacturer nor the lock customers. Publishing the configurations treats these parties as means to the end of making money.

Publicizing the lock configurations violates the very *raison d'etre* of the business, which is to protect property from theft. As locksmiths with the knowledge to penetrate the "secret," the Fanbergs seem to have a positive duty to protect the interests of the general lock customer. Instead, they sacrifice lock customers' interests altogether by making the lock combinations available to anyone willing to pay the price of the manual.

3 The Rawlsian approach to ethical decision making requires one to step behind a veil of ignorance and determine whether justice is served from this neutral position. In this case, the technique would require the Fanbergs to pretend that they might be tubular lock makers or tubular lock owners when their business plan was implemented. Would they still pursue it? Probably not, because the interests of those parties are harmed by this enterprise. Therefore, the decision appears to be unjust.

TWO

THE FOUNDATIONS
OF LEGAL SYSTEMS
AND BUSINESS

3

COMMERCIAL SPEECH:
Virginia State Board of Pharmacy
v. Virginia Citizens Consumer Council, Inc.

Susan E. Grady
University of Massachusetts

INTRODUCTION

One of the most important freedoms granted by the U.S. Constitution to people living in the United States is freedom of speech. The First Amendment to
the Constitution states, ''Congress shall make no law respecting an establishment of religion, or prohibiting the free exercise thereof; or abridging the freedom of speech, or of the press; or the right of the people peaceably to assem-
ble, and to petition the Government for a redress of grievances.'' These rights
are reinforced by the Fifth Amendment, which applies to the federal government, and by the Fourteenth Amendment, which applies to the state government. The relevant parts of the Fifth and Fourteenth Amendments use basically the same language, which states that no person can be deprived of
''liberty...without due process of law.''

For nearly two centuries the courts have struggled to define what free
speech is and what free speech is not. Court decisions have held that freedom
of speech involves freedom to think and believe as we choose; freedom to
speak by our voices and through writings, drawings, and films. Freedom of
speech even applies to our right not to speak.

However, all rights have limitations. Freedom of speech does not include
the slandering or libeling of others, obscenity, fighting words, or those words
that are a clear and present danger to the safety of others or which advocate
the overthrowing of the government by force.

One form of speech is commercial speech, that which advertises a product
or service for profit. Before the 1970s commercial speech was not protected by
the First Amendment because the courts did not consider it to be pure speech.

43

Commercial speech was suspect in a way because the motive of commercial speech was to make the speaker a profit.

The common law traditionally had laws that governed commercial speech, such as fraud and misrepresentation. These laws held that a plaintiff who was misled by the defendant's knowing or unknowing deceptive speech could recover his or her money damages. Note that deceptive speech would not necessarily have to be in the area of commercial speech, but a plaintiff would not be likely to have money damages unless it were.

The Federal Trade Commission (FTC) was established in 1914 by the federal government. One of its mandates was to prevent deceptive practices from occurring in commercial speech. Unlike the common law, which helped injured parties recover their damages, the FTC was designated to keep parties from becoming injured. Therefore, the FTC can review advertisements before they are published or aired on radio or television. The FTC can also request advertisers to withdraw an item of commercial speech because of a likelihood that a person may be deceived or injured by the speech.

VIRGINIA STATE BOARD OF PHARMACY v. VIRGINIA CITIZENS CONSUMER COUNCIL, INC.

In 1976 the U.S. Supreme Court held that certain types of commercial speech should be accorded First and Fourteenth Amendment protection. [*Virginia State Board of Pharmacy v. Virginia Citizens Consumer Council, Inc.*, 96 S. Ct. 1817 (1976).] The Virginia State Board of Pharmacy (hereinafter Board) licensed and regulated the pharmacists in the state. One of the regulations forbade pharmacists to advertise prices of prescription drugs. The rationale for this, from the Board's perspective, was that advertising was unprofessional conduct because it was too commercial and because advertising was beneath the dignity of specially trained pharmacists who were more than just sellers of medicines.

The Board could force a pharmacist to pay a fine or revoke his or her license if the Board found the person to be of poor moral character, negligent, fraudulent, deceitful with consumers, or guilty of unprofessional conduct such as advertising. Because only a licensed pharmacist could dispense prescription drugs in Virginia, the Board effectively prevented any advertising by pharmacists.

The attack on the ban of advertising in *Virginia State Board* was not made by the pharmacists, but by the Virginia Citizens Consumer Council (hereinafter Council), who claimed that prescription drug consumers were greatly injured by the lack of the advertising because it impeded consumers' ability to comparison shop. The Council also asserted that the First Amendment entitled the consumer to receive information that pharmacists wish to communicate to them about the price of prescription drugs.

A preliminary issue which the Court had to decide was whether First Amendment protection, if applicable in this case at all, extended to the recipients. The Court answered in the affirmative, reasoning that it is the communication that is protected under the right to free speech. Because there must be a sender and a receiver of a communication, both parties are given rights to sue if communications are withheld.

The major issue in the case, of course, was whether the advertising of prescription drugs was to be accorded First Amendment protection. The Board argued that the Supreme Court should follow precedent, which had inferred that First Amendment protection would not be granted to commercial speech.

First, the Court responded by discussing the content of commercial speech. The Court asserted that the content of commercial speech was not so different from speech of thoughts, ideas, or politics. Even though the speaker's interest in commercial speech is purely economic, there are paid political announcements that are protected by the First Amendment. Books, magazines, and films are "speech" sold for profit and protected by the First Amendment. Also, employees and employers in a labor dispute have an economic interest in the outcome of the dispute and their speech is protected by the First Amendment.

Second, the Court discussed the consumer's interest in the subject matter of commercial speech. The Court pointed out that oftentimes an individual may be more interested in the content of commercial speech than in the content of political speech. In this particular case, banning the advertising of prices of prescription drugs affects the poor, elderly, and ill. These classes of the population are the ones least able to travel from pharmacist to pharmacist to determine price differences in medicines.

Third, society in general may have an interest in commercial speech. Oftentimes advertisements contain policy arguments as well as information about a specific product. For example, commercial speech might urge the buying of American goods so that more Americans can keep working. Even if commercial speech does no more than promote a product's virtues, it is important to have an informed public. "Therefore, even if the First Amendment were thought to be primarily an instrument to enlighten public decisionmaking in a democracy, we could not say that the free flow of information does not serve that goal."

The Court then turned its attention to the arguments of the Board. The Board's major argument was that allowing advertising of the price of prescription drugs would lower the professionalism of the licensed pharmacists because consumers would seek out the lowest prices, oftentimes at the expense of the pharmacist-patient relationship. In order to compete, some pharmacists might begin to diminish the quality of their services. Publishing pharmaceutical advertisements could have the effect of driving smaller pharmacies out of business because they would be unable to compete with larger pharmacies.

The Court agreed that professional standards should be maintained. However, the Court argued that the banning of advertisements does not imply that standards would be lowered or that smaller pharmacists would be driven out of business. The only effect the advertising ban has had on the profession, as the Court saw it, was to permit some pharmacists to make an excessive profit.

The Court also stated that the Council had challenged the advertising ban on First Amendment grounds—and that was the issue the Court must decide. The Commonwealth of Virginia may set whatever professional standards it wishes to for its pharmacists, but not at the expense of suppressing information because they fear what the consumers would do with the information. "It is precisely this kind of choice, between the dangers of suppressing information and the dangers of its misuse if it is freely available, that the First Amendment makes for us." The Supreme Court held for the first time that commercial speech was entitled to the protection of the First Amendment.

The Court added that by according commercial speech First Amendment protection, it did not preclude the need for some regulation at times. The Court gave examples of four circumstances in which protected speech can be regulated. Because commercial speech has now been adjudicated protected speech under the First Amendment, it too could be regulated, if necessary.

The first type of regulation that could possibly be imposed on commercial speech is a time, place, and manner restriction. In the past the Court has approved legislation that limits speech to a certain time, place, or manner. In order for the legislation to be endorsed by the Court, legislators must show a "significant governmental interest" in restricting the speech. Legislators must also show that there are sufficient times, places, or manners in which the speech is allowable.

The second type of regulation are the restrictions prohibiting deceptive speech. As mentioned earlier, there are laws against fraud and misrepresentation as well as the FTC mandate to protect the public from deceptive practices. Even though commercial speech is protected by the First Amendment, laws against untruthful speech can and should be enforced.

The third type of regulation that may be imposed upon commercial speech are the laws forbidding illegal advertisements. The courts are not going to endorse advertisements for something that has been declared illegal. For example, advertising the prices of illegal drugs would not be tolerated.

The fourth type of regulation deals with special problems that electronic broadcast media might face. The precedent cited by the Court was the restricting of cigarette advertising on radio and television. These restrictions were limited to electronic broadcast media because those who operate radio and televisions are using the public airwaves. Therefore, broadcasters are subject to more federal regulations than book or magazine publishers.

Chief Justice Burger concurred with the majority opinion written by Justice Blackmun, but wished to emphasize the narrowness of the decision. He focused on the professionalism of pharmacists, noting that the decision dealt mainly with pharmacists' rights to advertise prepackaged drugs. This activity does not involve individual judgments, such as those that doctors and lawyers must use when confronted by a problem. Doctors must decide what course to take with a sick patient, such as what drugs to prescribe, if any. Lawyers must decide what to advise their clients, such as whether accepting an out-of-court settlement is a better strategy than going to court. Chief Justice Burger wanted to stress that the issue of other professionals' right to advertise must be brought forth in other cases.

Justice Stewart also concurred with the majority, but with his own reasoning. His concern with the result in this case is that the distinction between commercial speech and regular speech be preserved. Speech that contains ideological expression is protected by the First Amendment "whether or not it contains factual representations and even if it includes inaccurate assertions of fact." This is because the speaker is asserting ideas that sometimes cannot be proved to be true or false. In contrast, commercial speech asserts a fact that is provable, such as the price of a certain drug. If the statement in commercial speech is not provable and is considered deceptive, then restrictions should apply.

Justice Rehnquist dissented from the majority opinion. He argued that from his perspective the decision of the Court created two consequences that are extremely dangerous expansions of preexisting law. First, the decision extends standing to sue to consumers who have not been injured, and second, it extends First Amendment protection to commercial speech.

As to the first extension, Justice Rehnquist argued that the Virginia statute does not prevent consumers from finding out the prices of prescription drugs. It only prohibits the pharmacists themselves from publishing the prices. Consumers, including the poor, the ill, and the elderly, could telephone the pharmacies and inquire as to the price of a certain drug. In addition, a consumer group, such as the one bringing this action, could gather the information and distribute it themselves. That is, in fact, what the Council did when bringing this lawsuit. Justice Rehnquist argued that the Court is infringing upon the state legislature's right to regulate commercial information within the state. He quoted from a Supreme Court case decided 13 years earlier, where Justice Black stated in the majority opinion, "We have returned to the original constitutional proposition that courts do not substitute their social and economic beliefs for the judgment of legislative bodies who are elected to pass laws."[1]

Justice Rehnquist also argued that extending the right to sue to the consumer will bring about challenges to the bans on other professional advertising. Even though the Court had been careful to differentiate between the skills of pharmacists in dispensing prepackaged drugs and the creative skills of doctors and lawyers, there are standardized services in each of these fields. Thus, doctors and lawyers could be required to advertise the prices of such routine services as a physical examination or a title search for real estate.

The second objection Justice Rehnquist had to this decision is that it extends First Amendment protection to commercial speech. He argued that giving First Amendment protection to truthful commercial speech elevates it to the same plateau as thoughts, ideas, and political speech. The information that the public has a right to receive is of a higher nature than what type of pill to buy.

---

[1] *Ferguson v. Skrupa,* 372 U.S. 726, 730 (1963).

In addition, according to Justice Rehnquist, the Court has now set up a standard of protecting truthful commercial speech while disallowing deceptive commercial speech. This could encourage the widespread use of legal drugs by advertising the virtues of certain drugs and encouraging the consumer to pressure his or her doctor for a prescription. He also feared that advertising certain products, such as cigarettes, which the courts have limited, may have to be allowed as long as the advertising is truthful.

MANAGERIAL IMPLICATIONS

As with any Supreme Court decision that makes a radical change in the preexisting law, managers of businesses had questions and concerns as to how this decision affected them. Now that commercial speech was protected under the First Amendment, what exactly did this mean? It was obvious that deceptive commercial speech would not be tolerated, but there were other unanswered concerns. As a result, there was an increase in the number of cases dealing with commercial speech, which the Supreme Court agreed to hear in order to clarify and expand its decision in the case of *Virginia State Board*. The cases included realtors, attorneys, advertisers of contraceptives, electricity, and gambling establishments as well as billboard advertisers and sellers of household products through "parties" in a student's dormitory room.

These inquiries fall basically into one of two categories. One issue, as Justice Burger had predicted, was whether attorneys, like pharmacists, had the right to advertise. The Supreme Court held that they did. Consequently, consumers now saw advertisements on television and in newspapers for attorneys' services. Physicians and medical insurers also advertise in the same fashion as attorneys, concluding by analogy that they, too, have the legal right to have their commercial speech heard and seen by the public.

The second category of cases concerning commercial speech guidelines for managers were those dealing with governmental restrictions on truthful advertisements. *Virginia State Board* had held that any speech, as long as it was truthful, was protected by the First Amendment. What if a governmental agency, such as a municipality or a commission, banned truthful advertising for some reason? The Supreme Court held in 1980 that truthful advertising can be restricted. The Court created a four-part test to determine when the government can limit commercial speech. First, the speech must be legal and must not be misleading. Second, the restriction must serve a substantial interest. Third, the restriction must further the stated interest. Fourth, the regulation must be as narrow as necessary.

This four-part test has been applied when appropriate. For example, in *Posadas de Puerto Rico Associates v. Tourism Co. of Puerto Rico* (478 U.S. 328), a case decided in 1986, the issue was whether the Puerto Rico legislature could enact a statute that restricted gambling casinos from advertising to residents of Puerto Rico. The Court held that state and federal legislatures had the right to determine how to regulate potentially harmful businesses such as gambling. Thus, the Court held that the restriction must and did reflect a "substantial state interest" in protecting its citizens from the potential harmful effects of gambling. This was the first time the Court upheld a ban on *truthful* advertising for a legal product. More important, it indicated a shifting of the Court; some of the justices who decided *Virginia State Board* had retired and other justices had been appointed.

The decisions handed down from *Posadas* concerned many managers. They had believed that as long as the advertisement was not deceptive, the courts would interpret "substantial state interest" very broadly and allow the advertisement to be published or spoken.

In 1989 the Supreme Court modified one of the four criteria in *Board of Trustees of the State University of New York v. Fox* (109 S. Ct 3028). A student challenged a university regulation that restricted commercial speech in dormitory rooms. Previously, the Court had held that the last test of restrictive speech is whether the governmental interest could be served by the least-restrictive-means approach. Now, for the first time, the Court focused upon this issue and determined that "the reason of the matter requires something short of a least-restrictive-means standard." The Court cited several past decisions and came up with a standard of reasonableness. The other criteria are still (1) that the speech be about something which is legal and cannot be misleading, (2) that there must be a substantial state interest in restricting the speech, and (3) that the restrictions must further the state interest. But instead of the restrictions being required to be as narrow as possible, they now must be reasonable.

In summary, it appears that any group of businesspersons, including professionals, may advertise as long as the advertisement is truthful. There still are restrictions as to where the advertisements may be placed. Interestingly, cigarette advertisers, as Justice Rehnquist had predicted, did not fight to have their advertisements restored to television and radio. Moreover, the government may restrict any type of advertising as long as the four criteria mentioned earlier are met. However, the standards may be reinterpreted again in the future.

CONCLUSION

The Court's decision in *Virginia State Board* in 1976 has been expanded, explained, and modified since the decision was handed down. This is most often the case with any Supreme Court decision. Some of the justices who heard the case have retired and been replaced by other justices who see things in a different light. The interpretation of the decision has changed over time as different types of businesses have brought their particular types of problems to the Court's attention. Freedom of speech is an important constitutional right, but it carries with it responsibility. The Court's decisions involving both the protection of commercial speakers and their listeners often involve complex issues, and the passage of time is often the best judge of the Court's wisdom.

REFERENCES

Colford, Steven W., "Kennedy Has 'Paper Trail' on Ads," *Advertising Age,* November 16, 1987, p. 2.

DeVore, P. Cameron, "*Posadas de Puerto Rico v. Tourism Company of Puerto Rico:* The End of the Beginning," 10 *COMM-ENT,* Winter 1986, pp. 579–590.

Greenhouse, Linda, "High Court Returns Dormitory Case," *The New York Times,* June 30, 1989, pp. A8, B3.

Lipman, Joanne, "Case Fans Concern for Firms' Free Speech," *The Wall Street Journal,* September 12, 1989, p. B5.

Lively, Donald E., "The Supreme Court and Commercial Speech: New Words with an Old Message, 72 *Minn. L. Rev.* 289–310 (December 1987).

Nutt, Mary B., "Trends in First Amendment Protection of Commercial Speech" (case note), 41 *Vand. L. Rev.,* 173–206 (January 1988).

Pearson, Vernon R., and Michael O'Neill, "The First Amendment, Commercial Speech, and the Advertising Lawyer," 9 *Univ. of Puget Sound L. Rev.* 293–335 (Winter 1986).

"Symposium: Commercial Speech and the First Amendment," 56 *Univ. of Cincinnati L. Rev.,* 1205–1294 (Spring 1988).

Waterson, M. J., "A New Threat to the Freedom to Advertise; Report on Developments in the United States," *International Journal of Advertising,* Winter 1987, p. 67.

Wilcox, George H., "Toward a Definition of Commercial Speech," 23 *N.E. L. Rev.,* 595–614 (Autumn 1988).

DISCUSSION QUESTIONS

1 What are the different restrictions for noncommercial and commercial speech?
2 What concerns did the two concurring justices (Burger and Stewart) have with the majority opinion? What concerns did the dissenting justice (Rehnquist) have with the majority opinion? Which of the concerns were actually litigated?

SUGGESTED ANSWERS

1 Noncommercial speech is restricted in that one cannot slander or libel others or use fighting words or words that threaten the safety of others or advocate the overthrow of the government. Obscenity may be restricted by the government to certain times, places, or manners.

The same is true for commercial speech. However, commercial speech must be factually true or it is not protected by the First Amendment. This requirement does not apply to noncommercial speech because it is hard to judge if a person's beliefs or ideas are factually true. Many times, in noncommercial speech, one person's truth is not another's.

2 Chief Justice Burger was concerned that other professionals, such as lawyers and doctors, might assert that they also have the right to advertise. This was litigated, and the Court held that lawyers did have the right to advertise.

Justice Stewart was concerned that the distinction between noncommercial and commercial speech be preserved. This issue has never been litigated, and the difference remains.

Justice Rehnquist saw the majority decision as extending the right to sue to consumers and that this could bring consumer challenges to bans on other professional advertising. Justice Rehnquist was wrong in one sense, but right in another. The suit regarding the ban on attorney advertising was not brought by a consumer, but by an attorney. A case where a consumer sued protesting governmental restrictions on advertising was the college student who protested the restriction of no commercial speech being allowed in his dorm room.

Justice Rehnquist was also concerned that giving First Amendment protection to truthful commercial speech would allow certain products to be advertised. He specified cigarette advertising in particular. Although cigarette advertising is legal, it is still prohibited from television and radio. The cigarette advertisers never challenged this restriction.

INTERNATIONAL LAW:
Scherk v. Alberto-Culver Co.

Carolyn Hotchkiss
Babson College

INTRODUCTION

The emerging global operating environment for business in the United States presents new risks and opportunities for businesses of all sizes. Improvements in transportation and technology are leading to international customer bases for goods, services, and technology, as well as to international opportunities for investment of capital. Yet, these new markets may be relatively unfamiliar to U.S. traders, both in terms of the demand for products or services, and in terms of the political and legal environment.

Whatever the form of international trade or investment, the foundation of the international business transaction is the contract between the parties involved. Contracts in international business transactions serve several important functions. First, the terms of the contract set the parameters of the relationship between the parties. The specific terms detail what each party must do. Second, the contract serves as a method of risk reduction; it defines the scope of the obligations of the parties. Third, where risk is inevitable, the contract functions as a risk allocation device, putting the risks of nonperformance, nonpayment, or of unforeseen circumstances on one party or the other.

The contract makes up the primary legal environment for the parties to an international transaction. Its enforceability in the courts of any country involved with the transaction is an important factor in the success of the transaction. On a broader level, the enforceability of contracts is one of the elements influencing a country's ability to compete internationally. In the United States, courts have not always honored the intentions of parties to international contracts, preferring sometimes to substitute their standards of perfor-

52

mance for those of the parties. The Supreme Court's decision in *Scherk v. Alberto-Culver Co.,* 417 U.S. 506 (1974), stands as a landmark for freedom of contract and for the importance of international commerce.

The Conflict of Laws Problem

No matter how careful the parties are in drafting their contract, the terms will not cover all possible future events. Nor can the contractual promises of the parties violate other substantive laws, as would, for example, a contract agreeing to fix prices among competitors. In these circumstances, and for enforcement in the event of a breach of contract, the parties will have to look to the legal system for resolution of their disputes. The legal system provides both substantive and procedural ground rules for the business transaction.

By definition, the international business transaction involves business in more than one country. It thus involves more than one legal system and more than one set of possible rules for resolving disputes. These laws may vary widely, reflecting the different cultural and economic values of the countries involved. Where there is a potential conflict of law, the risk to participants in an international transaction grows in tandem with the level of legal uncertainty.

When two or more legal systems touch upon a business transaction, the contracting parties should be concerned about which set of laws will apply in the event of litigation. Different legal systems have no consistent solution to the conflict of law problem. In litigation, some courts apply the law of the place where the parties made the contract. Courts in other countries apply the law of the place where the parties performed their obligations under the contract. Still other courts look to the law of the place of the breach, and others analyze the contract and apply the law of the place with the most significant contracts. Sometimes, a court will apply the law providing the most favorable outcome for its nationals, whereas occasionally, a court will simply apply its own law, no matter what other law may have relevance to the transaction.

The uncertainty over which law applies to an international business transaction creates practical problems when a business deal sours. Each party may race to the courts of the forum most convenient to it, or with the most favorable substantive law. One party may find itself forced to defend a suit brought in a distant court, using unfamiliar legal practices, in a court that may or may not treat nonnationals fairly. The time and expense associated with defending an action in such a forum may make settlement at any cost a better alternative than pursuing a rightful claim.

The Contractual Solution

As part of the risk reduction and allocation functions of an international business contract, the parties will often include choice of forum and choice of law clauses, by which they will choose the setting for resolving disputes and the substantive law to govern their business relationship. For example, a contract might provide that all disputes arising from the contract will be brought before the courts of the state of California, and be governed by California law. A popular form of the choice of forum clause agrees to submit any dispute to binding arbitration. International disputes are often referred to the arbitration service of the International Chamber of Commerce in Paris, the American Arbitration Association, or, if one party is from a socialist country, to arbitration before the Stockholm Chamber of Commerce.

Enforceability

Choice-of-forum and choice-of-law clauses help achieve the goal of certainty in international business transactions. Yet their effectiveness is limited to the extent to which a judge in an inappropriate forum chooses to make the parties adhere to their contract. Suppose that a contract between a Swiss buyer and an American seller provides that all disputes will be brought in Swiss courts, and that Swiss law will govern the contract. If the American seller brings suit in its home state of New York, the effectiveness of the contract provisions is limited to the extent to which the New York court refuses to hear the case. If the court in New York decides the case, the contract has not served its intended function as a risk reduction and allocation mechanism. The same level of uncertainty exists when the parties have not attempted to structure the ground rules for their transaction.

Until the 1970s, the enforceability of choice-of-law and choice-of-forum clauses in the United States was erratic. Judges were particularly wary of arbitration clauses, as they sometimes put the interpretation of U.S. law into the hands of nonlawyers. In 1972, however, the Supreme Court sent its first message to lower court judges to enforce contractual dispute resolution clauses. In *M/S Bremen v. Zapata Off-Shore Co.*, 407 U.S. 1 (1972), the Court held that, ordinarily, a court should respect a contract clause choosing a forum and a law to resolve disputes.

The Bremen involved a straightforward contractual problem. A U.S. business chartered a German tug to tow an offshore oil rig from Texas to Italy. The contract provided that all disputes would be heard in court in London. When the rig suffered damage in a storm off the coast of Florida, the owners brought suit in Tampa.

In upholding the contract language, the Court recognized the choice of London as a reasonable compromise between the parties, even though the United Kingdom had no connection to the contract. The Court also recognized that the need for certainty in international contracts could outweigh the interest that the U.S. courts might have in deciding a contract dispute. The Court held that in order to overturn a choice-of-forum clause, a party would have to make a showing of some special circumstances outweighing the interest of certainty in the transaction.

The measure of the Supreme Court's commitment to freedom of contract in international transactions came two years later, in the case of *Scherk v. Alberto-Culver Co.*, 417 U.S. 506 (1974). The Court's decision in *Scherk* marked an important shift in the Court's view of the importance of certainty in international commercial transactions, relative to the importance of applying U.S. law to a transaction.

SCHERK V. ALBERTO-CULVER CO.

Alberto-Culver is a Delaware corporation, headquartered in Illinois, that is best know for its toiletries and hair care products. As part of an overseas expansion, it agreed to purchase three businesses from Scherk. The three businesses were organized under the laws of Germany and Liechtenstein for the purpose of marketing cosmetics in Europe. In 1969 Alberto-Culver signed a contract in Vienna to purchase all the stock and the assets of Scherk's businesses, including all of Scherk's trademark rights in his products.

The contract contained two clauses that would be central to the future dispute between the parties. First, it contained a warranty by Scherk that he held sole, unencumbered ownership of his trademarks. Second, the contract contained a clause requiring the parties to arbitrate all disputes arising from the contract or its breach before the International Chamber of Commerce in Paris, using Illinois law as the governing law of the contract.

About a year after the closing of the deal, Alberto-Culver discovered that Scherk did not have clear, unencumbered ownership of the trademarks he sold, and that other parties might be able to claim trademark rights superior to Alberto-Culver's. The company offered to rescind the contract, but Scherk refused. Alberto-Culver then sued Scherk in federal court in Illinois, charging in part that Scherk's guarantee regarding the ownership of his trademarks constituted fraud in connection with the purchase or sale of securities in violation of Rule 10b-5 under the Securities Exchange Act of 1934.

In response to the lawsuit, Scherk asked the court to dismiss the case pending arbitration in Paris under the contractual choice-of-forum clause. Alberto-Culver then asked the court to enjoin the arbitration, on the ground that the public policy interest of the United States in preventing securities fraud outweighed the interest in upholding the private agreement of the parties. The district court granted the injunction against arbitration, and the court of appeals affirmed.

The court of appeals' decision in favor of Alberto-Culver relied heavily upon the fact that the purchase of Scherk's businesses involved the purchase of securities. In drafting the securities laws, Congress provided investors with the protection of a forum in federal court. Parties should not be able to waive the protection Congress provided them through the use of contractual arbitration clauses. The respect that *The Bremen* indicated courts should ordinarily afford to freedom of contract should not apply when the Congress had expressed so clearly the public interest of the United States in the prevention of securities fraud. Where the contract clause would erode public policy, it should be invalidated.

The Majority Decision

In a 5-4 decision, the Supreme Court reversed the lower court decisions in favor of Alberto-Culver, holding that the intent of the parties, as expressed in the contract, should prevail, even when one party to the contract alleges securities fraud. The majority—Justices Stewart, Blackmun, Burger, Powell, and Rehnquist—looked to the special nature of the international contract as a foundation for their decision.

The Court first noted the risk to the parties caused by the possible application of more than one substantive law. This wasn't a contract between two U.S. businesses where federal law would certainly apply. Rather, the contract involved an American buyer and a German seller, transferring businesses organized in Germany and Liechtenstein. The contract was negotiated in the United States, England, and Germany and signed in Austria; the deal closed in Switzerland. The trademark rights at issue involved markets in several European nations. Any one of these legal systems could arguably provide the legal rules determining the rights of the parties. In these circumstances, the use of choice-of-forum and choice-of-law clauses was a sensible way to reduce the risk of conflict.

> Such uncertainty will almost always inevitably exist with respect to any contract touching two or more legal systems, each with its own substantive laws and conflict of laws rules. A contractual provision specifying in advance the forum in which disputes shall be litigated and the law to be applied is, therefore, an almost indispensable precondition to achievement of the orderliness and predictability essential to any international business transaction. Furthermore, such a provision obviates the danger that a dispute under the agreement might be submitted to a forum hostile to the interests of one of the parties or unfamiliar with the problem area involved.[1]

The Court, in reaching its decision in favor of Scherk, tilted the balance between national and international policy interests decidedly in favor of international interests. The Court envisioned the consequences of failing to uphold the contract choice-of-forum clause as creating "destructive jockeying by the parties to secure tactical litigation advantages."[2] If Alberto-Culver could go to court in the United States to prevent arbitration, what would prevent Scherk, in different circumstances, from seeking a similar court order in a European court? The Court recognized that what it called this "dicey atmosphere of such a legal no-man's land"[3] would have a negative effect on international commerce, possibly making traders less willing to enter into contracts with U.S. businesses.

[1] 417 U.S. at 516.
[2] *Id.* at 517.
[3] *Id.*

The Dissent

Justice Douglas, joined by Justices Brennan, White, and Marshall, in dissent would have balanced the public policy interests differently, favoring the application of the securities laws over the needs of international commerce. Justice Douglas' first concern was with the availability of a remedy under the securities laws:

> Those laws are rendered a chimera when foreign corporations or funds—unlike domestic defendants—can nullify them by virtue of arbitration clauses which send defrauded American investors to the uncertainty of arbitration on foreign soil, or, if those investors cannot afford to arbitrate their claims in a far-off forum, to no remedy at all.[4]

More significant to the dissenters was the notion that U.S. investors should receive the protection against fraud of U.S. law, no matter what the country of origin of the defrauder. "It is important that American standards of fairness in, security dealings govern the destinies of American investors until Congress changes these standards."[5]

Scherk's Significance

Scherk represented a real turning point for the Supreme Court in cases involving choice-of-law and choice-of-forum clauses. It marked, although by the narrowest margin, the demise of the viewpoint that only U.S. judges in U.S. courts could adequately protect U.S. business interests. The majority decision in *Scherk* also marked an acceptance of the role of arbitrators in resolving international business disputes. The decision sent a strong signal to lower court judges around the country to respect and enforce the choices expressed in contracts, even when the contract dispute involves public policy issues.

Perhaps of greatest significance for the long-term interests of U.S. businesses, the Court's decision sent a message beyond U.S. borders to the international business community. The Court recognized that the needs of international business might be different, at least in degree, from the needs of traders in purely domestic transactions. Because more than one legal system could exercise its authority over an international transaction, the potential for conflict would be much higher in an international transaction than in a domestic transaction. Because laws could vary substantially among legal systems, the parties would have a high need for negotiated certainty in their transaction. The Court's decision encouraging negotiated methods of dispute resolution encouraged international traders and investors to do business with U.S. businesses, with the knowledge that their contractual provisions would be honored in U.S. courts.

[4] *Id*. at 533.
[5] *Id*. at 528.

Recent Developments

The *Scherk* decision provided a foundation for a large number of lower court decisions upholding contractual choice-of-law and choice-of-forum clauses. In domestic transactions, *Scherk* has encouraged the enforcement of arbitration clauses in a variety of contexts. Recently, the Supreme Court used *Scherk* as a precedent in upholding arbitration clauses between customers and securities dealers. *See, Shearson/American Express, Inc. v. McMahon,* 482 U.S. 220 (1987).

In international transactions, litigants have continued to look for the kinds of special circumstances that will invalidate choice-of-forum and choice-of-law clauses, allowing litigation in federal court. The most important test of the Supreme Court's resolve to uphold *Scherk* in the international area came in *Mitsubishi Motors Corp. v. Soler Chrysler-Plymouth, Inc.,* 473 U.S. 614 (1985).

Mitsubishi was a joint venture between Chrysler International S.A., a Swiss corporation, and Mitsubishi Heavy Industries, Inc., a Japanese corporation. The purpose of the joint venture was to market Mitsubishi-made cars through Chrysler dealers. Soler signed a distributor agreement with Chrysler and a purchase agreement with Mitsubishi, allowing Soler to buy cars from Mitsubishi for resale in San Juan, Puerto Rico. The purchase agreement provided for arbitration in Japan by the Japan Commercial Arbitration Association.

Initially, sales of Mitsubishi cars were brisk, and the parties raised the minimum numbers of cars Soler would purchase under the contract. When demand slumped in 1979, however, the parties began to quarrel over contract performance. Soler sought delays in shipment, then sought to have some cars shipped for resale in the continental United States and in Latin America. Mitsubishi refused to comply with Soler's orders, and ultimately withheld shipment of nearly 1000 cars.

Mitsubishi sued in federal district court in Puerto Rico, seeking an order compelling arbitration, then filed a request for arbitration in Japan. Soler counterclaimed in federal court, asserting breach of contract, defamation, and antitrust violations, among other claims. The district court, relying on *Scherk,* ordered arbitration of all claims. The court of appeals affirmed, but it ruled that the antitrust claims were nonarbitrable. It based its decision against arbitrability on the public interest in the enforcement of the antitrust laws, holding that the public interest in adequate enforcement of antitrust protection was the kind of special showing needed under *The Bremen* and *Scherk* to invalidate a contractual choice-of-forum clause.

The Supreme Court, citing *Scherk,* ordered arbitration of the antitrust claims. Once again, the Court relied on the special nature of the international transaction:

> As in *Scherk v. Alberto-Culver Co.,* 417 U.S. 506 (1974), we conclude that concerns of international comity, respect for the capacities of foreign and transnational tribunals, and sensitivity to the need of the international commercial system for predict-

ability in the resolution of disputes require that we enforce the parties' agreement, even assuming that a contrary result would be forthcoming in a domestic context.[6]

Soler argued that the special nature of antitrust claims made them unsuitable for arbitration, especially in a foreign forum. The Court rejected the contentions that antitrust claims were too complex for arbitrators to understand, and too important to be entrusted to arbitrators who might not be lawyers. The Court further rejected the notion that allegations of antitrust violations made the entire contract suspect, including the choice-of-law and choice-of-forum provisions. Finally, the Court saw no reason to presume that arbitrators would not appropriately give effect to the antitrust laws.

Mitsubishi reaffirms and strengthens the *Scherk* decision in favor of freedom of contract. It signals the Supreme Court's support for negotiated dispute resolution in international commerce, even where one party alleges statutory causes of action, such as antitrust. It indicates that allegations that would invalidate choice-of-law and choice-of-forum clauses will get very close scrutiny from the courts, and that courts should only rarely overturn the parties' choices.

MANAGERIAL IMPLICATIONS

Choice-of-forum and choice-of-law clauses are common elements in international contracts. Often they are found buried deeply in the fine print, inserted by attorneys for one side, and accepted without negotiation by the other. They come into play only when there is a problem with the business transaction, so in the optimism at the start of every business dealing, the parties may assume that they will never need to use the clauses.

The lesson of *Scherk* for managers is that the fine print in an international contract is important. Absent some compelling, highly unusual circumstance, courts will presume that contract terms are the freely negotiated choices of the parties. Courts will enforce those choices, holding the parties to their bargain. Thus, if the protection of some U.S. law, such as the antitrust laws, the securities laws, or the Racketeer Influenced and Corrupt Organizations Act (RICO), is important, the choice-of-law clause must specify the applicability of a state or federal law. If a party does not want to have to litigate or arbitrate a dispute in a distant forum, it must negotiate a more convenient choice. Note that after the decision in *Mitsubishi*, Soler had to go to Japan to arbitrate its dispute.

Now that the enforceability of choice-of-law and choice-of-forum clauses is relatively certain in U.S. courts, a U.S. business might inquire about the enforceability of these clauses in courts in other countries. It does little good to negotiate an arbitration clause in a contract with a business in Australia if the Australian courts will hear a case brought in violation of the arbitration clause.

---

[6]473 U.S. at 629.

A second lesson of *Scherk* is that the enforceability of choice-of-forum and choice-of-law clauses is one factor in the risk analysis that every business should undertake before choosing to do business in another country.

The willingness of a nation to honor contractual dispute resolution measures is a good indicator of its status as a member of the international commercial community. Although acceptance varies among nations, most of the free-market industrialized nations willingly recognize private choices. Increasingly, socialist countries recognize the importance of contractual choice-of-law and choice-of-forum clauses in inducing Western nations to enter into trade and investment relationships. The difficult nations are those with unstable political and legal systems. Changes in political leadership, nationalist movements, and rebellions may make a written contract difficult to enforce or even lead to kangaroo court actions in the foreign nation and the seizure of assets abroad. A prudent business will assess the likelihood that courts in the countries with which it does business will enforce private contracts, before engaging in an international business transaction.

CONCLUSION

Scherk stands as a milestone in U.S. international trade law. It marks a new willingness of the U.S. legal system to participate in the international commercial community. By improving the ability of business to control the risks of their business transactions, *Scherk* invited foreign firms to participate in the U.S. market and opened the door to more U.S. participation in foreign markets. American courts now recognize that international commerce involves special considerations not always present domestically. *Scherk* sends the message that U.S. traders will honor their contracts.

REFERENCES

Branson, David, and Richard Wallace, "Choosing the Substantive Law to Apply in International Commercial Arbitration," 27 *Va. J. Int'l L.* 39 (1986).

Buchanan, Mark, "Public Policy and International Arbitration," 26 *Am. Bus. L.J.* 511 (1988).

Gabor, Francis, "Stepchild of the New Lex Mercatoria: Private International Law from the United States Perspective," 8 *Nw. J. Int'l L. & Bus.* 538 (1988).

Gilbert, James, "Choice of Forum Clauses in International and Interstate Contracts," 65 *Ky. L.J.* 1 (1976).

Greenberg, Marcia, "International Contracts: Problems of Drafting and Interpreting, and the Need for Uniform Judicial Approaches," 5 *B.U. Int'l L.J.* 363 (1987).

Gruson, Michael, "Forum-Selection Clauses in International and Interstate Commercial Agreements," 1982 *U. Ill. L. Rev.* 133.

Note, "Arbitration, Forum Selection, and Choice of Law Agreements in International Securities Transactions," 42 *Wash. & Lee L. Rev.* 1069 (1985).

Note, "General Principles of Law in International Commercial Arbitration," 101 *Harv. L. Rev.* 1816 (1988).

Salter, Leonard, "International Commercial Arbitration: The Why, How, and Where,"
88 *Comm. L.J.* 381 (1983).
Rhodes, James, and Lisa Sloan, "The Pitfalls of International Commercial Arbitration," 17 *Vand. J. Trans. L.* 19 (1984).

DISCUSSION QUESTIONS

1 What is the difference between a choice-of-law clause and a choice-of-forum clause?
2 Why are choice-of-law and choice-of-forum clauses so important in international business contracts?
3 Under what circumstances would parties to an international business contract choose to arbitrate disputes rather than use court systems?
4 What factors should a manager consider when negotiating choice-of-law and choice-of-forum clauses in international contracts?
5 After *The Bremen, Scherk,* and *Mitsubishi,* in what circumstances would a U.S. court tend *not* to uphold a contractual choice-of-law or choice-of-forum clause?
6 Under what circumstances would a foreign court fail to enforce a contractual choice-of-law or choice-of-forum clause?

SUGGESTED ANSWERS

1 A choice-of-law clause specifies the substantive law that will govern disputes between parties to a contract. A choice-of-forum clause selects the court or the form of alternative dispute resolution the parties will use to resolve contract problems. For example, the contract between Scherk and Alberto-Culver contained a clause choosing the law of Illinois as the substantive law of the contract. It also contained a choice-of-forum clause requiring arbitration of contract disputes before the International Chamber of Commerce.
2 These contract clauses offer managers predictability in the resolution of contract disputes. Predictability lowers the risk of doing business internationally, and thus helps managers control the costs of doing business.
3 Arbitration is a favored method of dispute resolution in international business for many reasons. It often costs less than litigation. Arbitrators, particularly in the major arbitral centers, tend to be more knowledgeable in the practices of international business than judges in local courts. Arbitration tends to be faster than litigation. Arbitration usually results in much less publicity than lawsuits.
4 The chief factor in negotiating a choice-of-law clause will be the differences in the substantive laws that might apply to the contract. Laws to consider would include contract law, products liability, business torts, and competitive practices. For a choice-of-forum clause, negotiators should consider first whether to use courts or alternative methods of dispute resolution, then look at the level of knowledge judges or arbitrators would have about business, the convenience to the parties of going to the forum, the cost and length of the process, and the likelihood of a fair hearing.
5 The answer is not entirely clear. However, the three court decisions and related law on the enforcement of foreign judgments would seem to indicate four situations in which a U.S. court would hear a case despite contrary contractual provisions. The first would require a party to show that honoring the clause would deny due process—that is, notice and an opportunity to be heard. This due process argument

might also cover instances of obvious corruption in the chosen forum. The second situation would involve a compelling U.S. government interest. The language of *Mitsubishi* leaves the door open for plaintiffs to make this argument, although what that compelling interest might be is unclear. The third situation would involve adhesion contracts, where the plaintiff had no real choice but to agree to the contract clauses. It would be unusual to find this circumstance in an international business transaction. The fourth situation involves subjecting a U.S. person or business to a forum obviously biased against the United States. This is essentially a political judgment by U.S. courts, and has arisen in past cases involving the Soviet Union and Iran, among others.

6 This risk is one a manager must evaluate when entering a business relationship involving a foreign country. A few countries freely state intentions to apply their law to a contract despite the intentions of the parties. In most cases, though, problems in the enforcement of contract provisions come about as a result of changes of government, revolution, war, or other major political change.

PART THREE

THE AMERICAN
LEGAL SYSTEM

5

THE CONSTITUTIONALITY OF REGULATING BUSINESS:
Judicial Review of the Interstate Commerce Clause Since *Gibbons v. Ogdon*

Carol J. Miller
Southwest Missouri State University

INTRODUCTION

The Interstate Commerce Clause, in Article 1, Section 8, Clause 3 of the U.S. Constitution, serves as the vortex for congressional regulation of business and commercial activities. With an ever-expanding definition of the nature of commerce and "that which affects commerce," and is thus "necessary and proper" to the regulation of commerce, Congress now legislates social agenda in the workplace. Use of the Interstate Commerce Clause in modern times has justified the application of the Civil Rights Act of 1964 to the private sector, mandating integration of hotels, race- and sex-neutral hiring practices, and affirmative action plans in the 1970s and early 1980s. The Supreme Court's view of the activities permissible for congressional regulation under this clause has broadened significantly since the turn of the century Gilded Age's narrow perspective. Areas formerly available for state regulation have been narrowed during the past 150 years and in some cases have been preempted by federal legislation. As long as the state regulation does not place an "undue burden on interstate commerce," state laws may still regulate some areas that "affect" commerce.

Regulation of the transportation industry is firmly linked to congressional power to regulate interstate and foreign commerce. Recognized early in U.S. history as constitutional subject matter for federal regulation, components of the transportation industry have often been a permissible area for expansion of regulatory power in interstate commerce. Federal licensing of steamboats formed the background for the first U.S. Supreme Court case which clearly upheld the power of Congress to regulate transportation. In the post–Civil War era, when rapid expansion of the railroads facilitated the market expansion and transportation of new industrialized goods to more remote markets, this form of transportation would be the subject of the first federal independent regulatory agency (the Interstate Commerce Commission). When laws focusing on economic regulation of the workplace were being struck down in the early 1900s, the first laws to be upheld were again directed toward the railroad industry (governing working conditions and hours restrictions). It would be the interstate transportation industry which served as a vehicle for expanding the federal civil rights agenda in the 1960s. By the 1970s and 1980s the emphasis shifted to the airline industry, and, as environmental concerns over second hand smoking became documented, smoking on flights of six hours or less on domestic airlines would be banned by 1990. After heavy regulation in the 1960s and 1970s, the routes of the airline and trucking industries were all regulated in the 1980s, leading to fierce competition, bankruptcies, and safety-impairment concerns.

The power of the Supreme Court to determine the constitutionality of congressional laws has long been recognized. In support of judicial review by the courts, Alexander Hamilton noted in THE FEDERALIST papers in the 1780s that "interpretation of the laws is the proper and peculiar province of the courts" and that "[n]o legislative act,...contrary to the Constitution, can be valid." At the height of political controversy between Federalists and Jeffersonians, a nonbusiness act of Congress was first declared unconstitutional in the landmark case of *Marbury v. Madison,* 5 U.S. (1 Cranch 137) (1803). The power of judicial review of legislation would be extended in future cases to the interpretation of state and federal regulation of competitive behavior and industry practices during the nineteenth and twentieth centuries.

GIBBONS V. OGDON

It seems only fitting that the first landmark case interpreting congressional power under the Interstate Commerce Clause was a transportation case. *Gibbons v. Ogdon,* 9 Wheaton 1, 6 L. Ed. 23 (1824) was the premier case upholding federal licensing practices on interstate waterways. Skeptical legislators granted Robert R. Livingston a 20-year license to navigate streams and rivers of New York State, provided that he could develop a boat that could travel at least 4 miles per hour. By 1807 Livingston and his partner, Robert Fulton, had successfully navigated New York's waterway with a steamboat. Renewal of this New York license and an exclusive license in the waterways of the Louisiana Territory gave Livingston and his partner, Robert Fulton, monopolistic control of much of commercial steam navigation. Other states passed retaliatory acts, and commercial warfare resulted. Ogdon had acquired a license from Fulton/Livingston, while Gibbons (partner turned rival) secured a federal license to operate steamboats between New Jersey and New York.

Because Gibbons was carrying human passengers rather than goods or commodities, Ogdon argued that Congress was without constitutional authority to issue Gibbons a license via the Commerce Clause. The Supreme Court under John Marshall did not adopt this narrow view of commerce, however, refusing to cripple federal power, in what was also hailed as the first "antitrust" decision. Commerce was viewed as more than trafficking goods; the regulation of commerce necessitated laws concerning navigation. Adopting the perspective of its advocate, Daniel Webster, the case of *Gibbons v. Ogdon* established the right of Congress to regulate activities of the transportation industry that involve movement of goods or people on navigable rivers or across state boundaries. A century later, the Tennessee Valley Authority's (TVA) federally sponsored dam-building activities would also be construed as within the federal government's power to provide for national defense and to regulate navigable streams.[1]

The importance of the *Gibbons v. Ogdon* case, as noted by historian Harry Scheiber, was that the United States would have an "internal common market."[2] Under the Articles of Incorporation, the United States had been a league of friendship, politically drawn together to provide for the common defense. Lack of economic and commercial cohesiveness was its major downfall, as each state retained its own authority to regulate business and economic practices. Even after the states were joined into a federal system under the Constitution, states maintained power to regulate matters of health, safety, and welfare under state police powers. Substantial control over regulation of commercial activities, however, was vested in the national government.

As the 12 countries of the European Community (EC) strive toward integration and free flow of goods, capital, labor, and services across their borders under "1992" policies, these country-states are also progressing toward an "internal common market." A federal system of sorts is developing in Europe for the regulation of business practices. What lessons can the Europeans learn from the evolution of a federal regulatory system in the United States? Firms in the United States need to consider what managerial adjustments need to be made to adapt to "1992" policies and establish a competitive foothold in the emerging European market regulated by both EC directives and nation-state laws.

APPLICATION OF GIBBONS V. OGDON

Although *Gibbons v. Ogdon* established the right of the federal government to regulate interstate commerce, rulings in the mid-1800s suggest that states also had some power to regulate interstate commerce. This perception would eventually develop into the "undue burdens" test. In the *License Cases*, 5 Howard 504 (1847), and *Cooley v. Board of Wardens*, 12 Howard 299 (1851), the Su-

---

[1] *Ashwander v. TVA*, 297 U.S. 288 (1936).
[2] Harry N. Scheiber, "The Road to Munn: Eminent Domain and the Concept of Public Purpose in the State Courts, *Perspectives in American History*, vol. 5, 1971.

preme Court ruled that states would continue to have a concurrent power to regulate interstate commerce in the absence of federal legislation.

With these cases in mind, states began to regulate unfair railroad practices after the Civil War through what became known as "Granger laws." Farmers and small businesspeople complained against discriminatory rebates (given only to large corporate shippers) and about unfair rail charges (which cost Iowa grain shippers more to ship goods from nearby farms to the Mississippi River than it cost to ship goods from the interior directly to Chicago). In response, Granger laws were passed by state legislatures in the 1870s, most notably in Illinois, Iowa, Minnesota, and Wisconsin. The railroads challenged these laws, temporarily without success on due process grounds, arguing that rate setting and regulation by the state was an unconstitutional taking of property and profits.[3] In what was considered "the Supreme Court's first major statement on the constitutionality of regulating the new industrial capitalization," this Chicago grain elevator case and the seven accompanying railroad cases were decided by the Supreme Court in the mid-1870s, temporarily upholding the constitutionality of the state statutes as within state's police power.

Interpretation of the Interstate Commerce Clause of the Constitution in *Walbash, St. Louis and Pacific RR Co. v. Illinois*, 118 U.S. 557 (1886), however, carved out an opportunity for expansive new federal legislation on rates of interstate shipments, while removing such regulatory power from the states. Congressional power to regulate interstate commerce was to be exclusive. In declaring the state Granger law legislation unconstitutional, the Supreme Court opened the door for the creation of the first federal independent regulatory agency, the Interstate Commerce Commission (ICC) in 1887 and for the passage of the Sherman Antitrust Act in 1990.

Most cases in the latter portion of the nineteenth century favored big business and management practices, limiting the application of business regulation and oversight. The category of "public enterprises," which *Munn* had recognized as suitable for regulation, was narrowed. Initially forestalling federal attempts to break up the American Sugar Refining Company sugar trust in the case of *United States v. E. C. Knight Co.*, 156 U.S. 1 (1895), the Court distinguished between "manufacturing and commerce." Despite one case invalidating a market-allocation scheme,[4] most early cases were not construed to break up managerial big business. Instead the Sherman Antitrust Act was initially directed against labor unions, alleging that they were a restraint on trade. In response, the Clayton Act in 1914 established some protection for the legitimacy of labor unions.

During the Progressive Era, the *Northern Securities* case returned to the more traditional area of regulation (transportation), and took a more expansive view of the Interstate Commerce Clause, striking down the monopolistic rela-

---

[3] *Munn v. Illinois*, 94 U. S. 113 (1877).
[4] *Addyston Pipe and Steel Co. v. U.S.*, 175 U.S. 211 (1899).

tionship of a railroad holding company under the Sherman Antitrust Act. Stock transactions that created illegal combinations were deemed to be in restraint of trade.[5] The ICC's regulatory power was also increased through the Elkins Act of 1903, the Hepburn Act, and the Mann-Elkins Act of 1910. More importantly, the ICC was granted the power to establish rates and issue binding orders, with the burden of proof and appeal shifted to the challenger of the regulation.

Other breakups of monopolistic interests under the Sherman Antitrust Act followed. With the breakup of Standard Oil, the Supreme Court announced its "Rule of Reason." Size was not to be the sole criterion used in determining whether or not a business violated the act. Only "bad" corporations that used anticompetitive devices to secure their monopolistic position would be broken up. "Bad" tactics presumably included price fixing, discriminatory freight rebates, predatory price cutting, exclusive dealing contracts, and tieing agreements—the kinds of activities determined to "substantially lessen competition" under the 1914 Clayton Act. In 1911, under the "Rule of Reason," Duke's American Tobacco Co. was subdivided into what constitute four of the Big 6 U.S. tobacco companies today,[6] and in 1905, the "beef trust" was found in violation of antitrust laws in *Swift & Co. v. United States,* 196 U.S. 375 (1905). The United Shoe Machinery Company (1918) and the United States Steel Corporation (1920) were allowed to survive, however, because they presumably had not engaged in prohibited practices to gain their dominant positions. Charged with the duty to regulate against "unfair methods of competition" (and later deceptive acts and practices), the Federal Trade Commission (FTC) was established in 1914.

Just as "bad" monopolies could be broken up, "bad" or dangerous products and practices could be banned from interstate commerce. In 1895 Congress banned the use of interstate commerce and mails for the distribution of lottery tickets. Finding these lottery tickets to be articles of commerce, the Supreme Court upheld the constitutionality of the law.[7] Muckraker journalism, such as *The Jungle* by Upton Sinclair, prompted the passage of the Pure Food and Drug Act in 1906 and the Meat Inspection Acts of 1906 and 1907, which banned misbranded, adulterated, or diseased food from interstate commerce.

Nonetheless, for almost a half century, narrow interpretations of the Interstate Commerce Clause would be a stumbling block to federal regulation of manufacturing practices. The distinction between "commerce" and "manufacturing," established in the 1895 case of *United States v. E. C. Knight Co.* gradually eroded to permit the regulation of the shipment of manufactured goods. Similarly, mining was distinguished from commerce in *Oliver Iron Mining Co. v. Lord,* 262 U.S. 172 (1923). Politics and policy would again be a source of controversy as the Supreme Court struck down several key pieces of

---

[5] *Northern Securities Co. v. United States,* 193 U.S. 197 (1904).
[6] *United States v. American Tobacco Co.,* 221 U.S. 106 (1911).
[7] *Champion v. Ames,* 365 U.S. 321 (1903).

New Deal legislation supported by President Franklin D. Roosevelt. In 1936 key acts were declared unconstitutional, including the Agricultural Adjustment Act of 1933[8] and the National Industrial Recovery Act (in the "Sick Chicken Case," *Schechter Poultry Corp. v. United States*).[9]

Faced with these constitutional challenges to his agenda, President Roosevelt threatened to pack the court with additional judges who were more judicially inclined to his perspective. The Supreme Court in the Marshall era had six judges; it had been expanded to nine judges by the twentieth century. Only some congressional reluctance toward political engineering of the Court and the Court's subsequent declaration of constitutionality of several laws prevented the expansion of the Supreme Court to 12 members. Relying on the Interstate Commerce Clause rather than on the taxing, spending, and general welfare clauses of the Constitution, the second Agricultural Adjustment Act of 1938 and its establishment of commodity quotas would withstand Supreme Court scrutiny in *Mulford v. Smith,* 307 U.S. 38 (1939). *Mulford v. Smith* permitted the establishment of marketing quotas for flue-cured tobacco, reasoning that it was regulating the "throat where tobacco enters the stream of commerce—the marketing warehouse."

Early cases also distinguished between "direct" and "indirect" regulation of commerce. Even as late as 1936, the Supreme Court struck down the Guffy Coal Act, declaring that the internal relations between management and workers did not have a "direct" effect on interstate commerce.[10] Further inhibiting federal legislation was the *Hammer v. Dagenhart* decision in 1918, which distinguished permissible regulation of "goods" flowing in interstate commerce from impermissible regulation of "conditions" under which those goods were produced.[11] In the latter case, federal legislation, aimed at restricting the use of child labor by banning the interstate transportation of goods manufactured with child labor, was declared unconstitutional. It was not until 1941 that the *Hammer* case's view of commerce would be explicitly overturned in *United States v. Darby,* 312 U.S. 100, 61 S. Ct. 451, 85 L. Ed. 609 (1941), a case upholding the constitutionality of the 1938 federal Fair Labor Standards Act.

In the interim, regulation of management practices was left primarily to the states. By 1917, 37 states had legislation limiting or banning use of child labor. Although even some early state laws were invalidated based on economic theory, as unlawful interference with the right to contract, most state laws were upheld. In *Muller v. Oregon,* 208 U.S. 412 (1908), the Supreme Court held that an Oregon law restricting the maximum number of working hours for women did not impair the Fourteenth Amendment's liberty of contract concept. Although the federal government initially had been limited in its extension of protective labor legislation to the private sector, Congress did pass laws in arenas

[8]*United States v. Butler,* 297 U.S. 1 (1936).
[9]295 U.S. 495 (1936).
[10]*Carter v. Carter Coal Co.,* 298 U.S. 238 (1936).
[11]247 U.S. 251 (1918), construing the Keating-Owen Child Labor Act of 1916.

more clearly within the traditional parameters of the Commerce Clause, such as the La Follette Seaman's Act in 1915 and the Adamson Act of 1916. The latter limited the maximum daily working hours of railroad employees to 8 hours a day [upheld in *Wilson v. New*, 243 U.S. 332 (1917)].

The case of *NLRB v. Jones & Laughlin Steel Corp.*, 301 U.S. 1 (1937), marked a turn of the tide for the constitutionality of labor relations laws. Shortly after the Supreme Court struck down the National Industrial Recovery Act, Congress passed the National Labor Relations Act (Wagner Act), designating a list of "unfair labor practices" and establishing the National Labor Relations Board (NLRB), which would have investigatory power and authority to issue "cease and desist orders" when it found the occurrence of egregious practices. As the premier act regulating the relationship between labor and capital, the Wagner Act targeted labor disputes that "burdened or obstructed interstate commerce." In upholding the constitutionality of this act, the Supreme Court allowed the Commerce Clause to be used to police business practices.

With the *Darby* case in 1941, Congress now had a mandate recognizing its duty to legislate in the area of social problems associated with business practices and a Supreme Court ready to recognize the Interstate Commerce Clause as the vehicle through which that social agenda could be realized. The first comprehensive federal wage and hour law was upheld as constitutional in the *Darby* case; this Fair Labor Standards Act of 1938 prohibited the shipment of products and commodities in interstate commerce if they were produced in violation of minimum wage and maximum hours requirements. An initial minimum wage of 25 cents was established, with a maximum of a 44-hour workweek before overtime pay. Recordkeeping became mandatory. The use of children in hazardous occupations was outlawed, and children under the age of 16 were banned from manufacturing and mining.[12]

In viewing the power of Congress to regulate interstate commerce, the *Darby* Court deemed this power to be plenary.

It extends to those activities intrastate which so *AFFECT interstate commerce* or the exercise of power of Congress over it as to make regulation of them appropriate means to the attainment of a legitimate end, the exercise of the granted power of Congress to regulate interstate commerce....(Emphasis added.)[13]

Activities whose impact on interstate commerce was indirect were now sanctioned for federal oversight. Regulation of that which was "necessary and proper" to regulate interstate commerce now facilitated the regulation of things "affecting commerce."[14] The extension of congressional authority be-

---

[12] *United States v. Darby*, 312 U.S. 100 (1941).
[13] *Id.*
[14] "Elastic Clause" or "Necessary and Proper Clause" of the Constitution, Article 1, Section 8, Clause 18.

yond pure transportation of goods to areas that "affect" commerce laid the foundation for extending the social agenda into the workplace.

The constitutionality of government restrictions on racially discriminatory business practices was slower to be recognized. Civil rights cases of the 1880s refused to forbid private discrimination under the Fourteenth Amendment, and the courts noted that Congress had no general "police power" under which it could regulate discrimination directly. After decades of upholding the "separate but equal" doctrine under the Fourteenth Amendment's Equal Protection Clause, the Supreme Court in 1954 overruled the discriminatory practice it had once condoned in the railroad car case of *Plessy v. Ferguson*.[15] Making inroads in the traditional area of interstate commerce (the transportation industry), the Supreme Court ruled in 1960[16] that a bus terminal was an "integral" part of interstate commerce and that passengers on interstate bus trips could not be segregated on the basis of race.

Passage of the Civil Rights Act of 1964 would mark a new era in government regulation of business practices. In the first significant attempt by Congress to ban race discrimination since the unconstitutional Civil Rights Act of 1875, the Civil Rights Act of 1964 has had a far-reaching effect.

Title II of the Civil Rights Act of 1964 required that:

> All persons shall be entitled to the full and equal enjoyment of goods, services, facilities, advantages, and accommodations of any place of public accommodation, ...without discrimination or segregation on the ground of race, color, religion or national origin.

Public accommodations included business establishments such as motels, restaurants, and theaters. This provision was upheld as a lawful exercise of congressional power under the Interstate Commerce Clause and the Equal Protection Clause of the Fourteenth Amendment in the case of *Heart of Atlanta Motel v. United States*, 379 U.S. 241, 85 S. Ct. 348, 13 L. Ed. 2d 258 (1964). In construing the act as constitutional, the Supreme Court also denied the appellant's contentions that depriving it of the right to choose its own customers and requiring it to rent rooms to blacks against its will was either an unlawful taking of liberty and property without due process of law or a form of involuntary servitude of hotel owners.

Transportation of passengers in interstate commerce had long been a subject of congressional regulation. In distinguishing the case from the 1875 Civil Rights Act and earlier decisions, the Supreme Court noted that "conditions of transportation and commerce have changed dramatically, and we must apply those principles to the present state of commerce." Testimony before Congress supported the contention that "denial of a substantial segment of the traveling public of adequate and desegregated public accommodations" ad-

---

[15] *Brown v. Board of Education of Topeka*, 347 U.S. 483, 74 S. Ct. 686, 98 L. Ed. 873 (1954), overturned *Plessy v. Ferguson*, 163 U.S. 537, 16 S. Ct. 1138, 41 L. Ed. 256 (1896).

[16] *Boynton v. Virginia*, 81 S. Ct. 182 (1960).

versely affected commerce and travel by such infringed upon groups. In the *Heart of Atlanta Motel* case, the Supreme Court reiterated the right of Congress to regulate intrastate activities that "affect" interstate commerce, noting in effect that regardless of how local a motel operation may appear initially, Congress may regulate its activities if interstate commerce is adversely affected by its policies.

MANAGERIAL IMPLICATIONS

Managerial decisions concerning hiring and firing practices, working conditions, and rendering of services must be made within the bounds of federal parameters. Freedom of businesspersons to establish their own policies has varied over the years. During the pro-manager eras of the late 1800s and 1920s, courts generally struck down attempts by the federal government to limit managerial discretion in economic decisions. By the end of the 1930s, however, legislation affecting wages and working conditions was deemed constitutional. By the 1960s the power of Congress to regulate intrastate activities that "affect" interstate commerce was firmly established.

Title VII of the Civil Rights Act of 1964, as amended, extended federal regulation to hiring, firing, and promotion practices, thus prohibiting discrimination on the basis of race, sex, religion, national origin, or handicap in employment. Employment practices with "disparate impact" on a protected class are forbidden if validity of job criteria cannot be shown. This has far-reaching implications, not only in employment practices, but also on recordkeeping expectations. Numerous other pieces of modern legislation regulate against discrimination in the workplace and business practices, including the Equal Pay Act, the Consumer Credit Protection Act, the Equal Credit Opportunity Act, Women's Business Ownership Act, and the Age Discrimination in Employment Act.

So pervasive is federal legislation today under the Interstate Commerce Clause, that it extends from the Insider Trading Sanctions Act of 1984 to the expansive Racketeer Influenced and Corrupt Organizations Act (RICO) to imposition of federal safety and health standards. Occupational Safety and Health Act, Mine Safety and Health Amendments Act, Railway Safety Act, Clean Air Act, Federal Water Pollution Control Act, the Safe Drinking Water Act, and Superfund legislation form just a sampling of legislation in the latter area. "Free enterprises" must adapt managerial practices under the guidelines of a regulatory environment.

Decisions of managers to expand businesses or merge with competitors is also subject to government scrutiny. Plans for expansion cannot substantially lessen competition or illegally restrain trade. Court-ordered antitrust breakups of powerful monopolies and oligopolies are no doubt a realistic shock to powerful entrepreneurs who may see themselves as above regulation. J. P. Morgan had mediated the power dispute between railroad kings Hill and Harriman to facilitate the creation of the Northern Securities Holding Company at the turn of the century and thought that he could bargain with the U.S. government to dismiss the *Northern Securities* case. After all, J. P. Morgan had been the primary financier of the Spanish American War and was a voice to be heeded. In finding the holding company to be an unconstitutional restraint of trade in 1904, the Court in effect had adopted the "Consent Theory" of corporate law rather than the "Contract Theory." Corporations were not merely created as a contractual, consensual relationship between investors, but had their origin from the state. During most of the 1800s, corporations were chartered by acts of state legislatures, rather than by administrative form filing, so there was a belief that corporations deriving their existence from the hands of the people must submit to regulation by the people.

To what extent can the federal government regulate managerial discretion in advertising and marketing techniques under the Interstate Commerce Clause? Marketers claim First Amendment rights when challenging legislative restrictions. In the *Virginia Pharmacy Board* case in 1976, commercial speech became an area of speech worthy of some protection.

> Advertising, however tasteless and excessive it sometimes may seem, is nonetheless dissemination of information as to who is producing and selling what products, for what reason and for what price. So long as we preserve a predominantly free enterprise economy, the allocation of our resources in large measure will be made through numerous private economic decisions. It is a matter of public interest that these decisions... be intelligent and well informed. To this end, the free flow of commercial information is indispensable.[17]

Commercial speech, however, is not accorded the same protection as political speech under the First Amendment, having a "subordinate position in the scale of First Amendment values."[18]

The power of the federal government to ban or restrict advertising of a misleading nature is well established. In recent years the FTC has prohibited companies from advertising health and superiority claims that they cannot scientifically substantiate, recognizing that commercial speech rights are not a license for misrepresentation of the truth.[19]

"When the nature of a product is such that it gives rise to a serious safety concern, advertisers are held to a high standard of care...."[20] If scientific evidence substantiates health hazards, Congress may mandate warnings of those health hazards on the packages of products, such as it has done through the Federal Cigarette Labeling and Advertising Act of 1965 and the Comprehensive Smoking Education Act of 1984. Cigarettes were banned from television

[17] *Virginia State Board of Pharmacy v. Virginia Citizens Consumer Council, Inc.*, 96 S. Ct. 1817, 1827 (1976).
[18] *Board of Trustees of the State University of New York, et al. v. Fox, et al.*, 57 U.S.L.W. 5015, 5017 (June 29, 1989).
[19] *Warner-Lambert Co., et al. v. FTC*, 562 F.2d 749 (D. C. Cir. 1977), *cert. denied*, 435 U.S. 950 (1978).
[20] *American Home Products Corp., et al.*, 95 F.T.C. 136 (1981).

advertising in 1970. Credibility of such a ban found constitutional recognition in the case of *Central Hudson Gas and Electric Corp. v. Public Service Commission,* 447 U.S. 557, 100 S. Ct. 2343, 2350 (1980), with the court recognizing that "[t]he government may ban forms of communication more likely to deceive the public than to inform it."

In 1986 government restriction on Puerto Rico casino advertising was accorded constitutionality under a First Amendment challenge.

[I]t is precisely *because* the government could have enacted a wholesale prohibition of the underlying conduct that it is permissible for the government to take the less intrusive step of allowing the conduct, but reducing the demand through restrictions on advertising.[21]

In recognizing the delicate balance between public health and welfare and propriety interest, the Supreme Court established a balancing test in the 1980s to weigh commercial speech interests against legitimate state interests of regulation. Government regulation of advertising should be "narrowly tailored to achieve the desired objective," but it does not have to be the "least restrictive means" of accomplishing the substantial government goal.[22]

CONCLUSION

As the Supreme Court construes the constitutionality of government regulation of business activities today, it takes an expansive view of the kinds of activities that can be regulated under the Interstate Commerce Clause and of the kinds of restrictions that can be imposed on commercial advertising of products and services. When the transportation industry is at issue, the constitutionality of federal regulation of the transportation of goods and persons has been recognized since 1824. Although slower to evolve, manufacturing is now considered a form of commerce subject to federal regulation, and practices that substantially lessen business competition can be prohibited. Since the late 1930s it is also clear that working conditions and labor practices that *affect* commerce can also be regulated by Congress as "necessary and proper" to the regulation of commerce itself. Even intrastate activities that serve as the origin for interstate transactions may be subject to federal regulation. Practices posing particular threats to health, safety, or morals can be regulated or even banned, and the federal government can constitutionally impose restrictions on deceptive advertising and marketing practices. Since the power of Congress to regulate under the Interstate Commerce Clause was first recognized in the 1824 case of *Gibbons v. Ogdon,* the Supreme Court has broadened its perception of interstate commerce and now upholds far-reaching regulation of business activities that "affect" interstate commerce.

---

[21] *Posadas de Puerto Rico v. Tourism Co. of Puerto Rico,* 106 S. Ct. 2968, 2979, 2980 (1986).
[22] *Board of Trustees of the State University of New York, et al. v. Fox, et al.,* 57 U.S.L.W. 5015, 5018, No. 87-2013 (June 29, 1989).

REFERENCES

Cushman, Robert F., *Leading Constitutional Decisions,* 14th ed., Appleton-Century-Crofts, New York, 1969.

Encyclopedia of American History, Richard B. Morris (ed.), Bicentennial Ed., Harper & Row, New York, 1976.

Friedman, Lawrence, *A History of American Law,* Simon and Schuster, New York, 1973.

Gibbons v. Ogdon, 9 Wheaton 1, 6 L. Ed. 23 (1824).

Heart of Atlanta Motel v. U.S., 379 U.S. 241, 85 S. Ct. 348, 13 L. Ed. 2d 258 (1964).

Horwitz, Morton, *The Transformation of American Law, 1780–1860,* Harvard University Press, Cambridge, Mass., 1977.

Hughes, Jonathan, *American Economic History,* 2d ed., Scott, Foresman, Glenview, Ill., 1987.

Hurst, James Willard, *The Legitimacy of the Business Corporation in the United States,* University Press of Virginia, Charlottesville, 1970.

Miller, Arthur Selwyn, *The Supreme Court and American Capitalism,* The Free Press, New York, 1972.

Northern Securities Co. v. United States, 193 U.S. 197 (1904).

Owen, Richard, *Times Guide to 1992—Britain in a Europe Without Frontiers,* Times Inc., Ltd., London, 1989.

Pusateri, C. Joseph, *A History of American Business,* 2d ed., Harlan Davidson, Inc., Arlington Heights, Ill., 1988.

Scheiber, Harry N., "The Road to Munn: Eminent Domain and the Concept of Public Purpose in the State Courts," *Perspectives in American History,* vol. 5, 1971.

Smith James M., and Paul L. Murphy (eds.), *Liberty and Justice, Forging the Federal Union: American Constitutional Development to 1869,* vol. 1, Knopf, New York, 1965.

United States Constitution.

United States v. Darby, 312 U.S. 100 (1941).

Walbash, St. Louis and Pacific RR Co. v. Illinois, 118 U.S. 557 (1886).

Articles, Hearings, and Collections

Advertising of Tobacco Products: Hearings on HR 4972 Before the Subcommittee on Health and Environment of the House Committee on Energy and Commerce, 99th Cong., 2d. Sess., *AMA Report* (1986).

Calingaert, "What Europe 1992 Means for U.S. Business," 24 *Business Economics* 30 (October 1989).

Federal Cigarette Labeling and Advertising Act, 79 Stat. 282 (1965), as amended by Pub. L. No. 98–474, 98 Stat. 2204 (1984) and Pub. L. No. 99–92, sect. 11, 99 Stat. 393, 402–04 (1985), current version at 15 U.S.C.A. 1331 (1985).

The Federalist vs. the Jeffersonian Republicans, Paul Goodman (ed.), Holt, Rinehart and Winston, Chicago, 1967.

Health Protection Act of 1987: Hearings on H.R. 1272 and H.R. 1532 Before the Subcommittee on Transportation, Tourism and Hazardous Materials of the Committee on Energy and Commerce, 100 Cong., 1st Sess.

Machado, P., and W. Mendelson, "Judicial Review: The Politics of Scholarship," 4 *Constitutional Commentary* 115 (Winter 1987).

Miller, Carol J., "Origins of American Judicial Review: Politics and Precedent," 7 *Midwest L. Rev.* 6–38 (Fall 1988).
"1992 and the United States," 9 *The Business Lawyer Update* 1, 4 (May/June 1989).
Notes of Debate in the Federal Convention of 1787 Reported by James Madison, intro. by Adrienne Koch, W. W. Norton, New York, 1966.
Scheiber, Harry N., "Federalism and the American Economic Order, 1789–1910," 10 *Law and Society* (Fall 1975).
The Federalist, nos. 78, 81 (A. Hamilton).
The Papers of Thomas Jefferson 440, J. Boyd (ed.), 1955.

DISCUSSION QUESTIONS

1 What seemed to be the constitutional stumbling blocks to early attempts by Congress to regulate wages, working hours, and working conditions in industries?

2 How is federal civil rights legislation justified as an extension of congressional regulation of interstate commerce?

3 Under what conditions can Congress restrict commercial speech (business advertising) without violating the First Amendment? What types of business are most vulnerable to restrictions and why?

4 Compare the legal environment for regulating the railroad industry in the late 1800s and early 1900s to regulation of the airline industry in the latter 1900s. Does the power of the federal government over navigation (cited in *Gibbons v. Ogdon*) extend to modern air and space traffic? Discuss the evolution of the federal government's rate and route control authority and the effect of the so called "deregulation" of the airline industry.

5 To what extent has the Supreme Court's exercise of judicial review helped shape congressional agenda for the regulation of business practices?

6 How does the evolution of the European Community in the 1990s compare to the evolution of U.S. political and economic development two centuries earlier?

SUGGESTED ANSWERS

1 Initially the federal courts distinguished between "commerce" and "manufacturing" and between "direct" and "indirect" regulation of interstate commerce. Although federal legislation regulating hauling rates and even working hours of interstate transportation workers (such as railroad workers and seamen) were upheld, restrictions on working hours and conditions in the manufacturing sector were viewed as outside of traditional federal jurisdiction under the Interstate Commerce Clause. Regulation of hours, wages, and working conditions was also viewed as an "indirect" rather than "direct" regulation of commerce. Structuring of hauling rates of shippers was deemed to be directly related to regulation of commerce, but regulation of employment conditions for child labor was indirect. Under this rationale, congressional legislation could not ban the interstate shipment of goods produced with child labor.

It was not until the National Labor Relations Act and the Fair Labor Standards Act were upheld in 1937 and 1941 that "unfair labor practices," wages, and hours could be constitutionally regulated by the federal government. In *United States v. Darby,* the Supreme Court recognized that congressional regulation of interstate commerce "extends to those activities intrastate which so AFFECT interstate commerce." Through the "Elastic Clause" of the Constitution, activities that relate to commerce could now be regulated in addition to regulation of commerce itself.

2 Rather than adopting a narrow "original intent" view of legislation and the Constitution, the Supreme Court of the 1960s recognized that "conditions of transportation and commerce have changed dramatically, and we must apply those principles to the present state of commerce." Under this philosophy, the Court rejected the narrow view of commerce that prevailed when the Civil Rights Act of 1875 was passed. Instead it viewed bus terminals and motels and employment opportunities as an "integral" part of interstate commerce. The Civil Rights Act of 1964 (as amended) had broad applicability, as public accommodations and employment opportunities were not to be denied on the basis of race, color, national origin, sex, or religion.

3 Free flow of truthful commercial information has received some First Amendment protection since 1976. Advertising that is false or misleading, however, can be banned or corrective advertising can be mandated by agencies such as the FTC. When products (such as cigarettes) pose known health threats, or when advertisers make health superiority claims without scientific documentation, such advertising can be banned. Advertising affecting health, safety, or morals can be restricted to designated media, or affirmative disclosures concerning contents and risks can be required.

4 The railroad industry was the first industry to come under substantial federal regulation. With the passage of the Interstate Commerce Act in 1887, the first giant federal regulatory agency had its origin. Its power was expanded through the Elkins Act of 1903, the Hepburn Act, and the Mann-Elkins Act of 1910, as the ICC was empowered to establish rates and issue binding orders. The burden of proof was on the challenger of the ICC regulations, as the railroads had to take the ICC to court to negate the implementation of its policies. Fierce competitive practices and attempts by powerful entrepreneurs to dominate routes lead to the enforcement of the Sherman Antitrust Act against the Northern Securities (Holding) Company in 1904. Although the once powerful railroad industry is a struggling remnant of its former self today, substantial federal regulation remains as a carryover from an earlier era. An underfunded attempt by the federal government to rejuvenate railroad passenger service via Amtrak was attempted in the 1970s and 1980s.

Regulation of the airline industry once witnessed rate and route restrictions, as was common in the railroad industry at its prime. Today smoking is banned on domestic flights and equal opportunity laws give older females and males the opportunity to fly the skies as flight attendants. Although the Civil Aeronautics Board is gone, federal investigations of accidents and federal monitoring of traffic patterns and communication frequencies remain.

Deregulation of the airline industry at the close of the 1970s led to initially fierce competition for previously restricted routes. As competition increased, rate discounts prevailed. A decade latter, however, some of the former giants of the industry were the subject of takeover attempts and labor unrest. Smaller arteries witnessed a cutback in available services. While customers flooded the system, air safety took a nose dive. Federal air traffic controllers went on strike in the early 1980s and were fired. The real loser was the airborne public, as overcrowded airport facilities and aging airplanes jammed the skies for understaffed, inexperienced air traffic controllers to monitor.

Railroad engineers, pilots, and bus drivers today may be subject to drug testing, as an attempt at increasing safe performance by employees in safety-sensitive jobs.

5 In 1886 only the state Granger groups and state legislatures seemed willing to take on the mighty railroads to regulate unfair business practices and rate policies. In recognizing the railroad transportation industry as a vehicle in interstate commerce, the Supreme Court stripped the states of power to regulate the railroads. Regulation of interstate commerce was the exclusive province of Congress. No federal legislation existed at that time. Congress reacted to that Supreme Court decision, filling the vacuum with the creation of the ICC and eventually empowering that commission to regulate railroad practices.

When the courts do not interpret legislation in the same manner as congressional leaders, passage of new laws, supported by new rationales, may result. Rather than follow the lead of the Supreme Court in the early 1930s, Congress sought new jurisdictional justifications for New Deal agenda. Eventually creative legislation prevailed, as Congress passed legislation that could withstand court scrutiny under the Interstate Commerce Clause while providing minimum standards for wages and working conditions for employees.

The Supreme Court of the 1950s and 1960s took an activist role as it overturned decades of precedent in striking down the "separate but equal" doctrine. Noting the Supreme Court's willingness in *Brown v. Board of Education of Topeka* to overturn discriminatory precedent, of the *Plessy v. Ferguson* railroad car case, and to require integration of buses in *Boynton v. Virginia* (1960), Congress passed the Civil Rights Act of 1964 to add legislative teeth to policies of antidiscrimination on the basis of race.

6 The American States perceived themselves as separate nations in the 1770s and 1780s, at the time the Articles of Confederation formed an alliance or perpetual league of friendship. It was only after these states realized the need for an economic union that the U.S. Constitution was ratified. Similarly, the countries of the European Community began their road to an economic union in 1954 and strengthened that pledge in 1985 by targeting 1992 as the date to harmonize free flow of goods, capital, services, and people across the borders on the 12 member nations. Just as several decades would be necessary to more clearly delineate the roles of the U.S. federal government and the state governments, the role of the EC is an evolving one as well. With the prodemocracy movement sweeping Eastern Europe, the EC is likely to play an ever increasing role in shaping the economic and political destiny of modern Europe.

6

ALTERNATE DISPUTE RESOLUTION

Debra Dobray
Southern Methodist University

INTRODUCTION

Our society has become increasingly litigious over the past three decades. Courts, through the common law and constitutional and statutory interpretation, have created new causes of action with respect to product liability, privacy rights, and employment relationships. In 1986 there was one civil lawsuit filed for every 15 Americans. The war against crime has taxed the court system as well, making the crowded civil docket take a backseat to the even more crowded criminal docket. In the federal court system, where district courts hear both civil and criminal cases, over 269,000 cases were filed in the year ending in 1988, an average of 417 for each of the nation's 575 federal district judges. As a result of the backlog that such congestion creates, the median wait for a case in the federal system is 14 months. Overall in the United States in 1988, over 22 million lawsuits were filed, and litigation costs exceeded $22 billion. Such costs not only burden the taxpayer whose taxes must support our justice system, but litigants, particularly with respect to the civil justice system, are finding legal expenses overbearing. As a result, alternate dispute resolution (ADR) frequently is viewed as offering relief for judicial delay and the increasing cost of litigation, and has been gaining popularity over the past 10 years.

Criticism of our jury system also has caused an increased interest in finding ways to resolve disputes out of court. Advantages of ADR seem to reflect conversely the disadvantages associated with the jury system. Juries and jury trials have been criticized as being time consuming, costly, inefficient in applying the law to facts in complex cases, and overly generous. For example, *Kemner v. Monsanto,* 492 N.E. 2d 1327 (1986), a toxic tort case, was the longest jury trial in our nation's history, lasting over 3 years. The cost of long trials and the expense of discovery incurred before the trial begins often preclude potential litigants from pursuing their claims in a court of law. In complex cases, juries have been criticized as being unable to understand the issues presented. Sometimes such confusion results in mistrials or inexplicable verdicts. The United States Third Circuit Court of Appeals in *In re Japanese Product Antitrust Litigation,* 631 F.2d 1069 (3d Cir. 1980), created an exception to the Seventh Amendment right to a trial by jury in cases where the law and evidence are so complex that due process would be denied if the case were tried by a jury. Juries also have been criticized for being overly generous in their damage awards. The jury in *Texaco v. Pennzoil,* 729 S.W.2d 768 (1987), awarded the largest amount of damages ever assessed, $7.53 billion in compensatory damages and $3 billion in punitive damages, although the punitive award was reduced on appeal. In contrast, ADR has been praised as being cost- and time-efficient as well as being more rational and proficient in the rendering of judgments and the awarding of damages.

Although there has been an increased attraction to settling disputes outside the court system, ADR or "informal justice" has been used in the United States since the beginning of the century. Alternate dispute resolution has been the preferred method of deciding international commercial disputes for some time. It has grown in importance in environmental and securities law, and historically has been utilized in labor disputes and controversies arising from construction contracts. Lately, bar associations and the judiciary have been recognizing that the burgeoning demands on the court system make it necessary for litigants with all types of claims to explore and use other dispute resolution mechanisms. Alternate forums are both practical and lucrative, because 90 percent of the cases filed eventually are settled out of court and 90 percent of such cases cost more to litigate than the amount of money at issue. This chapter will explore the various means of resolving disputes out of court through ADR along with the implications for managers of having such forums coexist with the court system.

ARBITRATION

Perhaps the most predominant form of ADR is arbitration. Often, parties will include an arbitration clause in their contracts that require disputes arising under the agreement to be submitted to arbitration. In the 1980s state and federal court decisions began giving more credence to such clauses, broadly construing the language of the contract in favor of arbitration. Federal and state statutes allow contracting parties to choose arbitration as a remedy and to enforce in court a motion to compel its use if it can be established that the parties agreed to handle the dispute in question through arbitration.

The Federal Arbitration Act was passed by Congress in 1925 to encourage the use of arbitration. It has succeeded through judicial interpretation and application in becoming a comprehensive national law for commercial arbitration, making all written agreements to arbitrate disputes enforceable so long as foreign or interstate commerce is affected and there are no legal defenses to the enforcement of the agreement. The breadth of the federal statute and the broad interpretation given by the Supreme Court to its provisions as to the arbitrability of disputes arising under the act is exemplified in *Shearson/American Express Inc. v. McMahon*, 482 U.S. 220 (1987). In *McMahon*, the Supreme Court had to decide whether claims brought under the Securities Exchange Act of 1934 and the Racketeer Influenced and Corrupt Organizations Act (RICO) must be sent to arbitration in accordance with the terms of an arbitration agreement. The McMahons were customers of Shearson/American Express Inc., a brokerage firm registered with the Securities and Exchange Commission (SEC). Two customer agreements signed by Julia McMahon provided for the arbitration of any controversy relating to the accounts the McMahons maintained with Shearson. Specifically, the arbitration provision provided that, "unless unenforceable due to federal or state law, any controversy arising out of or relating to my accounts, to transactions with you for me or to this agreement or the breach thereof, shall be settled by arbitration in accordance with the rules, then in effect, of the National Association of Securities Dealers, Inc. or the Boards of Directors of the New York Stock Exchange, Inc. and/or the American Stock Exchange, Inc. as I may elect."

In 1984 the McMahons filed suit against Shearson alleging that the requested representative who handled their accounts, with Shearson's knowledge, had violated the Securities Exchange Act by engaging in fraudulent, excessive trading on their accounts and by making false statements and omitting material facts from the advice given to them. They also alleged a RICO violation along with state law claims for fraud and breach of fiduciary duties. Shearson moved to compel arbitration pursuant to the Federal Arbitration Act relying on the two customer agreements. The district court held that the Securities Exchange Act claims along with the state law claims were arbitrable but concluded that the RICO claim was not because of the important federal policies inherent in the enforcement of RICO by the federal courts. The court of appeals affirmed the district court on the state law and RICO claims, but reversed it on the Securities Exchange Act claims. The Supreme Court held that all claims were arbitrable under the Federal Arbitration Act.

The Court noted that the act was designed to reverse centuries of judicial hostility to arbitration agreements by placing such agreements on the same footing as other contracts, and that the act accomplished that purpose by making arbitration agreements binding absent any legal or equitable grounds for the rescission of any contract. It further noted that the act established a federal policy favoring arbitration that requires courts to rigorously enforce agreements to arbitrate.

The Court did not distinguish statutory claims, such as those brought by the McMahons under the Securities Exchange Act and RICO, from any other type of dispute. The Court concluded that arbitration agreements should be enforced whether or not the dispute centers on a statutory right. Unless there was a valid claim that the arbitration agreement resulted from the type of fraud or excessive economic power that would be grounds for rescinding any other kind of contract, nonstatutory and statutory claims alike should be submitted to arbitration pursuant to the agreement. The Court reached this conclusion even though Congress did not specifically address the arbitrability of claims under the Securities Exchange Act and RICO.

In its decision, the Court stressed that the streamlined procedures of arbitration do not restrict substantive rights because there is no reason to assume that arbitrators will not follow the law. Even though judicial scrutiny of arbitration awards is limited, the Court felt that, nevertheless, judicial review was sufficient to ensure that arbitrators comply with the statutory mandates. In effect, the Court parted with the decision in an earlier case, *Wilko v. Swan,* 346 U.S. 427 (1953), which reflected a general suspicion of the desirability of arbitration and the competence of arbitral tribunals. The Court recognized that today, unlike when *Wilko* was decided, the SEC possesses expansive powers to ensure the adequacy of the arbitration procedures employed by self-regulatory organizations such as the national securities exchanges and registered securities associations. Thus, the integrity of the arbitration process would be preserved given that the SEC has broad authority to oversee and regulate the rules relating to customer disputes, including the power to mandate the adoption of any rules it deems necessary to guarantee that arbitration procedures adequately protect statutory rights. It concluded, therefore, that all claims were arbitrable under the terms of the Federal Arbitration Act and that the McMahons, having made an enforceable bargain to arbitrate, would be held to their bargain.

Justices Blackmun, Brennan, and Marshall concurred in the Court's decision to enforce the arbitration agreement with respect to the McMahon's RICO claim, but dissented with respect to the Court's decision holding the Securities Exchange Act claim arbitrable. The three justices felt that both the Securities Act of 1933 and the Securities Exchange Act of 1934 were passed to protect investors from predatory behavior by securities industry personnel and that the judiciary should not abandon its role in the resolution of claims, leaving such claims to the arbitral forum at a time when the industry's abuses towards investors were more apparent than ever.

The *McMahon* case demonstrates the willingness of federal courts to favor arbitration when the parties have bound themselves contractually to resolve their disputes in that manner and the issue is governed by the Federal Arbitration Act. Most state legislatures also have passed statutes that provide a framework for arbitrating disputes. Many of these laws track, with some modifications, the provisions of the Uniform Arbitration Act, a model statute. State courts, as well, have begun enthusiastically enforcing contractual provisions to arbitrate under these laws.

Usually the parties agree before a problem occurs that any dispute among them will be submitted to arbitration. However, an agreement to arbitrate may be reached after the controversy arises as well. In either case, the arbitration agreement usually specifies the number of arbitrators, one or three, and the process for selecting those arbitrators. For example, the agreement might state that each party will select one arbitrator and those two selected will choose the third. Absent an agreement to the contrary between the parties, there are no specific qualifications for arbitrators required. However, many are members of the American Arbitration Association (AAA), a national organization that trains persons in arbitration proceedings. The AAA also will assist in drafting the arbitration clause, formulating rules for arbitration, and supervising the procedure itself.

Arbitration is more informal than litigation. Both sides present their case to the arbitrator or panel of arbitrators. There are few procedural rules and no motions upon which the arbitrator must rule. Most discovery procedures are bypassed. Under the federal act only the arbitrator may order a deposition to be taken, and then only in limited circumstances. Often the proceeding is conducted after business hours at a time and place convenient to both parties. Venue rules need not be respected as the parties mutually agree upon a location for the hearing. Although representation by an attorney is allowed, there is certainly no requirement that a party be represented. As a result of these differences between arbitration and court proceedings, arbitration is assumed to result in a speedier resolution of the controversy.

The parties will specify whether an arbitrator's decision will be binding or nonbinding. If binding arbitration is agreed upon, there is limited judicial review of the decision. Generally, a court will not set the decision aside unless the arbitrator did not have jurisdiction pursuant to the agreement, the award violated public policy, or the award was obtained fraudulently. There is no review of the decision based on the merits of the case. Prolonged appellate review would defeat arbitration's goal of swift justice. Additionally, because arbitrators adhere to legal principles but are not strictly bound by precedent, being more outcome-oriented looking towards a fair resolution of the dispute, to review their decisions arguably would be superfluous second-guessing.

MEDIATION

Mediation differs from arbitration in that, rather than rendering a decision, the mediator guides the parties to a mutually agreeable resolution of their dispute. The mediator acts as a facilitator, suggesting avenues for compromise and noting common grounds for agreement. In the end, it is the parties themselves who reach the solution to their problem. Mediation is a particularly desirable type of ADR in those cases where the parties must continue their relationship as in a labor/management context or divorce/custody situation. Like arbitration, mediation is informal, lacks rigid procedural rules, and is less time consuming than traditional court adjudication.

MINI TRIALS

Mini trials are private proceedings loosely resembling a court trial. They are often used in cases involving complex corporate issues. Generally the parties resort to this ADR process after a lawsuit has been initiated and some discovery has taken place, but before the trial has commenced. In a mini trial both sides present shortened versions of their case before the person or persons having settlement authority, for example a CEO, and frequently before a third-party neutral adviser. Experts may testify and be cross-examined by the attorneys, or the presentation of evidence may be limited to depositions, interrogatories, and other discovery devices. The parties usually will specify the parameters of the process in a written agreement prior to the trial.

After the presentation of evidence, which may last 1 or 2 days, the principles will attempt to settle the dispute. If they cannot reach an agreement, the neutral adviser will issue an opinion as to the probable outcome of subsequent court litigation, including the resolution of evidentiary, factual, and legal questions. In short, a mini trial allows the parties to preview the trial in a nonbinding proceeding in order to assess the likely result. Because corporate decision makers are often insulated from information regarding the strengths and weaknesses of both sides of the controversy and the mini trial reveals such evidence to them, settlement may become more desirable and be reached before more costs are incurred and more time has passed.

SUMMARY JURY TRIALS

A summary jury trial is like a mini trial except that the case is presented to a jury. It is a nonbinding procedure designed to give both sides a sneak preview so as to encourage pretrial settlement of the case. Like a mini trial, a summary jury trial occurs after most of the discovery process is completed. It takes place in a courtroom with a judge or magistrate presiding. A mock six-member jury is impanelled after limited *voir dire* and preemptory challenges. Often the jury is not told that the trial will be nonbinding.

The attorneys for both sides are given an equal amount of time to make their presentations before the panel, generally 1 or 2 hours. Live testimony may not be allowed, and evidence presented will consist of that gleaned during discovery. The jury is then given instructions and renders its decision. This expedited ''verdict'' serves as a guide for settlement discussions. After it is rendered, both sides and their attorneys meet with the presiding officer to evaluate the jury's assessment of the dispute and to attempt to reach a formal settlement. Having some notion as to how a jury would decide helps both parties to judge realistically their chances should the litigation continue. Unlike mini trials, summary jury trials are not limited to complex corporate cases but can be used for other types of disputes. For example, this ADR device was used in Texas state courts to facilitate the processing of claims against asbestos manufacturers.

ADR CENTERS

Public or private ADR centers offer a moderately priced alternative to formal adjudication. Some public centers are funded by a percentage of court filing fees paid and are sponsored by various state and city bar associations. The procedure followed is like that of arbitration or mediation with attorneys conducting the review, often *pro bono*. Other centers, like the American Bar Association–sponsored Multi-Door Courthouse, aid the litigants in selecting the most appropriate forum in which to resolve their dispute and refer them accordingly. Neighborhood Dispute Resolution Centers represent such a potential forum and are often used to resolve controversies between neighbors, families, or landlords and tenants.

Traditional consumer ombudsperson groups such as the Better Business Bureau (BBB) and media action lines also serve as centers for grievance procedures. Most of these groups offer their services free; however, they lack the certainty of disposition that publicly funded ADR centers provide. In these situations generally only one party is complaining and there has been no agreement to resolve the dispute out of court.

In addition, more than 650 private companies offer ADR services. Firms such as United States Arbitration, Inc., EnDispute, Judicate, and Civicourt are handling civil disputes on a growing scale. United States Arbitration, Inc., conducts business through franchising with specialists in certain legal fields operating in different geographic areas, augmented by a referral system. Although not an ADR center per se, another private judging mechanism, "Rent a Judge," allows the parties to hire a retired judge to hear their case and render a decision. Like the firms' adjudication, these judges' decisions set no precedents and are binding solely by virtue of the parties' agreement. While such private systems of informal justice may be viewed as the capitalization of an important governmental function, proponents argue that they offer a less expensive and more practical alternative to the present judicial system.

COURT-ANNEXED ARBITRATION

Courts also have an interest in facilitating the disposition of cases. Some states have policy enactments that encourage the early settlement of pending litigation through settlement procedures. For example, Texas enacted the Alternate Dispute Resolution Procedure Act in 1987 whereby judges, the bar, and court administrators are mandated to encourage, although not compel, litigants to engage in the court's screening and referral process. Today over 100 court jurisdictions have some form of court-annexed nonbinding arbitration. Such programs are designed to decrease the time and expense of litigation without diminishing the quality or fairness of the process.

In the federal court system, there are currently 10 pilot projects of court-annexed arbitration with expansion to 20, depending upon the system's success. Under the federal program, certain civil cases involving contract or personal injury disputes of less than $150,000 are referred to mandatory, nonbinding pretrial arbitration. Those cases exceeding the jurisdictional limit are eligible for voluntary arbitration. The rules allow for a motion to be filed requesting that the case be excused from arbitration, and it is within the judge's discretion to grant that motion upon a proper showing of cause.

The hearing is conducted before three arbitrators chosen from a list of attorneys previously approved by the court. Five arbitrators are chosen randomly while each side is given one peremptory challenge and unlimited strikes for cause. Arbitrators who are not attorneys but who are experts in a given professional field may be furnished by the parties as well. Unless the parties stipulate to the contrary, the arbitration is nonbinding and either side may request a trial *de novo* after the decision is reached. Discovery is abbreviated, and most hearings last less than a day. The arbitrators follow the federal Rules of Evidence. Documents and witnesses may be subpoenaed and witnesses cross-examined under oath. The arbitrators' award is limited to money damages, although the rules may be amended in the future to include injunctive relief in those cases where it is appropriate, such as Title VII employment discrimination claims.

NEUTRAL CASE EVALUATION

Neutral case evaluation programs are another type of court-annexed ADR. They are designed to focus on the key issues in the case at bar in order to provide the parties with a realistic evaluation of their claims. The federal Rules of Evidence provide for both voluntary and involuntary fact finding by a neutral third party selected by the court or the parties to investigate, issue, and submit a report or testify in court. Neutral third-party case evaluation is employed in many state courts as well. For example, district and appellate courts in Houston use a moderated settlement conference to explore the issues of the case. The conference is conducted before a panel of three moderators who are court-appointed lawyers having some expertise in the area of law involved in the dispute. Each side is allowed to make a brief presentation of its argument as well as a brief rebuttal in an informal procedure where the moderators are allowed to question the attorneys. The moderators then advise the parties of their analyses of their arguments and their prediction regarding the probable outcome of the litigation. Their decision is merely a nonbinding, professional, and confidential opinion aimed at promoting settlement.

Other programs are conducted differently, but with the same goal in mind: to encourage settlement. In some jurisdictions, the moderators, or "neutrals" will give legal advice and help develop a plan for the litigation should settlement not be forthcoming. The Early Case Evaluation program in the Northern District of California uses only one third-party neutral who acts in this more flexible role. The Michigan Mediation Program employs a panel of experienced attorneys who evaluate a case after the advocates for each party have presented a short written summary. The mediators then suggest a settlement figure. This program also provides a penalty if the parties continue to litigate and the final award does not exceed the earlier settlement figure by 10 percent. Bankruptcy courts in the Southern District of California use third-party neutrals to objectively assess claims in certain contested matters.

These programs represent just a few examples of how many courts use one or more neutrals, be they called mediators or moderators, to help attorneys and their clients to evaluate their claims realistically to encourage settlement, functioning similarly to the mock jury in summary jury trials. Because more than 90 percent of cases filed are eventually settled prior to trial, such procedures should quicken that inevitability.

MANAGERIAL IMPLICATIONS

It can be argued that our justice system is on the verge of a revolution. Never before have there been so many alternatives to the court system for resolving civil cases. Never before have the judiciary and the bar supported, publicized, and encouraged the use of ADR. The support of the legal community along with the foresight of private enterprise in providing ADR foreshadows that alternatives to to court-adjudicated claims are soon likely to become the chosen route.

Why is it imperative for litigants, particularly those with disputes of a commercial nature, to recognize the availability of ADR? Our nation is probably the most litigious country in the world. The transaction costs of resolving the multitude of disputes before our courts increases each year and amounts to billions of dollars being spent annually. Other countries do not spend, arguably "waste," such vast resources solely on transaction costs. Although less populous, Japan still has a disproportionate fraction of attorneys as compared to the United States. It is also interesting to note that many other countries, including Great Britain, the birth place of our common law, have limited severely the role of juries in their justice system.

As other countries reform and streamline the mechanisms for dispute resolution so, too, must the United States in order to compete internationally. The potential for costly, elongated adjudication may discourage foreign investment in the United States. More important, the greater the share of revenues that U.S. companies must allocate to adjudicative expenses, the lesser the amount of revenues available for more productive enterprises, a situation which necessarily results in fewer profits being generated. The need to be able to efficiently compete in world markets will become even more apparent in the 1990s when Europe lowers its internal trade barriers to launch an economic campaign with its exterior borders. This challenge of increased international competition will prove difficult if U.S. businesses must spend enormous amounts of money on transaction costs associated with litigation.

In addition to the burden placed on business from such transaction costs, the delay that is presently inherent in our court system reduces productivity. As disputes linger for years, it is difficult to move forward with plans for future development. Several companies in the past decade filed for bankruptcy just from the threat of product liability lawsuits. Rather than hope that more tax dollars will be allocated to expand our court system in an effort to at least reduce judicial delay, businesses should begin to look to ADR for relief from both delays and increasing transaction costs. If ADR can be used to adjudicate those disputes conducive to out-of-court settlement, then the courts will be less taxed and more able to handle the controversies that need to be resolved in a judicial proceeding.

Moreover, successfully evaluating the likely outcome in any given case in order to accurately assess the viability of pursuing or defending a lawsuit is particularly troublesome given the difficulty of predicting jury verdicts or damage awards. This problem is exacerbated in terms of resource allocation and planning decisions when that final outcome, whatever it may be, takes years to be determined.

One way for businesses to bypass the court system is to include an arbitration or mediation clause in contracts with suppliers, distributors, consultants, or any of the myriad of people with whom their company conducts transactions. As the *McMahon* case illustrates, courts are increasingly likely to uphold these bargains to arbitrate or mediate unless a viable defense, such as unconscionability or fraud, is present to the extent that would justify the rescission of any other type of bargain. Companies also should open communication lines between their legal departments and those executives who are empowered to negotiate settlement agreements so that they might become more aware of the pending litigation in order to accurately access the avenues available for a swift resolution of the claim. Additionally, manufacturing companies, retailers, and other businesses interacting with consumers should anticipate the inevitability of lawsuits and prepare to handle them in advance with complaint departments headed by managers who have the authority to negotiate settlements. Finally, managers should acquaint themselves with the ADR available today and position themselves to utilize these forums whenever possible, as opposed to referring cases automatically to legal counsel. Certainly, many disputes will have to be litigated in a court of law; however, if managers can screen some claims for ADR, productivity should increase, transaction costs should decrease, and planning should be facilitated. The only challenge remaining will be to try to ensure that ADR does not become as adversarial as our court system. This temptation can be averted if an attitude of negotiation and conciliation is adapted, recognizing that confrontation often is more costly for all the parties involved in a dispute.

CONCLUSION

Although ADR boasts many advantages, this growing augmentation to our legal system is not without its critics. Some constitutional scholars fear that it threatens to usurp some of the powers of the courts conferred by Article III. Legal philosophers argue that traditional adjudication is more likely to render justice than ADR. Social commentators warn that ADR might become a second-class system of justice for the poor while the court system is reserved for the favored classes or in the extreme case, only for criminal trials. And there is always the threat that our common law system based upon precedent will be undermined by an adjunct system that does not necessarily adhere to those tenets.

However, proponents of ADR emphasize that some litigants face inaccessibility to the courts as a practical matter. They argue that our adversary system of justice must give way to a broader problem-solving orientation. Colleges and universities recognize such a need and are beginning to offer courses, even at the law school level, in settlement and negotiation. Whatever the academic struggles, ADR seems to be a permanent force in our society and growing at a fairly swift rate.

REFERENCES

Broderick, "Court-Annexed Compulsory Arbitration: It Works," 72 *Judicature* 217 (December–January 1988).

Buchanan, "*Public Policy and International Commercial Arbitration,*" 26 *Am. Bus. L. J.* 511 (1988).

Burton and McIver, "Evaluating the Impact of Court Annexed Arbitration," 18 *Colorado Lawyer* 879 (1989).

Campbel, "Arbitrating Lender Liability Claims," 18 *Colorado Lawyer* 879 (1989).

Cooke, "Court-Annexed Arbitration: Well Founded," 60 *N.Y.S. Bar J.* 10 (December 1988).

Dacks, "Arbitration v. Litigation," 200 *N.Y. L.J.* 3 (November 1988).

Dean Witter Reynolds, Inc. v. Byrd, 470 U.S. 213 (1985).

Katz, "Enforcing an ADR Clause—Are Good Intentions All You Have?" 26 *Am. Bus. L.J.* 575 (1988).

Kubasek and Silverman, "Environmental Mediation," 26 *Am. Bus. L.J.* 534 (1988).

Lipton, "Discovery Procedures and the Selection and Training of Arbitrators: A Study of Securities Industry Practices," 26 *Am. Bus. L.J.* 435 (1988).

Mitsubishi Motors Corporation v. Soler Chrysler-Plymouth, Inc., 473 U.S. 614 (1985).

Moses H. Cone Memorial Hospital v. Mercury Construction Corporation, 460 U.S. 1 (1983).

Nelson, "Arbitration Today," 52 *Tex. Bar J.* 1013 (1989).

Neslund, "Why Teach Conflict Resolution in Business Schools?" 26 *Am. Bus. L.J.* 559 (1988).

Penne, "Advantages of Institutional Arbitration," 200 *N.Y. L.J.* 3 (October 1988).

Rodriguezde Quijas v. Shearson/American Express, Inc., 109 S. Ct. 1917 (1989) [expressly overruling *Wilko v. Swann,* 346 U.S. 427 (1953)].

Scherk v. Alberto Culver, 417 U.S. 506 (1974).

Shell, "The Role of Public Law in Private Dispute Resolution: Reflections on *Shearson/American Express, Inc., v. McMahon,*" 26 *Am. Bus. L.J.* 399 (1988).

Siedel, "Present and Future Directions in ADR Research, 26 *Am. Bus. L.J.* 387 (1988).

Southland Corporation v. Keating, 465 U.S. 1 (1984).

Stipanowich, "Rethinking American Arbitration," 63 *Ind. L.J.* 425 (1988).

Weckstein, "The Purposes of Dispute Resolution: Comparative Concepts of Justice," 26 *Am. Bus. L.J.* 605 (1988).

Zollers, "Alternative Dispute Resolution and Product Liability Reform," 26 *Am. Bus. L.J.* 479 (1988).

DISCUSSION QUESTIONS

1 Compare and contrast the different forms of ADR.
2 What are some reasons for ADR's growth in popularity?
3 Discuss what type of disputes are most suitable for the different methods of ADR.

SUGGESTED ANSWERS

1 Arbitration differs from mediation in that with arbitration a third party arrives at a solution to the problem; with mediation, a third party helps the parties arrive at a mutually agreeable solution. Nonbinding arbitration and mediation are similar in that the parties are not bound to adhere to the solution reached. Private companies offer services such as mediation and arbitration. Court-annexed arbitration is similar to private arbitration services, although in some jurisdictions this preliminary review is mandatory.

   Mini trials and summary jury trials are similar; in both cases a sneak preview of the pending trial is presented in order to encourage settlement. However, in the mini trial that presentation is made before the corporate personnel who have the power to settle the dispute; in a summary jury trial, the presentation is made to a mock jury who renders a nonbinding verdict. Neutral case evaluation as annexed to some jurisdictions requires a similar type of presentation to neutral third parties who suggest possible settlement agreements.

2 The current backlog in the courts has spurred many litigants to seek a swift resolution of the dispute so that business may continue. The cost of a trial and the expenses involved in pursuing discovery, motion pleading, and appeals has become too great for many litigants to bear. The credibility of the jury system has also been undermined given the complex factual and legal issues present in many cases today. Lengthy trials and unpredictable verdicts and damage awards cause many litigants to opt for a more swift and predictable outcome to their dispute. In short, the primary impetus for the enhanced use of ADR has been the delay and costs involved in our current court system along with a questioning of the justice rendered by juries.

3 For small consumer complaints the Better Business Bureau and various media action lines offer a good start to resolving the controversy. Neighborhood centers for disputes offer a similar beginning for such complaints involving neighbors, landlords, and tenants. In the commercial world where the amount in controversy is greater, arbitration represents a viable alternative. With respect to commercial disputes between large companies, mini trials can be utilized to promote workable settlements. Mediation is a very appropriate way of resolving disputes in a less adversarial forum and is particularly attractive when controversies arise in a relationship which, by necessity, must continue, such as in custody and employment disputes. Summary jury trials are effective when courts must handle a large number of similar claims, such as in the asbestos litigation. Parties also may consult certain public ADR centers such as the ABA's Multi-Door Courthouse to determine what ADR forums are available and which ones are particularly suited to the controversy at hand.

7

TEXACO V. PENNZOIL AND THE UNHELPFULNESS OF BLACK-LETTER CONTRACT RULES

Charles C. Shepherd, Jr.
George Washington University

INTRODUCTION

In November 1985 a Texas jury returned a verdict for almost $11 billion for Pennzoil Company against Texaco Inc. for what amounted to Texaco's miscalculating whether Pennzoil had had a valid contract with another party. How could such an expensive error have occurred, given the many available experts and reference materials on contract formation? Couldn't Texaco just have looked up the rules of "offer" and "acceptance" in an ordinary business law textbook?

Although contract-law rules appear to be quite specific (and thus, for business law students, memorizable), their abstractness renders them of little use except in application. It is much more important to see how a judge, or jury, would apply a rule than it is simply to "know" the rule. That is, in part, inevitable because of the sheer complexity of some rules, but it is also a reflection of the societal drift to relativism, which disfavors universal principles and prefers situational decision making.

Black-letter legal rules are essential building blocks in lawyers' training. They are the language of argument for lawyers, serving as a shorthand for various logical and rhetorical devices used in the largely political contest of one party against another to see which has superior rights. However, for business students and other nonlawyers who need to understand the legal system, it would be much more important to describe, and then to study, the criteria that judges and jurors seem to use when they engage in situational decision making. Such criteria in the law of contract formation might sometimes refer to the legal rules of "offer" and "acceptance" but would include much more meaningful constructs that are *not* usually part of a business law course. I would like to offer several here, in the context of the *Texaco v. Pennzoil* case.

THE "CONTRACT" FOR GETTY OIL

In December 1983 Pennzoil, eager to acquire more oil capacity in a booming market, made a tender offer for 20 percent of Getty Oil, and later that month, executives of both companies worked out a "memorandum of agreement" by which the two firms would merge, with Pennzoil paying $112.50 per share. However, in early January 1984, Texaco, prodded by legendary takeover specialist Bruce Wasserstein (then of First Boston Corporation), announced a bid of $125 per share for Getty stock, and Getty (after securing a price of $128) accepted the offer. The jilted suitor filed a lawsuit in Delaware for intentional interference with a contract relation. The court refused to enjoin the Texaco-Getty merger, but when Texaco failed to respond to the lawsuit, Pennzoil seized the opportunity to refile in Texas (where a jury trial was available), commencing a $14 billion lawsuit in February. That November, the Texas jury returned a verdict against Texaco for $7.53 billion in compensatory damages and $3 billion in punitive damages for Texaco's willful interference with the "contract." (A necessary element of the cause of action is that Pennzoil prove that it had a contract with Getty despite the fact that both parties admitted they were "working on" the final contract when Texaco made its $125 offer.)

In classical contract law terms, there was no contract because Pennzoil's offer had not been formally accepted by Getty. That is, the document that both parties understood would "finalize" the merger had not yet been prepared when Getty received the better offer.

There are several logical reasons for this assumption. The dollar value of this transaction surely made it one in which a formal contract would be required to finalize the deal. For such an important decision, the board of directors should surely insist on a complete record before taking action that might incur for them legal liability. Furthermore, there is evidence that, within the industry that arranges mergers and acquisitions, the concept of "agreement" has a different meaning than the concept of a "contract." Thus, it can be assumed that both parties anticipated a final, signed contract, and since Getty was still several days away from signing (if at all), certainly Getty was free to take a better offer. In classical contract law, *an* offer may well have been "accepted," but it was not *the* offer to finalize the merger.

However, the jury (and probably the judge) found that a contract existed. Reference was made to various events and statements that indicated that a "meeting of the minds" had occurred.

• On January 3, 1984, Getty directors voted 15 to 1 to accept Pennzoil's merger offer. Pennzoil's lawyer, Arthur Liman, shook hands with all board members to signify that the deal had been struck. (But *what* deal? Just the price?)

• That evening, Gordon Getty toasted Pennzoil executives in the Pierre Hotel in New York City, signifying, according to those present, that a deal had been struck.

• Early the next day, Getty prepared a press release using terms almost identical to those in the agreement in principle (a document which, although not signed by anyone, came from the minutes of the board meeting the day before). Getty was, in a sense, partially performing on the "contract" by engaging in behavior it would not have undertaken absent a contract.

• Getty's press release said the firm "will receive" and did not use hypothetical language.

• Neither party took the rather routine step of insisting on being bound only by its signature on a final document.

• Despite specific questions at trial, no witness offered any other contemplated circumstance that might have derailed the Pennzoil-Getty arrangement between the time of the agreement in principle and contract. Only the relatively mindless mechanics of the deal remained.

Implicit in the consideration of these facts are the following assumptions—which tend to inhibit the usefulness of any universal principles in contract formation (implied by the primacy, in business law textbooks, of black-letter law).

First, the merger of two very large corporations arguably presents no single adequate "meeting of the minds" proxy opportunity. The transaction is too complex for the proxy of a written, signed contract. How many conditions would be necessary to ensure that the transaction could stand on its own as final? Three? Ten? Twenty? In such a case, oral recollections and memoranda of understanding might be just as useful as the "contract." A "meeting of the minds" *might* have taken place even though no final, formal contract existed.

Second, mergers involving publicly traded firms, by custom in the United States, often take place quickly because of the reaction of the stock market. In fact, when Texaco president John McKinley first spoke with Wasserstein early in the morning of January 4 about Wasserstein's hunch that Getty could still be purchased, Wasserstein told him that the window of opportunity might be open only 24 hours. Thus, some business transactions might have to occur so quickly that no formal contract could *ever* express precisely the minds of the participants.

Third, one view of the contract is that it is the last opportunity a party has to change its mind. (For some people; a metaphoric drum roll signals the arrival of the time to sign a contract. Palms perspire. Handwriting becomes unsteady. Some reassure themselves by the folklore that the contract won't be official until the pen is lifted from the paper.) However, the signing of the modern contract between two large firms is often little more than a photo opportunity and the document itself, a prop. Major decision making rarely takes place contemporaneous to the signing of the contract—implying that the "meeting of the minds" took place at some point (when?) before that.

THE UNSATISFACTORINESS OF BLACK-LETTER CONTRACT LAW

Acknowledging the primacy of situational decision making requires lamenting the growing unpredictability of legal decisions. The most predictable of all legal rules would be a universal principle that applies in every, or nearly every, case. An example would be a rule that allows a contract to be valid only as to those provisions agreed to in writing and signed by both parties. Universal principles are good in that they make it easier to predict outcomes and to order behavior. Reliance on a universal principle in contract law, however, might yield three kinds of unfair results:

• Some agreements made orally, or in writing but without one or both signatures, might deserve to be enforced if one party or the other has incurred some unfair risk.
• Some agreements (for example, stock market "buy" and "sell" decisions or taxicab rides) would be economically inefficient if they needed to be reduced to writing with specific conditions.
• Because only those terms unambiguously covered in the written contract could be used in the decision, whether or not to enforce the contract, any other situation would require methodology beyond the universal principle, or unfairness would result.

The response of contract-law scholars to these three problems has been merely to create a limited number of formal exceptions to the universal principle, in order to continue the illusion that universality exists. Thus, the Uniform Commercial Code, for example, lists 238,[1] and the Restatement of Contracts (Second), lists 1218 pages and 385 principles attempting to objectify the exceptions.

However, as the *Pennzoil* case illustrates, such a task is virtually impossible to accomplish meaningfully. The theoretical foundation for contract law, the "meeting of the minds," is not such a term that is inherently capable of objectification. Any such proxy for that instant would be highly idiosyncratic to the situation and/or to the decision maker and might even be arbitrary.

Black-letter contract law ("offer," "acceptance," and so on) in business law courses thus leaves students with the misimpression that cases usually have outcomes that are certain—if only the lawyer (or student) applies the law "correctly."

However, as Judge Jerome Frank wrote decades ago, the decision of a case quite logically is the application of facts (F) to the pertinent rules (R), or D (decision) $= F \times R$. Because F might be symbolically a zero, D can never be certainly determined just by knowing R. More important than rules, wrote Frank, is the skill of "fact characterization," or ordering the facts of the case as to their comparative significance. Without that skill, students are imbued

---

[1] Rules or exceptions to rules in Article 2 (Sales).

with a false knowledge about what the law "requires." In fact, many outcomes (including those of most cases that go to trial) are wildly unpredictable (because of fact characterization), even if *offer* and *acceptance* seem rather straightforward. Appreciation of the constructs used for situational decision making will assist (but not ensure) the successful prediction of the outcome.

A better exercise for those studying contract law would be to develop and consider some maxims of situational behavior by contracting parties according to how judges or jurors typically react to them, with the hope that such maxims might yield higher correlation to outcomes.

NEW "MAXIMS" OF CONTRACT LAW

If the determination is made that a contract existed when no final, formal document existed, *what criteria* could have been used to make such a determination? The business law class terms of *offer, acceptance,* and *consideration* are merely tautologies that invite *post hoc* rationalizing. Law should be at least *somewhat* predictable, lest people believe their behavior at any given time could be illegal even when much of the time it is not. Which criteria can we use to predict outcomes? Which criteria ought Texaco executives to have heeded?

Here are several that appear to be used often by judges and juries, even if they do not appear as memorizable principles in a business law course.

1 The more *voluntary* all aspects of the negotiation are, the better to infer a meeting of the minds. Even a signed contract can represent an involuntary decision, but voluntary behavior, without a signed contract, can signify a meeting of the minds.

2 The Uniform Commercial Code requirements of "good faith" and "reasonable" commercial behavior prevents judges and jurors from enforcing contracts that too badly disable one party unless that disability is a foreseeable result of a typical business risk undertaken by the victim.

3 Reasonable behavior should be defined in the first instance as that behavior typical in the industry or industries involved under the circumstances of the case, both normatively and as to its inevitability in free-market terms. (*Inevitability* is behavior which, under the circumstances, is dictated more by the need to remain strong in a competitive market than by the desire to defeat a competitor.)

4 Courts and jurors use comparative fault (comparative reasonableness) in judging which of the two parties' behavior was further from the socially imposed norm of conduct under the circumstances. Although that concept is associated with torts and not contract law, much has been written lately about the merger of the two doctrines.

Applying these constructs, rather than the sterile concepts of "offer," "acceptance," and "consideration," to the *Texaco v. Pennzoil* case makes the result, for Texaco, more nearly predictable.

• Pennzoil and Getty acted like willing, eager partners. They left no traces of issues on which they *disagreed*. The formal contract might not yet have taken place, but there was no evidence to suspect that a disagreement lurked ahead. Getty did not behave toward Pennzoil as though it believed its firm was worth more than $112.50 per share.

• Texaco appeared to be a ruthless party, entering negotiations after signs were present that the deal had been finalized. Getty appeared to be two-faced, taking all precautions to finalize one deal and then negotiating with another bidder without notifying Pennzoil. It is difficult to believe that, in good faith, Getty could so have undervalued its own company over a 24-hour period as to have settled on one price one day with Pennzoil, then the next day realized that there was a concrete case for valuing the firm higher.

• There is evidence to support Texaco's contention that all mergers and acquisitions players understand that deals move quickly and that nothing is final until it is final. On the other hand, judges and jurors retain, almost inherently, a sense of honor about reneging on one's word and of one party's "raiding" another's property right. At the least, Texaco should be on notice that judges and jurors might find it less reasonable than Pennzoil.

• Pennzoil is basically faultless in this transaction, whereas both Texaco and Getty have committed at least ordinary indiscretions of unfairness. On a comparative fault standard, to say that society believes more in the Texaco position is to endorse a legalistic, technical, Darwinian understanding of business transactions (including those between business and consumer).

MANAGERIAL IMPLICATIONS

For managers, insights from those four maxims are far more important than any that flow from the abstract rules of "offer," "acceptance," and so forth.

1 Parties wishing to maximize the probability that a contract will be enforced should elicit evidence of the other's eagerness to enter into the deal. For example, a stronger party that supplies a particularly hard-to-understand written contract should be able to demonstrate that it has explained the contract terms in great detail to the weaker party, and that the weaker party has a good reason (that is, one other than ignorance or fear) for agreeing.

2 Managers will find it difficult to make abnormal profits at the expense of another party if their only basis for doing so is a signature on a piece of paper. The party desiring enforcement should have left, at the scene of the contract, evidence that the risks involved in the contract were ordinary business risks that might be undertaken by other, even stronger and more prudent parties.

3 A party that wishes to engage in behavior different from that of its competitors should make it clear, at the time of the contract, why it is doing that. For example, if the standard in an industry is 60-day credit, a firm that will collect only in cash should give a reason (for example, ability to offer a discount) why a weaker party might voluntarily enter into such a cash contract when credit contracts are available elsewhere.

4 In fact, rarely are courts presented, in litigation, with a party that bears none of the fault for the spoiled contract relation; inevitably, judges and jurors must decide between two parties whose behavior could have been more prudent and "decent." Despite the clarity of black-letter contract law rules, decision makers necessarily factor in the respective degrees of fault of the parties, based on their departure from some unspoken standard of decent behavior for that circumstance.

Such evidence as noted here is now often produced in litigation. For managers, however, it is much better to produce such evidence at the time of the contract than to wait until the case arrives in litigation, when such evidence, even though accurate, might appear insincere and manipulative.

CONCLUSION

On February 12, 1987, the Texas Court of Appeals upheld the judgment and the $7.53 billion in compensatory damages against Texaco (although it reduced the $3 billion in punitive damages to $1 billion). In April Texaco filed for protection from creditors under chapter 11 of the bankruptcy code, in large part to avoid having to post a bond (equal to the amount of the judgment, which was $8.53 billion) in order to appeal the case to the Texas Supreme Court. After the trial court verdict, interest began to accumulate on the judgment, and by late 1987, when the two companies agreed to settle the lawsuit for what is believed to be around $3 billion cash, interest would have pushed the trial court judgment back to the $10 billion range. (Legal fees for the episode are believed to be in excess of $100 million, plus the contingent-fee arrangement of $600 million that has been reported for Pennzoil's lawyer Joe Jamail.) The Pennzoil lawsuit was filed against Texaco because, according to the merger agreement between Texaco and Getty, Texaco had agreed to compensate Getty in the event that Pennzoil sued for damages over the transaction.

Thus ended a lawsuit that was not only traumatic for Texaco but a loud clarion to the rest of the world of the unpredictability of U.S. legal decisions. When one of the very largest industrial firms can face bankruptcy because of indeterminateness of legal rules, it is time for a new approach to managerial education in the law. As to the law of contract formation, knowing the black-letter rules no longer properly serves the layperson and must be replaced by a quest for understanding the kinds of situations in which the "rules" will be applied.

REFERENCES

Petzinger, Thomas, Jr. *Oil & Honor*. G. P. Putnam's Sons, New York, 1987.
Texaco Inc. v. Pennzoil Company, 729 S.W. 2d 768 (Tex. Ct. App. 1987).

DISCUSSION QUESTIONS

1 Under what circumstances could your course syllabus be regarded as an enforceable contract, even though neither you nor your professor "signs" it or makes an express promise that it will be treated as a contract?

    a What if the professor "promised" to submit a course grade that reflects only exam grades but then gives a student a *B* for the course despite his or her having had *A*s on the only two exams given?

    b What if the professor "promised" to submit a course grade that reflects only exam grades but then gives a student a *C* for the course despite his or her having made an *A* on the final and a *C* on the midterm?

2 Suppose two graduate students were having a discussion in a study lounge.

    RAY: I'll give you $5000 for that pencil.

    NORM: $5000? It's just a pencil—19 cents each.

    RAY: Doesn't matter—$5000.

    NORM: Okay. You want to put it in writing?

    RAY: Yeah, sure.

Ray writes, "Ray promises to pay Norm $5000 cash for his Strathmore Number Two yellow pencil" and signs the paper. Then Norm signs it too.

    NORM: Okay, here's the pencil. Where's my money?

    RAY: I changed my mind.

    NORM: Tough. You signed the paper.

    RAY: Doesn't matter. Because of the societal drift to relativism, signed contracts don't matter anymore. As a practical matter, it's impossible for us to have an enforceable contract for your pencil for anything more than, say, a dollar.

    NORM: No way. You signed it.

    RAY: I know I did. Doesn't matter.

Who has the better position? Why?

SUGGESTED ANSWERS

1 Even though no signature appears on the syllabus, and even though the syllabus is not in the conventional form of a contract, courts have regarded similar documents as contracts in some situations. If the professor relied on the syllabus to govern students' conduct in the course (for example, used the stated course requirements to explain a particular grade given a student), the professor would be hard pressed to deny that the syllabus did not govern other aspects of the course. Any belief to the contrary by the professor should be stated in the syllabus. (By analogy, informal *employer* promises and conditions given to *employees* have in many cases been regarded as contractual in nature.)

    (In discussion of whether the syllabus is a "contract," it is not assumed that student and professor are in "equal" bargaining position. By the nature of the student's contract with the school, the professor stands in a superior bargaining position, and with good reason. However, the school's interests are not served by a professor's acting *arbitrarily* with regard to course requirements; rather, those interests are served only by the professor's reasonably choosing any of a variety of merit-measuring requirements and not arbitrarily changing them during the course. The discussion of "contract" in this question is limited to those instances in which the professor first establishes a condition by syllabus and then violates that condition.)

a Such a professor would probably be regarded as an "unfair" grader, but even more strongly stated, that professor might be in breach of the course contract. A professor does not have to award a final exam grade based only on the exams given, but once that condition is stated, and not modified in a timely manner by the professor, the condition should be enforceable.

b The professor might still be said to have breached the "contract." Because "custom" is one of the maxims by which judges and jurors give meaning to contract terms, the student could easily submit evidence that rarely is the midterm exam regarded as worth *more* than the final exam in a course. With no evidence to the contrary in the syllabus, it would be assumed that the midterm exam would be worth either *less than,* or *the same as,* the final exam. A professor could easily defeat this expectation by announcing in the syllabus that the midterm is worth more.

2 Ray is probably correct, but several interpretations are possible. In all likelihood, few judges would enforce the contract because it involves a huge profit to one of the parties (Norm) with virtually no loss or risk of loss on his part. If Norm had given more money so as to make it even arguably a "bargaining," or if Norm had gained his profit by virtue of having borne a risk that Ray was unwilling to bear, more judges would have enforced the contract.

Some courts might have focused on intention—on whether the parties had a "meeting of the minds." By virtue of his behavior, Ray might be said to have been joking and thus not having made a serious offer. However, the evidence is contradictory. (For instance, Ray states, "I changed my mind," which indicates that he believes that, shortly before, he did form the intent to contract.)

Many courts would use precedents for Ray (if they existed) or the statute of frauds (if the agreement had not been in writing) to avoid having to decide on the preceding abstract methods. But the common ground of the judges is that this is not a contract that the vast majority of judges would want to have enforced through the legal system.

8

BUSINESS AND THE LEGISLATIVE IMPERATIVE:
Gramm-Rudman-Hollings and the Budgetary Process

James P. Hill
Central Michigan University

INTRODUCTION

Oftentimes the publicity and subsequent analysis of celebrated decisions by the U.S. Supreme Court overshadow other significant aspects of a case, such as whether or not the legal questions raised were the product of a deliberative legislative process. Frequently, so little attention is paid to understanding the legislative origins of a case being analyzed by legal scholars that the average business person can be forgiven for discounting or even ignoring the legislative aspects of the case, the assumption being that bureaucratic regulations and court interpretations of business law are all that is worth studying.

The cursory attention paid by the media to the central role of state statutes in recent Supreme Court controversial rulings on the burning of the U.S. flag[1] and abortion[2] would seem to corroborate an increasingly held belief that legislative enactments are merely hortatory. How many people outside the legal community, for example, are aware or even care that the Court's opinions in these two cases were interpretations of Texas and Missouri statutes, respectively?

Yet both of these cases did not arise in a vacuum. The prior and subsequent deliberative actions by elected legislative bodies are still an important element in fully understanding the changing role of the law in business decision making. Unfortunately, it seems that discussion of the importance of the legislative process has largely been relegated to the political science and public administration arenas.

---

[1] *Texas v. Johnson,*—U.S.—(June 20, 1989).
[2] *Webster v. Reproductive Health Services,*—U.S.—(July 3, 1989).

THE FISCAL CRISIS

The advent of $200 billion U.S. deficits and the doubling and perhaps tripling of the national debt to $3 trillion in this decade alone, however, has gained the attention of businesses not only nationwide but internationally as well. Businesses are now becoming actively involved in deficit issues and asking how our nation has become so deeply indebted in such a short period of time. Consequently, members of the business community are beginning to realize the crucial impact of legislative macroeconomic decisions on the business environment, and how ill-prepared future business leaders are to effectively participate in resolving the deepening federal fiscal crisis.

The hard fiscal facts are indeed sobering. The U.S. government has operated in the black in only one year since 1961. Congress, which has the sole authority under the U.S. Constitution to borrow, spend, and tax, could convene and immediately adjourn without passing a single law and still spend approximately $500 billion.[3] What growing deficits mean in terms of interest rates, inflation, venture capital, and foreign investment will be explored in this article, as will the legislative actions that led to and continue to guide national spending decision making.

Hopefully, after reading this brief legislative case study, more attention will be given to the legislative aspects of court decisions in order to provide a more robust view of the business environment within which they must operate.

CONGRESS AND THE BUDGET

To demonstrate the importance of understanding the legislative process and the legislative origins of court cases, this chapter will focus upon congressional enactment of the Balanced Budget and Emergency Deficit Control Act of 1985, Pub L. 99-177 (amended November 9, 1987, Pub L. 100-158), 2 U.S.C.A. 901, hereinafter referred to as the Gramm-Rudman-Hollings Act—so named for the three key authors of the legislation. It also will analyze the U.S. Supreme Court case that overturned this law, *Bowsher v. Synar,* 106 S. Ct. 3181 (1986). (It should be emphasized, however, that this focus on the congressional level is merely a result of space constraints and is not meant to downplay the importance of state legislation on business decisions.)

To understand how the well-known Gramm-Rudman-Hollings law became the focus of national attention and a 1986 U.S. Supreme Court decision, some legislative background is needed as to how congressional budget decisions were made (or not made) that led to this new deficit reduction law. Particularly since World War II, congressional budget decision making had become largely a piecemeal, political process rather than a unified, fiscally responsible, decision-making process. The apparent emphasis in the budget process has

---

[3] Walter J. Oleszek, *Congressional Procedures and the Policy Process,* 3d ed., CQ Press, Washington, D.C., 1989, p. 47.

been on federal spending for re-election purposes, with little thought as to where the revenues to pay for new spending would come from. This spend now, pay later, attitude has resulted in perpetual deficit spending (in the past 39 years, the government has operated in the black only five times), a decision that may seem irrational to a business student but not to a member of Congress whose "profit" is measured in votes, not dollars.

Concern over the piecemeal budget process led Congress in 1974 to pass the Congressional Budget and Impoundment Control Act, 2 U.S.C.A. 631 (1982) (hereinafter referred to as the 1974 Budget Act). This 1974 Budget Act created budget committees in both houses of Congress, as well as a Congressional Budget Office (CBO), to monitor congressional spending and revenues. It was an attempt to force Congress to pass concurrent budget resolutions early in the budget process, to establish an orderly timetable for enacting appropriations legislation, and hopefully to constrain congressional spending habits as well.

However, the 1974 Budget Act did not work as well as its proponents had hoped. As Professor E. Donald Elliot described the situation, "The aggregate spending goals (under the 1974 Act) eventually became merely totals of the spending programs authorized by appropriations committees in various areas, rather than acting as genuine constraints."[4] He also described a further problem with the act; namely, that votes on revenue matters were still not tied to budget resolution votes, so Congress could continue to vote for costly new programs but against new taxes to pay for them.[5]

The decade of the 1980s brought a new administration to power that was determined to reduce taxes and increase defense spending at the same time that Congress was intent on avoiding cuts in domestic spending. The result was a major tax reduction law, increased defense spending, and an insufficient decrease in domestic spending to offset the lost revenues and increased defense spending. The consequence of this "policy" was huge annual deficits averaging over $200 billion between 1983 and 1986. The growing deficits resulted in what Chief Justice Burger was later to describe as "fiscal and economic problems of unprecedented magnitude."[6]

THE GRAMM-RUDMAN-HOLLINGS SOLUTION

It was apparent as the deficits grew that the 1974 budget law was not an effective constraint on congressional spending. A credible mechanism was necessary to enforce budget targets, and the eventual result was passage of the Gramm-Rudman-Hollings law in 1986, a major revision of the budget process.

It should be noted, however, that Gramm-Rudman-Hollings was not a piece of legislation deliberated over a period of 2 years as was the 1974 Budget Act.

---

[4] E. Donald Elliot, "Regulating the Deficit after *Bowsher v. Synar*," 4 *Yale Journal on Regulation* 356 (Spring, 1987).
[5] *Ibid.*, p. 356.
[6] *Bowsher*, 106 S. Ct. at 3193.

Instead, it was an amendment to an emergency national debt ceiling increase bill that was introduced on the Senate floor without prior committee hearings and enacted into law only 3 months later.

A further curiosity about the Gramm-Rudman-Hollings law was that it was approved not so much for creating a new budget process but rather as a means to force the president to negotiate over deficit reduction by use of a draconian automatic sequestration (budget cancellation) procedure. Some members of Congress voted for the bill thinking the president would never sign it, because if it were triggered, it would require that half the budget cuts be from defense programs while exempting nearly 70 percent of all federal spending.

Essentially, the bill established annual budget reductions in order to eliminate the deficit by 1991. The (CBO) and the Office of Management and Budget (OMB) were to make independent estimates of across-the-board-spending cuts if Congress did pass a budget within $10 billion of those annual targets, and these estimates were to be sent to the comptroller of the General Accounting Office (GAO) for reconciliation. The comptroller was then to send the reconciled report to the president listing the percentage reduction for each federal program that would be necessary to meet the annual target, and the president was required to issue a sequestration order implementing the comptroller general's cuts without change.

A weak fallback provision was included in the bill in the eventuality that the law was declared unconstitutional. The provision required the CBO and OMB to average their deficit estimates and automatic cut projections differences and submit their report to a joint House-Senate budget committee. That committee was to translate the report into a joint resolution and report it to each house of Congress no more than 5 calendar days later. No more than 5 days after that, both houses were required to vote on final passage of the joint resolution.

For obvious political reasons, many members of Congress preferred the automatic comptroller approach if politically damaging spending cut decisions were to be made, rather than taking a vote to cut pet programs as provided in the fallback provision. In addition, the Gramm-Rudman-Hollings bill indirectly did what the 1974 Budget Act did not do; namely, tie spending decisions to revenue decisions, because deficit targets took into account expected annual revenues.

Gramm-Rudman-Hollings also had the effect of neutralizing new spending programs by allowing points of order against any new spending legislation that did not indicate the source of new revenue to fund the new program. However, the threat of across-the-board automatic cuts if Congress did not act to meet annual deficit reduction targets was to be crucial for maintaining fiscal responsibility in Congress.

BOWSHER V. SYNAR

It was the key power vested in the comptroller that was challenged by Congressman Charles Bowsher and 11 other congressmen, along with an employees' union and the support of the executive branch. The suit was against the leadership of the House and Senate, as well as the comptroller. The result was the *Bowsher v. Synar* decision overturning the Gramm-Rudman-Hollings law.

Upholding a three-judge district court ruling, *Synar v. U.S.*, 626 F. Supp. 1374 (DC 1986), the Supreme Court ruled that the law violated the separation of powers doctrine. Acting with unusual speed, because the first significant application of the draconian provision of the law was to occur in the summer, the Court found that "[b]y placing the responsibility for execution of the Balanced Budget and Emergency Deficit Control Act of 1985 in the hands of an officer who is subject to removal only by itself, Congress in effect has retained control over the execution of the Act and has intruded into the executive function."[7]

Much has been written about what the Court did and did not decide in this case—from the inflexibility of the Court's use of the separation of powers doctrine to the "executive" nature of the position of comptroller general. But, as important as the invalidation of the role of the comptroller in the law may seem from a short-term perspective, what is overlooked in many analyses is how much the Court relied upon the fallback provision of the law to strike down the comptroller's "executive role," rather than take the less drastic remedy of invalidating the statutory removal provisions of comptroller general law enacted 65 years ago, a provision in the eyes of the Court that made the office appear to be controlled by Congress.

The Court quoted with approval the district court's conclusion that the grant of authority to the comptroller general under Gramm-Rudman-Hollings was a "carefully considered protection against what the House conceived to be the pro-executive bias of the OMB. It is doubtful that the automatic deficit reduction process would have passed without such protection."[8] A more thorough understanding of the legislative history of the budget process should have raised doubts by students about the Court's conclusion that there was careful congressional consideration of the Gramm-Rudman-Hollings law. Furthermore, subsequent congressional action amending this new law one year after the Court's *Bowsher* decision and granting final authority for spending cuts under the revised law to the OMB would seem to contradict the Court's conclusion that Congress feared granting such power to the OMB.

In addition, the Court, in striking down what Justice White in dissent called "one of the most novel and far-reaching legislative responses to a national crisis since the New Deal,"[9] likened their action to their previous decision in *INS v. Chadha*, 462 U.S. 919, 103 S. Ct. 2764 (1983). In *Chadha*, the court struck down a one-house legislative veto provision that Congress previously had enacted in nearly 200 laws to exercise a more efficient means of control over burgeoning growth of regulatory agencies. The Court in *Bowsher* ruled that "[t]o permit an officer [in this case the comptroller general] of Congress to execute the laws would be, in essence, to permit a congressional veto."[10]

[7]*Id*. at 3192–93.
[8]*Id*. at 3192.
[9]*Id*. at 3205.
[10]*Id*. at 3188.

The Court then went on to quote *Chadha* in restating that "the fact that a given law or procedure is efficient, convenient, and useful in facilitating functions of government, standing alone, will not save it if it is contrary to the Constitution. Convenience and efficiency are not the primary objectives—or the hallmarks—of democratic government."[11] Thus, despite acknowledgment by the court of the unprecedented economic problems facing the nation and Justice Blackmun's acknowledgment in dissent that the Gramm-Rudman-Hollings Act "unquestionably ranks among the most important federal enactment of the past several decades,"[12] the Court continued its hostility to new legislative procedures devised to handle both extraordinary regulatory and fiscal problems. The operative principles of business—efficiency and usefulness—were not by themselves considered to be significant in the legal environment, an important lesson for those in the business community who propose strictly business solutions to the complex deficit crisis.

As far as the argument that the *Bowsher* decision forced Congress to accept responsibility for budget deficit, again reference to the evolution of the budget process and subsequent legislative revision of Gramm-Rudman-Hollings in 1987 to grant spending cut authority to the OMB would tend to severely discount this particular impact of the *Bowsher* case.

But perhaps the most significant impact of the *Bowsher* case was not the Court's initial ruling that the comptroller's role violated the separation of powers doctrine, but the fact that it forced Congress to reconsider Gramm-Rudman-Hollings, resulting in a revised law that significantly enhanced executive authority at the expense of Congress. Under the revised Gramm-Rudman-Hollings law (hereinafter Gramm-Rudman II), not only was the timetable for eliminating the deficit extended for 2 years until 1993, but also the role of the pro-legislative CBO became primarily advisory, whereas the pro-executive OMB was empowered to determine the scope of spending cuts if it finds that budget targets are not likely to be met by Congress.

Thus, a clear shift away from the dominant legislative role in budget process has occurred as an aftereffect of the *Bowsher* case, a shift much more significant in terms of long-run national spending policy than the short-term effect of invalidating the role of the comptroller general—an important impact that would have been overlooked if analysis of the *Bowsher* case ignored the legislative process aspects of this case.

MANAGERIAL IMPLICATIONS

In addition to providing a more robust understanding of the political impact of the *Bowsher* case and providing managers with a better understanding of the new realities of the budget process and how they can influence federal spend-

---

[11]*Id.* at 3193.
[12]*Id.* at 3124.

ing decisions, there are also several direct economic reasons for seeking to understand the legislative underpinnings of Gramm-Rudman-Hollings.

First of all, the continued growth of the federal deficit reduces the amount of funds available to business for capital formation and investment purposes, thereby inhibiting business growth. As Leonard Silk explained in an article in the *New York Times,* government's borrowing keeps real interest rates artificially high, causing an overvalued U.S. dollar, aggravating the U.S. trade deficit, and making the United States an increasingly heavy debtor both at home and abroad.[13]

Significantly reducing the U.S. deficit, according to a number of economists, would lower interest rates around the world, leading to a decline in the high value of the U.S. dollar and a subsequent increase in U.S. exports.[14] With these positive macroeconomic benefits to business, why hasn't the deficit been quickly reduced?

One obvious reason gleaned from an understanding of the legislative process and the approach of Congress to budgetary decisions is the recognition that reduction of the deficit is not likely to be resolved according to traditional management practices nor endorsed by the Court because the method chosen by Congress is efficient. The budget deficit process is fraught with political problems, making a quick and efficient resolution both unlikely and unpredictable. Merely striking down the comptroller general's role in the Gramm-Rudman-Hollings law does little by itself to resolve the underlying deficit crisis, for the budgetary process is riddled with gimmicks to avoid politically painful spending cuts.

The most common budget gimmick is to balance the budget on paper through rosy forecasts of the economy. By predicting increased revenues through a high rate of economic growth, lower interest rates during the year, thereby lowering the cost of federal borrowing, and lower inflation and unemployment rates in order to reduce projected costs of federal social programs, the OMB can reduce the short-term political fallout of meeting annual budget targets in the early years of the Gramm-Rudman-Hollings Act.

However, fudging on cuts in the early years only increases the difficulty of meeting more stringent budget targets in the early 1990s. Thus, business ought to be concerned that the future impact of the Gramm-Rudman II deficit reduction plan ironically may be an adverse one. It might result in either further delaying the deficit elimination date beyond 1993, which will only prolong the adverse effects on business of large U.S. deficits, or it may result in requiring the enactment of new revenue sources to meet the later budget deficit targets. The latter course translates into possible new taxes, user fees, or import fees that will likely be targeted at business.

---

[13]Leonard Silk, "Stock Market Gets the Jitters" *The New York Times,* January 10, 1986, p. D2.

[14]For a general discussion of the economic impact of Gramm-Rudman-Hollings, see *The Gramm-Rudman Budget Proposal,* Joint Economic Committee, 99th Congress, 2d Session, U.S. Government Printing Office, 1985.

Thus, the potential adverse long-term effect of this act on business, when viewed from the legislative/political vantage point rather than from a case-analysis approach, ought to be of deep concern to U.S. business. Hopefully, this understanding of the new budget process will dispel any complacency in the business community as to the need for a credible budget reform mechanism in order to avoid the steep economic costs that will accompany continued delay in reducing the deficit.

The short-term effects of the Gramm-Rudman-Hollings law on business are also apparent. On the positive side, some analysts have argued that the law, despite its loopholes, has helped keep a tight rein on spending by applying the concept commonly referred to as "deficit neutrality" to new tax and spending measures. The blossoming of such a requirement under Gramm-Rudman-Hollings, so that legislation proposing new programs or tax cuts must be accompanied by measures that will indicate how to fund these bills, has led to the defeat of costly new programs and tax credits/deduction legislation that might have further exacerbated the budget deficit. In addition, the concept has been credited with keeping the 1986 landmark overhaul of the tax code (Pub. L. 99-514) on track.[15]

On the negative side, confidence or the lack of confidence in Congress's ability to control the deficit has resulted in wild gyrations in the stock and bond markets. Articles in the *Wall Street Journal* credit bond price rallies to reports that Congress plans to strengthen Gramm-Rudman-Hollings,[16] while blaming the plunge in the value of the dollar to European and trader reactions to a U.S. district court ruling that the Gramm-Rudman law is unconstitutional.[17] Chad Dickson, vice president of foreign exchange at Salomon Brothers Inc., makes the case for Gramm-Rudman-Hollings internationally: "The international market views Gramm-Rudman as the last bastion of responsibility. The world views it as an enforcing measure on what has been a cowboy atmosphere.[18]

Perhaps the most dramatic short-term impact attributed in part to the Gramm-Rudman-Hollings law and its 1987 revision was the October 19, 1987, crash of the stock market, resulting in the worst point drop in the Dow Jones industrial average history and eclipsing Black Tuesday, October 28, 1929, which signalled the start of the Great Depression. Although other reasons were also cited for the 1987 crash of the Dow, Martin and Kathleen Feldstein pointed the finger clearly at the deficit: "Make no mistake, the federal budget deficit was the fundamental cause of the recent stock market crash."[19]

Some economists have been quick to tie the crash to a lack of investor con-

---

[15]See "Gramm-Rudman: A Year of Mixed Success," *1986 CQ Almanac,* p. 579.

[16]"Bond Prices Rally, Sparked by Reports Congress Will Fortify Gramm-Rudman," *Wall Street Journal,* July 30, 1987, p. 37 (E).

[17]"Dollar Plummets, Led by a Sell-off by Europeans," *Wall Street Journal,* February 11, 1986, p. 36 (E).

[18]*Ibid.*

[19]"For Healthy Economy, Extend Budget Cuts Years Ahead," *Los Angeles Times,* November 9, 1987, sec. II, 7.

fidence in the political will of Congress to implement Gramm-Rudman II so as to continue reduction of the deficit. Accordingly, a white house fiscal summit was called to address the deficit issue shortly after the October 19 crash, an event that changed the political climate of deficit reduction. Gramm-Rudman-Hollings had framed the process, but as Congressman Barney Frank noted, "The crash did what Gramm-Rudman was supposed to do but never did, force everyone to negotiate."[20]

CONCLUSION

Emphasis on court cases without an adequate understanding of legislative enactments and the legislative processes that frame the legal issues before the courts provides only a partial understanding of the true dynamics of the decision and its impact on business. The *Bowsher* case is important not only because it invalidated a key provision of the Gramm-Rudman-Hollings Act, but also because of the political dynamics it stimulated that have had significant short- and long-term effects on the business climate in the United States and international markets.

More important, managers need to acquire an understanding of the political/legislative process as well as the legal nuances of each case if they are to fully appreciate future macroenvironmental impacts. If investors are convinced that congressional attitudes toward fully implementing Gramm-Rudman II provisions and continuing reduction of the national debt have indeed been strengthened in light of the crash of 1987, then positive business prospects are possible.

If, on the other hand, Congress reverts to its old behavior of avoidance and budget gimmickry to meet deficit reduction targets, then investor confidence will deteriorate, and the negative impacts of a long-term deficit will follow. If political will does indeed sag, the long-term economic prospects for business are grim indeed.

REFERENCES

Abikoff, Kevin, "The Role of the Comptroller General in Light of *Bowsher v. Synar*," 87 *Columbia L. Rev.* 1539 (1987).

Elliot, E. Donald, "Regulating the Deficit After *Bowsher v. Synar*," 4 *Yale Journal on Regulation* 317 (1987).

Eskridge, William, and Philip Frickey, *Cases and Materials on Legislation: Statutes and the Creation of Public Policy*. West Publishing Company, Minneapolis, 1988.

Gifford, Daniel J., "The Separation of Powers Doctrine and the Regulatory Agencies after *Bowsher v. Synar*." 55 *Geo. Wash. L. Rev.* 441 (1987).

Levinson, L. Harold, "Balancing Acts: *Bowsher v. Synar,* Gramm-Rudman-Hollings, and Beyond," 72 *Cornell L. Rev.* 527 (1987).

Oleszek, Walter, *Congressional Procedures and the Policy Process*, 3d ed., CQ Press, Washington, D.C., 1989.

[20]Oleszek, *op. cit.*, p. 69.

Rauch, Jonathan, "The Thickening Fog," *National Journal,* July 12, 1986, pp. 1721–1724.

Redman, Eric, *The Dance of Legislation,* Simon and Schuster, New York, 1973.

Stockman, David, *The Triumph of Politics,* Harper and Row, New York, 1986.

DISCUSSION QUESTIONS

1 Discuss the similarities and differences between a legislative veto in *Chadha* and the "veto" power that Congress has over the comptroller general in *Bowsher.* Do you find the majority or Justice White's dissenting opinion more convincing as to the "veto" issue? Explain.

2 What are the positive and negative aspects of the Supreme Court's refusal to accept new legislative vehicles such as the legislative veto and the sequestration process to handle increasingly complex legislative duties?

3 Because the courts seemingly have only a negative influence on congressional budgetary decision making, how can business be effective in the legislative arena in order to affect budget deficit decisions?

SUGGESTED ANSWERS

1 The focus of this question rests upon Congress's historical hands-off policy as to the comptroller General's removal power versus the more recent use by Congress of the legislative veto power to control agency actions. Then it should be pointed out that the comptroller can be removed only by joint resolution, meaning the president must concur, as contrasted with the concurrent resolution process of the legislative veto that does not require presidential presentment.

2 Focus upon the struggle between a flexible constitutional interpretation so as to keep up with new economic and technological developments that require novel legal solutions with the problem of losing checks on the balance of power between the three branches of government so as to create a dangerous concentration of power in one branch of government. Then discussion could turn to what the proper constitutional role of "independent" agencies as opposed to executive branch agencies should be in light of *Bowsher,* since these independent agencies also seemingly exercise executive power. The *Bowsher* decision is silent on this point.

3 It is here that discussion can center around the enhancement of executive authority in the budget process under Gramm-Rudman II, and how this change offers business an alternative executive branch input that is more centralized than merely lobbying 535 members of Congress or working through three unelected bureaucracies (OMB, CBO, GAO). With this change in the political terrain, it is possible that business can be more effective in seeking national coalitions in order to put pressure on a president with enhanced agency authority to seek real deficit reduction without the need to pursue the more costly and less predictable route of working through the congressional budget maze.

9

ADMINISTRATIVE LAW:
United Technologies Corp. v. U.S. EPA

Renee D. Culverhouse
Auburn University at Montgomery

INTRODUCTION

It would be impossible today for the federal government and its expansive programs to operate without the benefit of administrative agencies. Even though the government's administrative agencies are scarcely 100 years old, they have exerted and will continue to exert a large effect on business and its legal environment. Indeed, it is often said that administrative agencies "have become a veritable fourth branch of the Government."[1] Virtually all business activity, both inside and outside of the United States, is regulated by 50 or so federal agencies.

It is rare to hear praise for a federal agency. Indeed, all one needs do is pick up a daily newspaper or turn on the television to see and hear about abuses of power by various federal agencies. That is probably the exception, however, rather than the rule. With cries of excessive regulation, inadequate regulation, industry collusion, and inattention to public opinion, many seek to derail the federal regulatory process. The truth is that with the complexities of business today, it would be impossible for the government to function without those agencies. Although there is always talk about abolishing this or that federal agency, without them, the burdens of Congress would increase, because the task of passing each and every administrative rule as a law would fall to Congress. No other work could be handled by the Congress, and they would lack the expertise, knowledge, and time to operate the agencies.

---

[1] *FTC v. Ruberoid Co.*, 343 U.S. 470 (1952).

111

ADMINISTRATIVE LAW

Administrative agencies are created by legislation. The powers and functions of each agency are contained within the legislation creating it. Because of the numbers and size of the administrative agencies within the federal government, it would be difficult for all the procedural rules and formalities to be uniform. Congress recognized that difficulty and, in 1946, enacted the Administrative Procedures Act (APA). This law governs the general operations of all federal agencies and covers all phases of the administrative process, imposing uniform guidelines and procedures on those operations and, in the process, protecting private rights.[2]

Agencies engage in prodigious and surprising amounts of legislative activity, adopting rules that affect millions of people and which operate as laws. The rules adopted by those agencies fall into three groups: (1) the internal operations and structure of the agency are governed by *procedural* rules, (2) the meanings and effect of statutes applicable to that agency are set forth in *interpretative* rules, and (3) the exercise of the agency's lawmaking power comes about in *substantive* or *legislative* rules.

To rein in some of the power of those federal agencies, the APA requires all substantive or legislative rules to be presented to the public before they are enacted. The agency must provide both notice of the proposed rule and an opportunity for interested or affected parties to comment on the consequences of the rule. That is done through a hearinglike procedure where those interested parties can present evidence for or against the rule. If there is a need for immediate action, however, an agency may invoke the "good cause" exception to the APA and simply publish a statement, along with the new rule, explaining why normal notice and comment procedures are not necessary.

As you can understand, the process and procedures required for new legislative rules are costly and time-consuming. That, of course, is not the case with interpretative rules. These rules are exempt from the notice and comment requirements of the APA, and no advice must be sought from those affected by the rule. Thus, the classification of a rule as either legislative or interpretative becomes very important for both the agency and those affected by it. That distinction was the subject of the following case.

UNITED TECHNOLOGIES CORPORATION v. U.S. EPA

821 F.2d 714 (D.C. Cir. 1987)

In 1982 Subtitle C of the Resource Conservation and Recovery Act (RCRA),[3] set up a regulatory structure that would oversee the safe treatment, storage, and disposal of hazardous waste from creation to removal. The Envi-

---

[2] See Table 1 for a summary of the major provisions of the APA.
[3] 42 U.S.C. §§ 6921–6934 (1982).

TABLE 1
ADMINISTRATIVE PROCEDURES ACT

Summary of Major Provisions		
APA Section	U.S. Code	Substance of Provision
2	5 U.S.C. § 551	Terms and coverage of the act are provided by definitions.
3	5 U.S.C. § 552	Publication requirements (in the *Federal Register*) for agency rules and regulations are set out.
4,5,6,7,8	5 U.S.C. §§ 553, 554, 555, 556, 557, 558	Procedures and regulations for actions by agencies are established. Specifically covered are functions of rulemaking, adjudication, and review of agency decisions.
10	5 U.S.C. §§ 701, 702, 703, 704, 705, 706	Judicial review of agency decisions is established.

ronmental Protection Agency (EPA) was required to identify the solid waste classified as hazardous waste regulated by the statute and to issue regulations that would establish performance standards for owners and operators of new and existing facilities for treatment, storage, and disposal of hazardous waste. The act required owners and operators of such facilities to obtain operating permits from the EPA. However, this only applied to new facilities.[4] Existing hazardous waste management facilities were allowed to operate on an interim basis until procedures could be implemented for issuing those permits.[5]

The RCRA, as originally enacted, did not require seekers of permits to take significant remedial action to correct past mismanagement of hazardous waste. This was taken care of in 1982 by the Comprehensive Environmental Response, Compensation, and Liability Act (CERCLA), which addressed the cleanup of hazardous disposals not covered by other programs;[6] CERCLA included a "Superfund" to pay for corrective cleanups pending recovery of those costs from the owner or operator originally responsible for the release.

In 1984 the RCRA was amended, requiring: (1) that every landfill or surface impoundment unit seeking a permit after November 8, 1984, meet certain design and monitoring requirements;[7] and (2) that owners and operators take corrective action for all releases of hazardous waste from any solid waste management unit at a facility regardless of the time at which the waste was placed in the unit.[8]

Regulations were then proposed by the EPA to implement the 1984 amendments. Issuing a Final Rule on July 15, 1985, the EPA incorporated into the

---

[4] Section 3004(a) of the act, 42 U.S.C. § 6924(a) (Supp. III 1985).
[5] Section 3005(a) of the act, 42 U.S.C. § 6925(e) (Supp. III 1985).
[6] 42 U.S.C. §§ 9601–9657 (1982).
[7] Section 3004(o) (1) (A), 42 U.S.C. § 6924 (o)(1)(A) (Supp. III 1985).
[8] Section 3004(u), 42 U.S.C. § 6924(u) (Supp. III 1985).

existing regulations a set of requirements from the new RCRA amendments.[9] That Final Rule became effective immediately, without prior notice or an opportunity for comment by interested parties.

Several groups united and filed a petition for review, contending that the Final Rule was invalid because it was promulgated without notice and comment under the APA. The EPA, however, maintained that the Final Rule was not legislative but interpretative and, therefore, outside of the APA's notice and comment requirements. The EPA further contended that, even if the Final Rule were adjudged to be legislative, the "good cause" exception was properly invoked.

The court noted that the APA specifically excludes interpretative rules from its notice and comment procedures.[10] Amplifying on the meaning of such exclusion, the court cited the principles to be used in determining whether or not a rule is interpretative. The characterization of the rule by the agency is certainly relevant to the determination, although not dispositive. Citing its decision in a 1979 case,[11] the court noted that an interpretative rule merely says what the administrative agency thinks the statute means, whereas a legislative rule creates new law, rights, or duties. Under that view, the Final Rule was seen by the EPA as being a codification of the 1984 amendments. In fact, the EPA had carefully separated out proposed rules that dealt with new provisions and had subjected them to the notice and comment procedures.

According to the court, interpretative and legislative rules can be distinguished from each other by looking at the legal base of the rule. If the basis of the rule is specific provisions in a statute and the validity of the rule is determined by the correctness of the agency's interpretation of those provisions, the rule is interpretative. If the basis for the rule is the agency's power to exercise its judgment in implementing a general statutory mandate, the rule is legislative. Because the Final Rule was an attempt to construe specific statutory provisions and its validity depended on whether or not the EPA had correctly interpreted the 1984 amendments, it was clearly interpretative.

The court then went on to address the "good cause" exception invoked by the EPA, noting that its invocation did not automatically cause a rule to be classified as legislative. In citing the "good cause" exception to the notice and comment requirement of the APA,[12] the EPA stated that the requirement would be impracticable, unnecessary, or contrary to the public interest, in that: (1) Congress had explicitly authorized such exception in the promulgation of the regulations, (2) immediate action was not a necessity, and (3) the EPA would not be likely to gain anything from public comment because of the na-

---

[9] 50 Fed. Reg. at 28,703.
[10] 5 U.S.C. § 553(b)(A) (1982).
[11] *Citizens to Save Spencer County v. EPA*, 600 F.2d 844 (D.C. Cir. 1979).
[12] 5 U.S.C. § 553(b)(B) (1982).

ture of the regulations. Thus, the court noted that the EPA decision not to use notice and comment procedures was reasonable under the circumstances.

IMPLICATIONS FOR BUSINESS

It should be clear, then, from this case that there is a lot at stake, both from the standpoint of the agency and from the standpoint of industry, when a new regulation is promulgated by that agency. Because the notice and comment requirements of the APA involve a big commitment of both time and money on the part of an agency, it is much simpler either to declare the new rule to be interpretative or to declare it an exception to the notice and comment requirements of the APA than to declare it legislative and go through the process of a public hearing with evidence being presented both for and against the new regulation.

Indeed, the courts say that the agency's characterization will be relevant to a determination of the regulation as legislative or interpretative. In some cases, an agency may be willing to take the chance that its classification of the new regulation as interpretative won't be challenged. Even if it is, an agency will likely hedge its bet by noting that the proposed regulation is an exception to the notice and comment requirements because those procedures would be either impracticable, unnecessary, or contrary to the public interest.

If an agency chooses to proceed in that direction, what does a business lose? It loses the opportunity to challenge the regulation *before* it goes into effect. The notice and comment procedures provide interested parties with an opportunity to present their objections so that adverse effects can be considered prior to implementation. Once the new regulation is implemented, the business will then bear the burden and costs of the new requirements, as well as the expense of a challenge. Unless a temporary restraining order can be obtained, staying the effects of the new regulation, a business may be faced with years of being saddled with new rules before its objections can be heard in court. (Note that it took until 1987 for the case discussed earlier to be heard by an appellate court. The new rules went into effect in 1985.)

A business also loses the opportunity to join together with other enterprises that will be similarly adversely affected by the new regulation. Its voice must be heard alone, rather than in concert with others, as it would be at a pre-implementation hearing. Agency administrators and court personnel are like anyone else; numbers talk.

Finally, a business loses its due process rights guaranteed under the U.S. Constitution. Because the new regulation will adversely affect a property interest in the business, either by the loss of profits and/or customers, or the inability to compete through increased costs of operation, the business deserves an opportunity to address those concerns. When a regulation is declared to be interpretative, due process does not attach, and those rights to be heard are lost or never materialize. Because the regulation was not voted on either by Congress or the people it represents, an important safeguard is bypassed.

Much of the way an agency handles its dealings with the businesses it affects depends upon the attitude and atmosphere of the prevailing administration. A spirit of cooperation and openness on the part of those in charge of the agency will result in more public hearings and requests for input than will an adversarial outlook. Business and agencies must work together to foster an attitude of mutual understanding and cooperation so that everyone will benefit.

MANAGERIAL IMPLICATIONS

Because managers can't always rely on the "notice and comment" procedures to give them advance knowledge of the particular rules and regulations of a federal agency which will have an impact on those managers, it becomes important to develop strategies to deal with that eventuality. Managers must develop an aggressive attitude in dealing with the regulatory process. They must also be knowledgeable about the remedies available for administrative acts that are improper. Both of those strategies are discussed hereinafter in some detail.

Aggressive Attitude

Managers can no longer occasionally monitor the climate of Congress or a regulatory agency. "Once in a while" lobbying activities and "lip-service" support of trade associations won't put managers in a position to know what is about to happen. Managers who will be affected by new agency regulations must anticipate those regulations and try to shape and mold them in a way that will be favorable to business in general. Issues of crucial importance to managers and to business must be anticipated. In fact, in some companies and businesses it might be very useful to a manager to have a government relations office in Washington, which can feed critical information back to the manager. Some tactics that might prove helpful include strengthening trade associations, forming political action committees, and seeking alignment of stockholders and other special interest groups in fighting or supporting proposed regulations.

Knowledge of Remedies

If those actions fail and unfavorable regulations are passed without proper notice and comment procedures, the manager must then be informed about and be prepared to act on the remedies available for improper agency action. The action may be challenged in a variety of ways. A manager may want to seek to involve his or her company in a civil lawsuit, alleging monetary damages for the offending regulation. Alternative legal relief might come in the form of an injunction, ordering the agency to cease and desist enforcement of the challenged regulation. Sometimes, the declaratory judgment may be useful so that a company's rights in relation to the agency, and its questioned regulation, can be clarified by the court.

No manager these days, however, can afford to be uninformed about his/her business, how it affects society, and how it may be affected by regulation. Those are issues of crucial importance in fighting the battle against government regulation. The more managers know about all these matters, the less likely the chance that they will be caught off-guard and unaware by new administrative requirements or procedures.

REFERENCES

FCC v. Pacifica Foundation, 98 S. Ct. 3026 (1978).

Fleming, John, "Linking Public Affairs with Corporate Planning," *California Management Review,* Winter 1980, vol. XXIII, no. 2, p. 35.

Gelhorn, Ernest, *Administrative Law and Process in a Nutshell,* West Publishing, St. Paul, Minn., 1972.

General Motors Corp. v. Ruckelshaus, 742 F.2d 1561 (D.C. Cir. 1984) (*en banc*); cert denied, 471 U.S. 1074, 105 S. Ct. 2153, 85 L. Ed. 2d 509 (1985).

Greene, James, *Regulatory Problems and Regulatory Reform: The Perceptions of Business,* The Conference Board, New York, 1980.

Koch, Charles, "Business Can Have Free Enterprise—If It Dares," *Business and Society Review,* Winter 1978–1979, no. 28, p. 54.

McGrath, Phyllis, *Redefining Corporate-Federal Relations,* The Conference Board, New York, 1979.

Royster, Vermont, "'Regulation' Isn't a Dirty Word," *The Wall Street Journal,* September 9, 1987, p. 30.

Weidenbaum, Murray L., *The Future of Business Regulation,* AMACOM: American Management Association, 1979.

DISCUSSION QUESTIONS

1 What is the difference between an interpretative rule or regulation and a legislative one?

2 On what general basis did the court say it was possible to distinguish the rule in the *UT* case as an interpretative rule rather than a legislative one?

3 What factors should be considered, according to the court in the *UT* case, in deciding whether an agency regulation is interpretative or legislative?

4 What difference does it make to a business affected by an agency whether that agency's new regulation is interpretative or legislative?

5 It has been said that corporate managers are whores, not caring who is in office, to what party they belong, or what they stand for, so long as they can buy a politician. Do you agree or disagree with that characterization? Why or why not? [The statement was made by Representative Robert F. Dorman (R-Calif.).]

SUGGESTED ANSWERS

1 Interpretative rules are the agency's idea or interpretation of the meaning of the statutes that govern it. These rules tell interested and affected parties what the agency expects and requires of them with respect to the governing legislation. Legislative or substantive rules, on the other hand, have the effect of law. These rules are policy expressions of the agency.

2 The court in this case looked at how the EPA had separated out some of the proposed rules and subjected them to the notice and comment procedures of the APA. Clearly, the EPA thought that the Final Rule challenged here was interpretative. Also, it attempted to construe specific statutory provisions, and its construction of those provisions may or may not be correct. If the EPA did not interpret the 1984 amendments correctly, the Final Rule will not be valid.

3 To distinguish between interpretative and legislative rules, it is necessary to look at the legal base of the rules. If an agency rule is interpreting specific provisions of the governing statute, merely stating what the agency thinks the statute means, it is interpretative. If the agency is exercising its power and judgment to issue a mandate, thereby creating new law, rights, or duties, it is legislative. Aiding in this determination is the agency's idea of into which category the rule falls.

4 If a rule is legislative or substantive in nature, the agency is required to follow the "notice and comment" provisions of the APA. This allows those affected by the proposed regulation to appear at a hearing and give testimony and evidence in support of or against it. They are afforded an opportunity to change the rule by changing the thinking of the agency. When a rule is interpretative, those safeguards do not apply, and there is no opportunity for a business to object to the rule before it goes into effect.

5 This question is designed to provoke discussion among students relative to the strategies discussed in the final section of the chapter. Are business managers as corrupt as Mr. Dorman says? Are members of Congress any less corrupt?

PART FOUR

THE COMMON LAW FOUNDATIONS OF CAPITALISM

10

THE CONTRACT LAW DUTY TO READ

E. Elizabeth Arnold
University of San Diego

INTRODUCTION

> "Wait a minute! I did not agree to do anything like that!"
>
> "Yes you did. It says so right here on the paper we both signed."
>
> "Well, I did not read that part. I would never have signed if I had seen that part."

Parties to contracts play out variations on the foregoing scenario all too of-ten. One or both of them did not read the entire writing, signed it anyway, and, after the fact of signing, did not want to do what the writing they signed said they would do. Also all too often, the parties end up asking a court to decide whether one of them is bound by a term he or she did not read. This chapter examines the circumstances under which a court will hold a party responsible for a contract term even though that party did not read the term. This chapter also details the circumstances under which a court will *not* hold a party re-sponsible for a contract term the party did not read.

The importance of understanding the difference between the two almost goes without saying. A business that wants to enforce a written contract term does not want find that, because of some factor related to the other party's failure to read that term, the business cannot enforce it. Yet, all of us, including judges, can probably relate to the surprised party in the preceding scenario. For one reason or another, we have probably all put off doing some reading we wished later we had not put off. Taking as fact the commonality of this kind of human conduct, should contract law allow it as an excuse to escape from liability? What would allowing the excuse do to the viability of written contracts? In the discussion that follows, we will see that when the law does impose liability despite failure to read, it tries to reconcile these tensions.[1]

THE DECIDING RULE

Interestingly, nowhere in written, black-letter contract law can one find an express, affirmative rule requiring parties to read contract documents before they sign or accept them. Moreover, the courts will only enforce contract terms to which the parties have *actually* agreed. It is well settled, however, that a party is deemed to have actually agreed to all the terms of a writing which he or she signs or accepts. That a party may not, in fact, have read the writing generally does not provide an escape from liability. Lack of escape for failure to read then, by implication, imposes a duty to read.

Reported case decisions to this effect fill the shelves of law libraries. Law summaries devote considerable attention to it. A venerable California case, *Greve v. Taft Realty Co.*, 101 Cal. App. 343 (1929) (review denied by the California Supreme Court on December 16, 1929), illustrates. In *Greve,* Frank H. Greve, a real estate broker, sued Taft Realty to recover a commission of $6266.50. Greve based his cause of action on the following signed writing:

"Hollywood, Calif. 6/6/23

"It is understood and agreed that Frank H. Greve is to receive 2% of the gross sales made by us in the Greve Tract at the S. W. intersection of Pico Blvd. and Preuss Road, known as Tract No. 6800, in consideration of his getting this tract for us to handle.

"We also agree that he shall be paid 2% gross on sales from any other acceptable tract he secures for us to handle, or any other person bringing us an acceptable tract shall be paid the same amount.

"Taft Realty Co.
"By B. Y. Taft.
"Mildred Taft Tinkham.
"George W. Zent.
"Chester A. Taft."[2]

---

[1] Generally, states, instead of the federal government, regulate contract law. This chapter cites California law almost exclusively. Admittedly, California has a reputation for leading the way in breaking new ground for law. California is, however, mainstream in the area of the law discussed in this chapter. Thus, the concepts presented here generally apply throughout the nation.

[2] These signatures reveal the second major issue in this case, that is, the question of whether the corporation is bound when the signatures of its agents are not accompanied by statements

On June 14, 1923, Greve succeeded in getting the tract for Taft Realty. Taft Realty then sold Greve tract lots for a total gross of $328,725 on which it received a 15 percent commission. Taft Realty paid Greve no commission whatsoever. At trial B. Y. Taft and Chester A. Taft both testified that they did not read the agreement before signing it and neither of them intended to bind Taft Realty by their signatures.

In deciding it could give no legal effect to the testimony of B. Y. and Chester, the court cited, among others, the following California Supreme Court precedent:

> If a person enters into a contract with another, between whom and himself no relation of a special trust or confidence exists, and it is reduced to writing by such other person, and the means of knowledge of the terms of the writing are equally open to both, and he signs it without reading or having it read by someone for him, he cannot avoid a liability created by the writing.[3]

The court then ruled: "These cases and others which might be cited clearly establish the law that the testimony of the witnesses Taft that they did not read the commission agreement is wholly insufficient to support the finding of the (trial) court that the corporation was not bound by the agreement."[4]

Thus, in *Greve* we find both an implicit statement of the duty to read and the limits of that duty. The court does not expressly say the parties must read. The court says, instead, that parties may not use evidence that they did not read to support a conclusion that the written agreement does not bind them. By implication, then, the court says: "Read, for the agreement you sign or accept does bind you." The court does limit application of the rule to the usual, competent parties entering a truly voluntary, arms' length agreement. In actuality, then, the duty applies in most contract situations. Factors such as fraud and confidential relationships are the *unusual;* not the usual. One condition precedent must first be satisfied. The parties must have the means of knowledge of the written terms.

THE CONTINUING DISPUTE AND RESOLUTIONS FOR IT

Despite *Greve* and many, many similar court decisions, to this day parties continue to raise their own failure to read as a defense to liability. After all, they really had not agreed and contract law centers on real mutual meeting of the minds. In effect parties often claim the natural human tendency not to read causes a failure of the condition precedent; that is, by reason of human nature they do not have the means of knowledge of the written terms.

The problem with taking this claim at face value is obvious. Any time parties decided they did not want to perform a particular term, they would need

---

showing the nature of their representative capacity. As that question is an agency law question, and not a contract law question, we will consider the question no further here than to note that the court ruled that the corporation *was* bound by these signatures.

[3] *Hawkins v. Hawkins,* 50 Cal. 558 (1875).
[4] *Id.*

only to claim they had not read the term to nullify it. No contract would be worth the paper it was written on.

Court Solutions

Over the years, courts have struggled to reconcile the mutuality and duty to read requirements. They have also tried to deal fairly with both parties while at the same time recognizing the above-mentioned natural tendency of people *not* to read all the words on papers they sign or accept, as well as recognizing the opportunity for abuse should the excuse be allowed. Thus, in *Ames v. Southern Pacific Co.*, 141 Cal. 728, 721 (1904), the court ruled that a passenger *is* responsible for terms printed on a ticket accepted by that passenger *if* those terms were brought to the passenger's notice. Similarly, in *Laurrus v. First National Bank,* 122 Cal. App. 2d 884, 889 (1954), the court held a customer was liable for a term printed on a signature card. The term consisted of one sentence printed in readable type size and the customer had overnight possession of the card at home before signing and returning it. The average reasonable person would have read the term and, thus, Laurrus—being within that class of persons—was liable on the term with, or without, actually personally reading it. In both cases, then, the parties had the means of knowledge of the written terms.

Legislative Solutions

The Uniform Commercial Code. Drafters of the Uniform Commercial Code confronted the problem in a number of sections. Basically, the code does implicitly impose a duty to read on the parties—particularly when the parties are merchants. For illustration consider Section 2-201, Statute of Frauds.[5] Section 2-201 allows a merchant who receives a written, signed confirmatory memorandum of an oral agreement 10 days in which to give written notice of objection to the memorandum. A merchant who does not object is bound by the memorandum, and it satisfies the code's Statute of Frauds even though the party to be charged with breach of contract has not signed it. Implicitly, then, that section tells merchants they have 10 days to get their reading done or else accept the consequences of failure to read—here losing a Statute of Frauds defense.

Code Section 2-207 provides a second illustration in its treatment of additional terms in the acceptance. As between merchants, additional terms in the acceptance become a part of the contract unless the offeror gives notice of objection to the terms in a reasonable time. Again, implicitly that sections tells

---

[5] In general, statutes of frauds provide that certain classes of contracts are *unenforceable* in a court of law unless those contracts are evidenced by a writing signed by the party to be charged with breach of contract. The code so provides for contracts for the sale of goods for $500 or more.

merchants they have a reasonable time to get their reading done or else accept the consequences of failure to read—here losing control of the contract terms.

Generally, the code approach comports with the previously described approach of the courts. Before liability attaches the party must have the means of knowledge of the written term at issue. Consider Section 2-205, Firm Offer,[6] for example. Frequently *offerees* supply the forms containing firm offer terms. Section 2-205 mandates for an offeree-supplied form, as a prerequisite to enforceability of the firm offer term, that the *offeror* sign separately *on the term*. In effect, the act of signing separately at the term, as well as at the bottom, calls the offeror's attention to the term. The condition precedent is then satisfied and the duty to read activated.

The code's provision for effective disclaimer of implied warranty[7] gives an additional example. According to Section 2-316(2) a written exclusion of the implied warranty of merchantability or the implied warranty fitness takes no effect unless that exclusion is "conspicuous." Section 1-201(10) defines as "conspicuous" a term that when "so written...a reasonable person against whom it is to operate ought to have noticed it." The format of the writing, then, should call the other party's attention to the writing.

Experts recommend boldfaced, capital letters of a strongly contrasting color for the *entire* text of the disclaimer language. These same experts also counsel caution in placement of the disclaimer. Although placing an otherwise effective disclaimer on the back of a page does not automatically invalidate the disclaimer, courts have invalidated disclaimers so placed—particularly when no "conspicuous" language on the front directs the reader to the back for disclaimer provisions. *See,* for example, *Massey-Ferguson v. Utley,* 439 S.W.2d 57 (1969). Assuming the seller complies with these requirements, however, the buyer then does have a duty to read, for the buyer will be bound by the term. The reasonable person would have noticed it.

Other Statutory Solutions

In wrestling with human nature and the need for parties to quickly deliver effective communication, legislatures have turned more and more to statutory solutions similar to that of the code's "conspicuous" requirement. In one instance, the California legislature addressed the problems of parking lot operators who wanted to limit their contract liability for bailed[8] automobiles. The

---

[6] A "firm offer" is an offer the merchant-offeror cannot revoke for the time specified or, if no time is specified, for a reasonable time not to exceed 3 months.
[7] When making a warranty, a seller assumes responsibility for one or more features of the goods or services sold. If the goods or services sold do not measure up to the warranty, the seller is liable for the value of the deficiency. When the code implies a warranty, to sell goods is to automatically make the warranty unless the seller effectively nullifies, that is, disclaims, the warranty.
[8] To "bail" an auto the owner delivers custody of the auto to another who has an ultimate duty either to return the auto or satisfactorily explain why the auto cannot be returned. Park

1957 California Civil Code, Section 1630, as amended in 1970, permits a binding term of limitation if the printed bailment contract says (1) in 10-point type or larger, "THIS CONTRACT LIMITS OUR LIABILITY—READ IT; (2) all provisions are printed in 8-point type or larger; and (3) a copy of the contract printed in large type in an area 17 inches by 22 inches is conspicuously posted at each entrance.

California and other states have similar "conspicuous" requirements for retail credit or installment sales (Calif. Civ. Code Section 1803.2), subordination agreements[9] (Calif. Civ. Code Sections 2952.2 and 2952.3), sale of motor vehicles pursuant to a financing agreement (Calif. Civ. Code Section 2981), health studio services (Calif. Civ. Code Section 1812.85), and home solicitation contracts (Calif. Civ. Code Section 1689.7). Provisions in the California Insurance Code require varying type sizes, colors, and intensities of darkness for different categories of insurance contracts. Ten-point type tends to be the size of choice, and perusal of California's statutes leads one to the conclusion that California has left no kind of written agreement untouched by a "conspicuous" requirement. Nevertheless, the failure-to-read problem persists.

In its Civil Code Section 1860, California tries to solve the problem by requiring "conspicuousness" in sign placement instead of type size. California Civil Code Section 1860 provides that hotels have no liability to guests for loss of valuables left in the guests' rooms if the hotel keeps a separate, fireproof safe and *prominently* posts signs in those rooms—signs that announce availability of the safe for valuable repository and disclaimer of liability for valuables left in the rooms.

Requiring conspicuous type and positioning of written terms does not solve the problem of how to establish binding written terms with parties who do not read English. Some legislatures have developed a partial solution. In its Civil Code Section 1632, California requires tradespeople and businesspeople who conduct most of their negotiations in Spanish to supply, on request, Spanish translations of most commercial contracts and of contracts providing that the prevailing party, in a suit to enforce the contract, shall be entitled to attorney's fees. Civil Code Section 1632 seeks to ensure that parties are informed of their right to request a Spanish translation. The statute requires covered tradespeople and businesspersons to display conspicuously a Spanish-language notice of the right.

This solution is only partial, of course, because it does not cover negotiations conducted primarily in some language other than Spanish or English. Also, it does not address the problem of illiteracy. In 1875 the *Hawkins* court

---

ing lot operators want to avoid liability for autos or property stolen while in the operators' custody.

[9] In a "subordination agreement," one lender who holds a priority security interest in the property of another agrees that a second lender shall have a better security interest in that same property. In other words, the first lender agrees to subordinate its security interest to that of the second lender. Often the first lender has advanced funds for the purchase of unimproved land and the second lender will advance funds for the construction of a building on that land.

used this approach to the problem of illiteracy: "The fact that the plaintiff was illiterate, and could read manuscript only with difficulty, did not render this precaution (to read the term or have it read for him) less necessary. Judgment affirmed."

An exemption in California's Civil Code, Section 1632, perhaps provides a key to the solution. When the other party negotiates through his or her *own* interpreter, the tradesperson or businessperson need not supply a Spanish language translation. Relying on Section 1632 for guidance, tradespersons or businesspersons who negotiate primarily in languages other than English or with the illiterate can seek to protect themselves by insisting those persons provide their own interpreters or readers.

CONTRACT INTERPRETATION AND THE DUTY TO READ

Rules for court interpretation of contracts also impose on the parties a duty to read. The parol evidence rule requires the courts to determine the intentions of the parties from the writing alone when the parties have an integrated agreement—that is, a writing the parties intend as a complete and final expression of their understanding. Reported case decisions often say the rule limits court inquiry into intentions of the parties to the "four corners of the contract." By prohibiting oral testimony, the rule mandates reading the writing, for the writing alone "testifies" in litigation. If the writing must stand on its own, then it should say what all the parties want it to say. Only by reading the writing can the parties know whether the writing does state all the terms as the parties orally agreed to them.

Rules for court interpretation of writings also implicitly require the parties to do more than just read; they require parties to both keep abreast of trends in their respective trades or professions and to read those writings with care. Courts interpret ordinary words according to their ordinary meaning and technical words according to their technical meaning. The problem is that some apparently ordinary words have special technical meanings in particular lines of work. To sort out things out in these circumstances, the courts use the meaning that people in the particular profession or trade normally use. Thus, for example, use of the ordinary word *assignment* can lead to trouble for the uninformed and/or careless reader. It can technically mean "homework" or it can mean "transfer of contract rights."

MANAGERIAL IMPLICATIONS

Business managers can derive several implications from these materials. First, to create enforceable contracts, managers need to satisfy the condition that gives rise to the duty to read. Managers must ensure that their intended audiences have the means to know the terms managers want enforced. Second, in today's environment of heightened concerns for consumers and others with whom business deals, managers must give more than lip service to calling attention to terms. They must take every reasonable measure necessary to cause actual reading and comprehension at the formation of the contract. In so doing, management must take into account the human tendency not to read carefully. Third, management should recognize that the rules work both ways. In most cases, management has the means to know the terms of proffered written contracts. Thus, management, too, has a duty to read.

The foregoing materials show that management can and should look both to the statutes and published case decisions for guidance in creating enforceable contracts. Management can also look to communication experts for guidance. As we have seen, the statutes often contain specific instructions for designing and drafting contract terms. Through their written decisions, the courts instruct as to both acceptable and unacceptable efforts to truly communicate contract terms. In effect, the statutes and the cases urge effective business writing. Thus, experts in business communication can provide valuable assistance to the business manager.

In light of management's duty to read and the natural human tendency not to read—a tendency as commonly found in business managers as in others—managers should seek to institutionalize reading. Reliance on the assumption that members of a business organization will read would be misplaced.

CONCLUSION

By implication, contract law imposes on parties a duty to read. We draw the implication from the long-standing rule that competent parties to an arms' length bargain are deemed to have accepted all written contract terms they had the means to know. Parties have the means to know terms that are actually called to their attention orally or by a writing. With the means to know a term and, thus, with acceptance established, liability for failure to honor the term follows. With the means to know a term obscured and acceptance, thus, not effective, no liability for failure to read ensues.

REFERENCES

Ames v. Southern Pacific Co., 141 Cal. 728, 721 (1904).
Calif. Civ. Code § 1632
Calif. Civ. Code § 1639
Calif. Civ. Code § 1644
Calif. Civ. Code § 1645
Calif. Civ. Code § 1689.7
Calif. Civ. Code § 1803.2
Calif. Civ. Code § 1812.85
Calif. Civ. Code § 1860
Calif. Civ. Code § 2952.2
Calif. Civ. Code § 2952.3
Calif. Civ. Code § 2981
Calif. Comm. Code § 1630

THE CONTRACT LAW DUTY TO READ

Calif. Comm. Code § 2-201
Calif. Comm. Code § 2-207
Calif. Comm. Code § 2-205
Calif. Comm. Code § 2-316
Calif. Comm. Code § 1-201 (10)
Greve v. Taft Realty Co., 101 Cal. App. 343 (1929) (review denied by the California
  Supreme Court on December 16, 1929).
Hawkins v. Hawkins, 50 Cal. 558 (1875).
Laurrus v. First National Bank, 122 Cal. App. 2d 884, 889 (1954).
Massey-Ferguson v. Utley, 439 S. W.2d 57 (1969).
White, James J., and Robert S. Summers, *Handbook of the Law Under the Uniform
  Commercial Code,* § 12-5.
Williston 3d §§ 90A–90E
1 Witkin 9th § 119–127.

DISCUSSION QUESTIONS

1 Betty owns and operates an antique shop. A sign on one wall of her shop proclaims:
  "All sales final and 'as is.' Seller makes no warranties of any kind, express or implied." A customer purchased what both the customer and Betty thought was an antique diamond ring. The ring proved to be a fake. The customer attempted to return
  the ring and obtain a refund. Betty refused pointing to the sign on the wall. The customer had not read the sign. If the customer sues, will the customer prevail? If you
  need more facts to resolve the issue, what additional facts do you need?
2 After protracted negotiations, Widgets Inc., and one of its suppliers agreed to a contract for the sale by the supplier to Widgets of widget-making materials. The supplier
  reduced the agreement to writing. Both parties signed at the bottom of the writing.
  Both initialed each paragraph in the writing as well. During the signing and initialing
  process, both parties joked about that fact that Widgets did not actually read any of
  the terms. It later turned out that the writing contained a payment-on-delivery term
  that Widgets did not believe the parties had agreed to during their negotiations. If
  Widgets refuses to honor the term and the supplier sues to enforce it, who will prevail? What about the fact that the supplier knew Widgets did not read the contract
  before signing it and initialing each of its paragraphs?
3 Compare and contrast the contract law duty to read with constitutional due process
  requirements.

SUGGESTED ANSWERS

1 Betty has attempted to include the disclaimer as a term of the sale. Under the basic
  duty-to-read rule, the customer will be bound by the term if it was called to her attention or the reasonable person would have noticed it. No facts show that Betty
  literally called the customer's attention to the sign. Whether the reasonable person
  would have noticed the sign is problematic. The sign needs to be conspicuous. We
  are not told anything about the size or color of the sign's text, nor are we told where
  the sign was placed in the store. The courts would certainly view a sign placed in a
  dark corner at the back of the store quite differently from a sign placed in a well-

lighted, eye-level spot right next to the cash register where every customer is sure to pause.

2 Widgets signed the contract at the bottom and initialed each contract paragraph. No facts show fraud or any type of confidential relationship. That the supplier and Widgets joked about the fact that Widgets did not read what it signed provides Widgets no relief. The supplier did not prevent Widgets from reading the contract. Each term, including the term in dispute, was called to Widgets' attention. The reasonable person, under these circumstances—particularly in light of the fact that negotiations were protracted—would have read the contract. Thus, Widgets is deemed to have agreed to it and be responsible for it.

3 Due process requires fair play and ensures fair play by denying enforcement against parties who have not had notice and opportunity to respond. No duty to read exists unless the party has the means of knowledge of the terms. Without such means, the party has no notice and no opportunity to respond. It would offend our sense of fair play under these circumstances to hold the party responsible for the term. Fairness requires notice as a precondition to the duty to read. Thus, the duty to read exists only if the concepts essential to those of due process have been satisfied.

11

WRONGFUL DISCHARGE AND THE *FOLEY* CASE

Maria Boss
California State University at Los Angeles

INTRODUCTION

The At-Will Doctrine: Overview

The concept of wrongful discharge evolved as a response to the harshness of the at-will employment doctrine. This doctrine, an aspect of the laissez-faire economic philosophy of the nineteenth century, provides that in the absence of an employment contract an employer can fire an employee for good cause, no cause, or even bad cause. Cases reflecting the at-will philosophy specifically state that the presence of improper motive or ill will on the part of the employer is irrelevant. Conversely, the at-will employee is free to quit at any time. Note that it is assumed that either party in an at-will relationship will provide proper notice of intent to terminate. The at-will principle demonstrates the mutuality concept in contracts: Because an employer can never force an employee to work owing to the U.S. Constitution's prohibition against involuntary servitude, the employee should not be able to force the employer to accept him or her as a worker if the employer does not wish to do so.

Erosion of At-Will Concepts

Despite this tradition of at-will employment, legislatures and courts began to erode the doctrine in recognition of the vulnerability of U.S. workers and of the overwhelming importance of a job in a worker's life. Having a job usually ensures not only economic survival and stability, it also contributes to one's sense of self-worth and status in the community. Thus, a significant encroachment on the at-will doctrine was federal and state legislation limiting an employer's ability to discharge an employee for a discriminatory purpose. The most important federal law prohibiting such discrimination is Title VII of the Civil Rights Act of 1964, which protects persons from discharge based on their race, color, religion, sex, or national origin. There is wide variation among state and local government statutes in the scope of classes of persons who are protected from discriminatory discharge. For example, a state statute or municipal ordinance may be broader than the federal law and prohibit discharge based not only on race, religion, color, national origin, or sex but also on categories such as ancestry, physical handicap, medical condition, sexual orientation, and marital status.

Other significant restraints on the employer's right to fire an employee are set forth in union contract provisions and in civil service protections. However, despite these restraints, it has been estimated that at least half of all employed Americans are governed by employment at-will.

In order to provide protection to those workers who were not specifically covered by antidiscrimination legislation, some state courts began to carve out exceptions to at-will employment, and, thus, a body of case law has evolved that supplements the federal, state, and local government statutory protections. Such case law exception in California has even been made in the face of a California Labor Code provision, which creates a presumption of at-will employment. ("An employment having no specified term may be terminated at the will of either party.")

Judicial Activism Versus Judicial Restraint

In taking such an aggressive approach, the California courts were following the philosophy of judicial activism: that is, it is up to the courts to implement social change if the legislatures refuse to make laws reflecting current social and economic realities. By contrast, courts following the philosophy of judicial restraint adhere to the traditional separation of powers set forth in the Constitution and believe it is wrong for courts to usurp the legislative function by making law. Under a philosophy of restraint, the proper judicial role is only to interpret the law.

The issue of judicial activism versus judicial restraint received a good deal of publicity in 1988 during the U.S. Senate confirmation hearings of Justice Bork, who had been nominated to the U.S. Supreme Court by President Reagan. There was never any allegation made that Justice Bork had any ethical violations or improprieties in his background; rather, the entire reason for his rejection by the Senate was based on his well-known record as a vigorous advocate of judicial restraint. The Bork nomination was the first time in U.S. history that a Supreme Court nominee was rejected based on his or her judicial philosophy. Although it is true that a judge or justice's bias regarding activism or restraint can influence his or her decision making, critics of the Bork hearings argued that such influence should not disqualify one from judicial service.

State courts that refuse to create any exceptions that would erode in any way the at-will doctrine are following the philosophy of judicial restraint. For example, the Louisiana judiciary made it clear that it was hesitant to circumvent the at-will doctrine established in the Louisiana civil code. Thus, in a case where an employee was discharged for revealing wrongdoing by his employer ("whistleblowing"), the court affirmed for the employer even though many state courts have created a public policy exception to at-will employment in such a situation. The Louisiana court specifically noted "Louisiana's traditional and unique deference to legislative authority" in reaching its decision. At least one-quarter of U.S. state courts appear to follow this philosophy of strict judicial restraint and recognize no exceptions to the employer's right to discharge.

Because the decisions of California courts, particularly its supreme court, have an important influence on the rest of the country, this article will focus on the California Supreme Court case of *Foley v. Interactive Data Corporation,* 47 Cal. 3d 654 (1988), decided in December 1988, which reflects the reluctance of the current California high court to impose burdensome damages on business defendants. Note that state court decisions are so significant in this area, because there is no federal law regarding at-will employment (aside from antidiscrimination and regulatory statutes). Federal courts apply state law in wrongful discharge litigation.

Wrongful Discharge Legislation

At least one state legislature has taken an assertive position regarding wrongful discharge: A Montana statute protects workers from arbitrary dismissal but limits the damages that can be collected in a wrongful discharge suit. The *Wall Street Journal*[1] quoted an attorney as stating that the law was passed partially in response to fears that an increasing number of large jury verdicts for employees would drive business away from Montana. The statute was upheld by the state supreme court and, thus, may serve as a model for other states to follow.

THE *FOLEY* CASE

Facts

Daniel Foley worked in Los Angeles as a product and branch manager for Interactive Data Corporation, a wholly owned subsidiary of Chase Manhattan Bank, which markets computer-based decision-support services. During his almost 7 years of employment, he had a superior record and consistently received salary increases, promotions, bonuses, awards, and outstanding perfor-

---

[1] A. Dockser, "Wrongful-Firing Case in Montana May Prompt Laws in Other States," *The Wall Street Journal,* July 3, 1989, p. 11, cols. 4–5.

mance evaluations. However, after a routine management shift where Foley got a new supervisor, Foley expressed concern to his former supervisor when he heard that the new supervisor was under investigation for embezzlement from his previous employer. He was told not to spread rumors. Two and one-half months later, just 2 days after he had received a merit bonus of $6,762, the new supervisor fired him for "performance reasons." The new supervisor did later plead guilty to embezzlement.

Procedural Background

The trial court sustained the employer's demurrer without leave to amend, thus, in essence, holding that Foley had no case. The appellate court affirmed this dismissal with a classic statement of the at-will philosophy: "Neither employer nor employee should be locked in an unwilling embrace." The California Supreme Court granted appeal to consider each of the appellate court's conclusions regarding the three distinct theories asserted by Foley: (1) a tort cause of action alleging a discharge in violation of public policy, (2) a contract cause of action for breach of an implied-in-fact promise to discharge for good cause only, and (3) a cause of action alleging a tortious breach of the implied covenant of good faith and fair dealing.

As will be discussed in detail hereinafter, the California high court's resolution of each of Foley's theories of recovery has considerably undermined safeguards provided to at-will employees in earlier California cases.

THE SIGNIFICANCE OF *FOLEY*

The Public Policy Exception

An exception to employment at-will is the public policy exception where the discharged employee alleges that the employer's conduct in firing him or her violates public policy. This court-created exception should not be confused with specific legislation that has been passed to protect employees who whistleblow (that is, disclose illegal conduct of their employers) under a wide variety of state and federal law (for example, the National Labor Relations Act and the Environmental Protection Act). In theory, the possibilities for use of this exception are almost limitless, because the concept of public policy is so broad. Indeed some cases involving public policy are so egregious that even a conservative court that believes in judicial restraint might find an exception to at-will principles. For example, an at-will employee who was fired for refusing to commit a felony might be able to convince even a conservative court that such a discharge is harmful to society as a whole and cannot be tolerated.

The scope of the public policy exception is still evolving, owing to increased public concern and awareness of white-collar (business-related) crime, particularly in areas such as environmental protection and securities regulation. California courts have taken a leading role in defining the scope of this exception. For example, early appellate cases from the late 1950s and early 1960s held that an employer may not discharge an employee for refusing to commit perjury or for exercising a statutory right (for example, signing a union card).

However, the most significant California case dealing with wrongful discharge is *Tameny v. Atlantic Richfield Company,* a 1980 state supreme court case. There the court held that the employer's firing of Mr. Tameny in retaliation for his refusal to participate in an illegal price fixing scheme (a violation of antitrust law) violated public policy. The *Tameny* case holds that such violation is the tort of wrongful discharge, thus subjecting the employer to liability not only for the general or compensatory damages available in a contract cause of action, but also to the punitive or exemplary damages available in tort. The latter damages are used to punish the defendant for reprehensible behavior and to make an example of the defendant to deter others from similar behavior. The business significance of the availability of tort remedies will be discussed more thoroughly hereinafter with regard to the covenant of good faith and fair dealing.

Although the *Foley* court did not directly reject the *Tameny* precedent of allowing tort remedies in a wrongful discharge suit alleging violation of public policy, it did considerably narrow the type of activity that would be protected under the umbrella of public policy. Although Mr. Foley argued that there is a duty imposed on employees to report relevant business information to their employers, and that Interactive Data Corporation violated public policy by firing him for performing that duty, the California Supreme Court rejected his argument, stating that public policy issues only arise when the public at large is being protected by the employee's action (such as whistleblowing about hazardous working conditions). Here Mr. Foley's disclosure of the information served his employer's private interest only and, thus, did not invoke public policy issues. Note that the *Foley* reasoning would protect an employee in a *Tameny* situation, because price fixing involves the public at large. However, the *Foley* analysis clearly eliminates a considerable portion of employer behavior from public policy concerns.

The Implied-in-Fact Contract Exception

The strongest basis for a wrongful discharge suit after *Foley* is for the employee to bring a claim for breach of an implied-in-fact contract to discharge only for good cause. Mr. Foley had argued that Interactive Data Corporation's actions throughout his employment and its personnel policies resulted in an implied oral contract not to fire him without good cause. The California supreme court was unanimous in holding that Mr. Foley was entitled to have a jury determine whether or not there was an implied-in-fact contract limiting his employer's right to discharge him arbitrarily.

The appellate court had rejected the oral contract argument based on the statute of frauds, holding that any implied contract was unenforceable because the contract would be for more than 1 year and, thus, would be required to be in writing under the California statute of frauds. It concluded that because Mr. Foley had been employed almost 7 years, his oral employment contract was obviously for more than 1 year and, thus, barred by the statute of frauds.

If the California supreme court had accepted this argument, it would have as a practical matter put an end to wrongful discharge litigation in California, because most of the cases being litigated do not involve written contracts. It might have made it much more difficult for wrongful discharge plaintiffs in other states to prevail when relying on an implied-in-fact contract, because employers would have been able to argue that the influential California supreme court applied the statute of frauds to implied-in-fact contracts.

However, the California high court accepted long-standing precedent holding that indeterminate term employment contracts can be performed within 1 year and, thus, are not within the statute of frauds. This is true even if the parties spoke in terms of "permanent" or "lifetime" employment, because the statute of frauds only applies to contracts that have no possibility of being performed within 1 year (for example, a contract with a 2-year term). As long as there is some possibility of performance within 1 year (for example, if the employee died), the oral contract should be enforceable.

The California supreme court relied heavily upon an earlier state court of appeals case in deciding that the employer's behavior, including oral statements and employee handbooks, can create a reasonable expectation of continued employment, thus creating an implied-in-fact contract to not discharge the employee arbitrarily. In the earlier case, an employee who had been fired after 32 years of employment with continual promotions and no oral or written criticism of his work was held to have demonstrated a *prima facie* case of wrongful termination in violation of an implied promise by his employer that it would only terminate him for good cause.

Therefore, it may be very important for an employer to examine its employee handbook and its personnel policies and procedures to ensure that no promise of continued employment is implied. Employers should review offers of employment, whether oral or written, as well as subsequent oral or written communications to employees to see whether there is any basis whereby an employee could reasonably believe continued employment was implied. It is advisable for employers to thoroughly document progressive discipline of employees. With such a paper trail of warnings and/or probation, it is much harder for an employee to argue that he or she reasonably relied upon an implied contract not to arbitrarily be discharged. Length of employment is significant; a long-term employee will have a stronger argument for an implied contract. Practices in the particular industry in which the employment relationship takes place are also important. Some employers also provide clear statements in their employee handbooks or in job offer communications that employment is at-will and that there is no express or implied promise of continued employment. Employees are sometimes asked to sign statements acknowledging that their employment is at-will.

Breach of the Implied Covenant of Good Faith and Fair Dealing

In holding that tort damages are not recoverable for breach of the implied covenant of good faith and fair dealing, the *Foley* decision will have its most significant impact upon businesspeople. In California and elsewhere, courts have stated that there is an implied covenant of good faith and fair dealing in every contract. Although the concept was first formulated by the California courts in insurance contracts, it was later extended to all contracts, including employment contracts. By precluding tort recovery in this area of wrongful discharge litigation, and limiting a plaintiff's recovery to contract damages of lost pay and attendant economic losses, the court removed a powerful incentive for plaintiffs' attorneys to take cases. The *Wall Street Journal*[2] has referred to punitive damages as the "jackpots in litigation," and there is no doubt that the availability of punitive damages has provided a powerful incentive for attorneys to take cases on a contingency fee basis. In such a fee arrangement, the plaintiff does not make payment for the attorney's services directly. Rather, the attorney is paid a percentage of the plaintiff's recovery. Contingency fee arrangements are extremely common in personal injury litigation. If only compensatory (or general) damages are available (primarily lost wages), lower- and middle-income discharged employees will find it much more difficult to find attorneys to represent them because their damages would be too small. Commentators have noted that only the highly paid executive will have general damages sufficient to sustain a wrongful discharge lawsuit if punitive damages are precluded. Moreover, by limiting recovery for breach of the implied covenant of good faith and fair dealing to contract damages, the court precluded tort damages for emotional distress, which are often extremely significant.

In justifying its conclusion that tort remedies are inappropriate, the California Supreme Court clearly stated its belief in judicial restraint, noting that "in the absence of legislative direction to the contrary contractual remedies should remain the sole available relief for breaches of the implied covenant of good faith and fair dealing in the employment context."[3] It also unequivocally expressed its concern that the business community should have predictability relating to the consequences of employment contracts for "commercial stability." Employers will be unduly deprived of their discretion to dismiss an employee if they are afraid of potential tort damages, thus causing commercial instability, according to the California high court.

MANAGERIAL IMPLICATIONS

Clearly the *Foley* decision represents a victory for management in reversing the judicial erosion of at-will employment in California. It should be noted that the appellate court in *Foley* had stated that at-will employment is actually more favorable to the employee, because it prevents employers from using adhesion contracts with employees. (An adhesion contract exists when one party with greatly superior bargaining power dictates the terms of a contract to the party in an inferior bargaining position). However, in reality, the unfettered

---

[2] R. Schmitt, "California High Court Makes Mark on Law by Limiting Damages," *Wall Street Journal,* July 11, 1989, p. 1, col. 1.

[3] 88 Daily Journal D.A.R. 16079, 16089 (1988).

right to discharge is a significant advantage to the employer. The California Supreme Court expressly recognized this reality when it noted the importance to employers of "freedom to make economically based decisions about their work force." It also made pointed reference to its concern for "the stability of the business community."

Of course the rebuttal to management's concern about business stability and freedom from burdensome restraints and regulations is that job security promotes employee morale with, consequently, more efficient performance. Commentators have criticized the harshness of at-will employment, noting that the United States is out of step with much of the industrialized world where legislation exists to protect employees against unfair dismissals. Managers in the United States will need to carefully balance the advantage of managerial discretion in employment at-will relative to the alleged increased productivity owing to improvement in employee morale when legislation exists protecting employees against unfair dismissals, particularly in view of the fact of the economically united Europe.

CONCLUSION

Clearly California employers now have a respite from what many in the business community perceived as a deluge of wrongful discharge litigation, particularly in light of a subsequent California Supreme Court decision holding that the *Foley* decision is retroactive. In other words, the *Foley* holding will apply to cases already filed, not just to cases filed after it was decided. *Foley* will serve as a strong argument for employers in other states to use in opposing wrongful discharge litigation.

Although, in theory, tort remedies are still available when an employee argues that his or her discharge violated public policy, in reality, such cases have been relatively uncommon and not of great significance. In order to have tort remedies available, a discharged employee may be able to allege such tort causes of action as fraud, defamation, and infliction of emotional distress. It remains to be seen how such litigation will be treated by the courts in California and elsewhere. In the meantime at-will employees in California, and by analogy in other states also, can hope that their state and local legislatures will take an assertive position in defining the respective rights of at-will employees and their employers if the state courts have failed to do so in a satisfactory manner.

REFERENCES

Cal. Labor Code § 2922.
Cleary v. American Airlines, Inc., 111 Cal. App. 3d 443, 168 Cal. Rptr. 722 (1980).
Dockser, A., "Wrongful-Firing Case in Montana May Prompt Laws in Other States," *The Wall Street Journal,* July 3, 1989, p. 11, cols. 4–5.
Foley v. Interactive Data Corporation, 47 Cal. 3d 654 (1988).

Gil v. Metal Service Corporation, 412 So. 2d 706 (La. App.), *cert. denied,* 414 So. 2d 379 (La. 1982).

Glenn v. Clearman's Golden Cock Inn, 192 Cal. App. 2d 793, 13 Cal. Rptr. 769 (1961).

Pugh v. See's Candies, 116 Cal. App. 3d 311 (1981).

Schmitt, R., "California High Court Makes Mark on Law by Limiting Damages," *The Wall Street Journal,* July 11, 1989, p. 1, col. 1.

Tameny v. Atlantic Richfield Co., 27 Cal. 3d 167, 620 P. 2d 1330 (1980). See also *Peterman v. Int'l Brotherhood of Teamsters, Local 396,* 174 Cal. App. 2d 184, 344 P. 2d. 28 (1959).

42 U.S.C. §§ 2000e, *et seq.*

DISCUSSION QUESTIONS

1 You are the vice president for human resources for a Fortune 500 company. You are asked to review your company's practices in light of the large number of wrongful discharge cases that have been filed in state court recently. What should your approach be?

2 What steps should you take if you were an at-will employee of a major government contractor who discovered that your immediate supervisors were falsifying important documents submitted to the government?

SUGGESTED ANSWERS

1 First, review all company policies and procedures, particularly employee handbooks, to ensure that there is no basis whereby an employee could reasonably conclude that there was an expectation of continued employment under the implied contract exception to at-will employment.

   Then speak to managers, and confirm in follow-up memos, to ensure that no oral representations regarding continued employment are made during the hiring process or in offer letters. Explain to managers that it is their responsibility to communicate to the employees reporting to them that their employment is contingent upon good performance. Prepare memos from corporate headquarters under your signature emphasizing that employment is at-will and is subject to the company's profitability requirements. Consider having employees sign statements acknowledging that employment is at-will.

   Establish clear procedures for progressive discipline and be sure all reporting units are following them. Emphasize to managers the importance of the "paper trail" in supporting termination decisions. Try to keep current regarding what other employers are doing as well as what law is developing in other states. You should be aware of countrywide trends in this area, particularly if your company has offices or divisions in other states.

   Finally, try to ensure that managers and other persons in authority are fully aware of the importance of their compliance with your instructions. Have corporatewide training sessions, including discussion of the significance of public policy in this area.

2 Because your supervisor is committing a crime, you have a duty to promptly report his/her wrongdoing to the appropriate authorities within the organization. You cannot ignore such white-collar crime and, indeed, could have criminal liability yourself

for not reporting the wrongful activity. Such reporting by an employee of wrongdoing by the employer is known as whistleblowing.

Document as thoroughly as possible what your supervisors are doing so that when you speak with the appropriate people you can clearly support your concerns. Keep a private journal at home setting forth your observations and what you are doing about the problem.

If you are dissatisfied with the corporate response, take your charges to an outside government agency. However, it is very unlikely that you will need to do so, because management will very likely initiate an investigation of your charges and, if true, most likely will commend you for your action. Many government contractors have lost important contracts because of such fraud by employees. If, for some reason, your employer takes retaliatory action against you, immediately report your situation to the appropriate governmental agency. You should have a very strong public policy argument to challenge your employer's action. Employers who retaliate against whistleblowing employees are often dealt harshly with by courts, even by conservative courts who believe in judicial restraint.

PART **FIVE**

LEGAL ASPECTS
OF THE FIRM
AND THE REGULATION
OF ITS POWER

12

CORPORATE PROPERTY RIGHTS IN INFORMATION:
Misappropriation by Insiders after *Carpenter v. United States*

John W. Bagby
Pennsylvania State University

INTRODUCTION

Insider trading enforcement has assumed increased prominence in recent years. Considerable controversy has arisen over the efforts of the Securities and Exchange Commission (SEC), the Congress, the courts, and private litigants to police the financial markets and preserve the markets' integrity. Several major issues are presented in the litigation, legislation, and administration of insider trading, including the definition of *insider* and the need for insider trading enforcement. This chapter addresses these controversies and reviews the *Carpenter v. United States* Supreme Court decision that has endorsed the misappropriation theory of insider trading.

Adoption of the misappropriation theory of insider trading has an important impact on managers. It requires them to design procedures to safeguard corporate assets. Confidential corporate information is the firm's property irrespective of any employee's participation in its creation. Managers should set an ethical tone that discourages subordinates from misusing corporate information for personal purposes.

Who Is an Insider?

At first glance, it may seem simple to define *insiders*. However, difficulties arise because there are various laws that apply to insider trading. Additionally, there are many avenues to gain access to inside information. It is also necessary to identify which of insiders' trades violate the securities laws. The Securities and Exchange Act of 1934 (the 1934 act) originally restricted insider trading by insiders in three fairly precise categories: corporate officers, directors, and 10 percent shareholders. Although these "statutory insiders" may generally trade in their corporation's securities, "short-swing" profits are prohibited. Section 16(b) of the 1934 act defines short-swing profits as any purchase *and* sale or sale *and* purchase made by the designated insider within a 6-month period. The unlawful profits may be recovered by the corporation or by any shareholder(s) suing on the corporation's behalf. Another basis for insider trading enforcement arose in the 1909 case of *Strong v. Repide,* 213 U.S. 419 (1909). This case established the state common law "special circumstances" doctrine that restricts insider trading. The insider's fiduciary duty was combined with the tort of deceit (fraud) to restrict insider trading.

Contemporary insider trading enforcement is brought under various provisions of federal law: Section 10(b) of the 1934 act, SEC Rule 10b-5, SEC Rule 14e-3, the Racketeer Influenced and Corrupt Organizations Act (RICO), the federal mail and wire fraud statutes, the Insider Trading Sanctions Act of 1984 (ITSA), and the Insider Trading and Securities Fraud Enforcement Act of 1988 (ITSFEA). These seemingly diverse liability provisions actually take a rather homogeneous approach to insider trading enforcement. Persons in possession of nonpublic confidential information have two choices: either disclose the information publicly before trading or abstain from trading altogether (the "disclose or abstain" rule). Under the *misappropriation theory,* an insider is any person with access to confidential, nonpublic information that would affect a reasonable investor's decisions to buy, sell, or hold securities.

The misappropriation theory expands the definition of an insider well beyond the traditional statutory insiders to include lower-level employees of the firm whose shares are traded. Even the trading of some nonemployees is prohibited. Therefore, the "insider" designation no longer accurately identifies either the type of unlawful trading or the individuals who are prohibited from trading. This chapter reviews how insiders and their illegal trading are identified in light of the landmark Supreme Court case *Carpenter v. United States,* 484 U.S. 19 (1987). However, first the controversy over the restriction of insider trading is discussed.

Controversy over Insider Trading

A considerable debate has emerged over the justification for insider trading and the need for vigorous enforcement of the insider trading restrictions. Opponents of insider trading contend that insider trading is inherently unfair and harmful to the "integrity of the securities markets." These forces, including Congress, the SEC, the Justice Department, the presidential administration, and most investors, advocate strong enforcement to curb the practice.

Advocates of insider trading enforcement argue that insider trading is unfair because it violates the insider's basic fiduciary duty of loyalty to shareholders. If insiders were permitted to trade freely, they might manipulate the disclosure of information to take full advantage of the nonpublic information. Investors without access to inside information cannot overcome the insider's informational advantage through diligent research. Therefore, the proliferation of insider trading creates a widespread loss of confidence in the securities markets. Loss of public confidence from various causes followed the Great Depression and the 1987 market crash, making it difficult to raise capital efficiently in the securities markets.

Opponents of Insider Trading Enforcement. Another group opposes strict enforcement of insider trading. They attack the unfairness and market integrity arguments mentioned earlier by asserting that insider trading is a victimless crime and may sometimes be beneficial. The insider usually trades with an unknown party over the impersonal securities markets. The victimless crime argument suggests that this trading partner previously decided to trade based on "fundamentals" or for personal reasons unrelated to the insider's short-term information. However, this argument ignores that the insider's trading partner would undoubtedly insist on trading at a price reflecting the insider's nonpublic information. The price should rise for positive information or decrease for unfavorable information. Shareholders are beginning to recognize this condition, and they are indirectly insisting their corporations prohibit employees from insider trading.

Opponents of strict enforcement correctly recognize that it is costly for the government to police insider trading. Strict enforcement also may serve as a disincentive to securities analysts who sell their confidential "stock pick" recommendations. Without investment analysis, the markets would become inefficient and eventually deteriorate. Although individual investors openly condemn insider trading, most candidly admit they would trade on inside information if given access to it.

Opponents of trading restrictions also argue that insider trading is a traditional "emolument," benefit, or implied element of compensation for corporate employees. Indeed insider trading has been tolerated in most foreign countries for this reason, although in recent years, most foreign countries have made "insider dealing" technically illegal. These advocates argue that corporate management produces the inside information, so they have a greater right to use it than do outsiders. Of course, this line of reasoning ignores these managers' fiduciary duty to use corporate information only for corporate purposes and to the benefit of all shareholders equally. Instead, insider trading permits managers to benefit themselves at the expense of some or all other shareholders.

There is a more limited and reasonable view of this emolument theory. It suggests that insider trading provides a missing link between the creative efforts of managers and their incentive compensation. If the securities are genuinely efficient, then a corporation's stock price will rise when entrepreneurial managers are successful at innovating. If these managers are permitted to conduct insider trading, they could be rewarded more quickly than under traditional compensation systems. However, such a limited tolerance for insider trading ignores that unproductive employees have no right to incentive "bonuses'' yet they would have many of the same trading opportunities as do innovative managers. Additionally, any employee with negative confidential information could profit from bad news. Neither of these latter two outcomes are consistent with managers' fiduciary duties or the incentive theory.

Insider Trading and Market Efficiency. A final argument concerning insider trading addresses how the practice affects the securities markets' efficiency. Insiders who trade on accurate nonpublic information send a ''signal'' to other traders in the market. The message is optimistic when prices rise and is pessimistic when prices fall. If accurate information is best to maintain efficient capital markets, this suggests an important policy choice between two methods to deliver information to the market. First, information could be indirectly communicated through ''inference.'' Investors would observe market price movements and thereby deduce that there is positive nonpublic information when prices rise or negative nonpublic information when prices fall. Of course, investors would not know the actual underlying information and would be unable to verify its accuracy. This policy is apparently favored by opponents of insider trading enforcement. Alternatively, information could be more directly revealed to the market, such as through corporate disclosure. The securities laws strongly favor direct disclosure, preferring that investors be given the opportunity to assess corporate information personally and directly. Despite the controversy over restricting insider trading the practice is illegal. There are several important contemporary issues in identifying (1) what is inside information, (2) who are insiders, and (3) when is trading restricted.

THE MISAPPROPRIATION THEORY

The focus of inquiry is broadening in insider trading cases brought under the securities laws, particularly under SEC Rule 10b-5. Conventional wisdom suggests that the original source of the information subject to the insider trading restriction must be from within the corporation whose shares are traded. However, the advent of rampant insider trading during tender offers and takeovers has caused a flat rejection of this restrictive interpretation. Increasingly, ''outsider trading'' based on confidential information is also classified as unlawful insider trading.

Classifying Information

Traditionally, concern has centered on the source of inside information in insider trading analysis. Many people assume that the suspect information must come from within the corporation. However, the advent of outsider liability for insider trading requires consideration of the various classifications of information. The public versus nonpublic distinction suggests that publicly available information cannot be misused by insiders. ''Public'' information contained in the corporation's press releases, disclosed in government filings, or reported by the press is presumably unsuitable for insider trading. However, securities analysts often produce nonpublic information through their research and assessment. Their trading or tipping of such information is not generally unlawful.

The inside versus outside dichotomy might appear sufficient to define the permissible scope of insiders' trading. Inside information pertains to the corporation's internal business affairs that affects its assets, liabilities, or earning power. Outside information is produced by persons outside the corporation whose shares are traded. However, outside information may nevertheless affect the corporation's stock price. Outside information can be specific to the corporation, such as when the information is produced by employees of institutional investors, judges, tender-offer bidders, financial printers, investment bankers, government officials, the press, law firms, accountants, or securities analysts. Outside market information about the corporation may be known by various stock exchange professionals including specialists, market makers, floor traders, transfer agents, big block traders, or odd-lot traders. These persons often have direct knowledge of the volume of trading, price direction, and the identity of purchasers and sellers. This market information can be used to interpret either publicly available information or confidential proprietary information (for example, trade secrets), creating insider trading opportunities.

Confidential outside information may concern the outsider's dealings with the corporation. For example, the corporation's stock price could be affected materially by a prospective customer's decision to award a lucrative contract to the corporation, a supplier's inability to satisfy demand for a scarce resource, a regulator's or court's decision affecting the corporation, a tender offeror's decision to purchase the corporation, or a consultant's advice to a takeover bidder who is considering a purchase of corporate stock.

Outside information might not concern the corporation specifically. For example, information about the corporation's industry, a related industry (for example, suppliers, customers), the financial markets generally, or the whole economy may have an impact on the corporation. An employee of a bank or the Federal Reserve Board might know of an impending interest rate change. Alternatively, a regulator or court might know of a new regulation or precedent with an impact on the corporation's stock price.

The Misappropriation Rule

Clearly these traditional information distinctions are too simple to accurately distinguish between the type of information that is available for trading from information that cannot be the basis for trading. This imprecision has led to a better method of separating legal from illegal trading. It is based on the ability of any market participant to gain access to or separately produce similar information.

The misappropriation rule abandons the customary labels of inside, outside, public, and nonpublic information in favor of protecting "confidential" information. The "disclose or abstain" restriction applies to any person, from inside or outside the corporation, who has access to confidential, nonpublic information that belongs to someone else. The misappropriation rule was originally suggested in the landmark Supreme Court case of *Chiarella v. United States,* 445 U.S. 222 (1980). It was later adopted by several lower federal courts permitting the SEC to pursue insider trading enforcement using the theory. The *Carpenter v. United States* case reinforces the misappropriation theory more fully, yet it also raises some disturbing paradoxes.

Carpenter v. United States

The *Carpenter* case involved *Wall Street Journal* columnist, R. Foster Winans, former author of the "Heard on the Street" column. He regularly evaluated in the column various stocks, taking points of view on their investment potential. Often Winans' column affected stock prices of the corporations he discussed. He violated the *Journal's* policy requiring confidentiality of unpublished commentary by trading in the stocks featured in upcoming articles. Winans tipped his cohorts, David Carpenter and Kenneth Felis, who also traded and shared their profits with Winans.

Information is "Property."   Winans' trading was in direct violation of the *Journal's* confidentiality policies. Winans contended that only the *Journal* could be a victim of their alleged fraud, and because it had no financial interest in the stocks traded, the *Journal* suffered no damage. However, the Supreme Court reasoned that the *Journal* has a property interest in maintaining the prepublication confidentiality of its "Heard" column. Confidential business information is private property. "News matter" is the "stock in trade [of a newspaper] to be gathered at the cost of enterprise, organization, skill, labor, and money, and to be sold to those who will pay for it." The owner of information has an exclusive right to decide how to use information produced by its employees in the course of their employment. If an employer is deprived of its exclusive use of proprietary confidential information, the employer becomes a victim of the misappropriation. The fact that information is intangible is irrelevant, "property" rights permit the owner to exploit either tangible or intangible assets.

Intangible property has an important difference from tangible property. Tangible property is totally exhaustible. This means that when it is misappropriated, the rightful owner loses all its value to the misappropriator. For example, when a thief steals an automobile, the owner is completely deprived of the asset because the thief's possession is complete, only one individual can possess an automobile at one time. Misappropriation totally exhausts the owner's value in the tangible asset.

By contrast, when an intangible is misappropriated, it is only partially exhausted. For example, when Winans misappropriated the *Journal's* proprietary stock analyses, the *Journal* still had the information. A similar problem exists with computer software or sound and video recordings. When a misappropriator takes a "copy," the owner still retains the original. Of course, eventually if too many illegal "copies" of the original are misappropriated, the owner loses all the property's value. For example, if all the fans of a rock group receive illegally pirated copies of the group's latest record, the group will become unable to sell any legitimate records. Thereafter, the group cannot profit from the record sales because the property's value becomes exhausted. A similar problem exists for the owner of computer software if an excessive number of unauthorized copies are distributed. This principle also applies to nonpublic information about stocks. The market price of a stock eventually adjusts to reflect the good or bad nonpublic information. When enough insiders trade, the market adjusts to it, and the information's value is steadily lost.

Most people understand that misappropriation does not completely exhaust intangibles because unauthorized copying of information or intellectual property often goes undetected. Some people believe that if the owner is unaware a copy was misappropriated, then no harm is done. However, each misappropriation of intangible property reduces the owner's value somewhat until the information or recording eventually becomes worthless. The *Carpenter* decision clearly recognizes that despite the seemingly inexhaustible nature of intangible property, the owner still retains exclusive rights to exploit its value by deciding how and when it is used and who uses it.

Work Rule Violations as Fraud. An employer who owns the information produced by its employees has a choice of keeping the information confidential or making it freely available to employees and the public. However, the employer retains exclusive rights to the information when it establishes workplace rules prohibiting misappropriation or stock trading based on information discovered at the workplace. Today, confidentiality is required of all employees working for participants in the financial markets. Additionally, corporate consultants and their employees are prohibited from tipping or trading on nonpublic confidential information. This rule restricts investment bankers, law firms, audit firms, and financial printers who serve takeover target corporations or takeover bidders from insider trading on information misappropriated from a client. The 1983 Supreme Court case of *Dirks v. SEC,* 463 U.S. 646 (1983) reinforced this concept by suggesting that such outsiders become "temporary insiders" to the corporation whose shares are traded.

IMPACT OF THE *CARPENTER* DECISION

The *Carpenter* decision is a mixed blessing for advocates of stricter insider trading enforcement. The Supreme Court voted unanimously to adopt the misappropriation theory of insider trading when the Justice Department is prosecuting it as a form of mail and wire fraud. Thereunder, criminal prosecutions of insider and outsider trading are permissible when (1) there is a *confidential source* of information, (2) the owner has *rights* in the information, (3) the owner has an *intent* to maintain its confidentiality, and (4) the owner has undertaken *efforts* to do so.

However, the Supreme Court did not unequivocally approve the use of the misappropriation theory when based on SEC Rule 10b-5. The Court was split evenly, four justices approving and four disapproving outsider trading cases predicated on SEC Rule 10b-5. The SEC has no power to prosecute outsider trading with the mail and wire fraud statutes; only the Justice Department may prosecute criminally. This leaves a curious gap in insider trading enforcement. The SEC is the independent regulatory agency with superior expertise in stock market regulation. Without clear Supreme Court guidance sanctioning the use of the misappropriation theory, the SEC will be more cautious in pursuing novel outsider trading cases. This is inconsistent with congressional intent found in two laws passed during the 1980s to crack down on insider trading: the ITSA and the ITSFEA.

Insider Trading Sanctions Act of 1984

With passage of the ITSA, Congress gave the SEC exclusive jurisdiction to use a new triple-penalty provision to challenge insider and outsider trading under this new act. The legislative history accompanying the ITSA shows that Congress approved of the developing pattern of insider trading enforcement established in the past 40 years of litigation. Congress's deliberate refusal to define insider trading more precisely illustrates its desire to have the definition evolve in the case law. Indeed, the House of Representative's report accompanying the ITSA referred to the misappropriation theory with approval.

Insider Trading and Securities Fraud Enforcement Act of 1988

The ITSFEA further reinforces the developing case law of insider and outsider trading enforcement. The ITSFEA increases criminal penalties, provides for the payment of bounties to informants, and requires brokers and investment bankers to supervise their employees to prevent insider or outsider trading and unlawful tipping. It also codifies individual investor's rights to sue for damages. In this act, Congress has removed several obstacles to effective insider and outsider trading enforcement. The uncertainty over the SEC's enforcement powers raised by the *Carpenter* decision seem somewhat inconsistent with congressional intent in the ITSA and ITSFEA.

MANAGERIAL IMPLICATIONS

The traditional form of insider trading involves officers, directors, and controlling shareholders who generally have regular access to confidential corporate information. Section 16 of the Securities Exchange Act of 1934 restricts these insiders from trading in their employer's stock by requiring them to report their trades and by recognizing that inside information is a corporate asset that should not be converted for personal use. However, Section 16 is not fully effective to eliminate insider trading. Many statutory insiders fail to report their trades in a timely manner. Additionally, Section 16 is inapplicable to lower-level employees and most outsiders.

The insider trading laws suggest a need for managers to adopt company-wide codes of conduct prohibiting employee misconduct. There is tremendous growth in the explicit adoption of work rules that prohibit insider trading and the misappropriation or revelation of confidential corporate or client information. Separately, there are specific federal and professional regulations applicable to independent accountants, investment banking firms, stock brokers, and law firms that require imposition of control mechanisms to prevent mishandling of clients' confidences. For example, brokerages must install *Chinese walls* that separate the underwriting and trading departments to prevent the internal communication of confidential client information that could lead to illegal insider trading. Managers of all firms should install these control devices and monitor their employees to ensure compliance.

Managers may be held responsible for failing to adequately supervise their employees to prevent insider trading. Employees should be influenced to resist the temptation to use valuable proprietary information for personal, noncorporate purposes. Such misuse is a breach of the employee's fiduciary duty of loyalty that can damage the firm's shareholders whose shares are traded. Trading in the stock of a client firm or takeover target by employees of an outside consultant or the takeover bidder directly damages the outside firm. Insider trading injures the reputation of an outside consultant as a safe repository for its client's confidences. Insider trading by employees of a takeover bidder signals the market of the potential takeover, raising the eventual takeover price the bidding firm must pay. Managers have a clear responsibility to prohibit insider trading and monitor employees' misuse of valuable corporate confidences.

CONCLUSION

Despite some arguments in support of insider trading, the preponderance of public policymakers (Congress, the SEC, the Supreme Court, and the presidential administration) all oppose insider trading because it undermines public confidence in the markets. The uncertainties of insider trading enforcement have been substantially reduced through legislation and court decisions.

The most important development has been an expansion of the persons restricted from insider trading. The distinction between "inside" and "outside" information or between "public" and "nonpublic" information are no longer useful in identifying insider trading. Indeed, numerous outsiders are restricted from trading particularly when they obtain "confidential" information that belongs to a takeover target, takeover bidder, a corporate or takeover consultant, or the corporation whose shares are traded. The misappropriation rule ignores whether the information is sourced from within the corporation whose shares are traded. The focus is on whether confidential information is misappropriated. After this determination, the information is considered tainted, making any trading based on such information illegal.

The *Carpenter* case reinforced application of the misappropriation theory to outsider trading. Perhaps most important, there was a general recognition that information is property and, therefore, worthy of legal protection. If an employer's work rules are intended to maintain confidentiality of information produced for a corporate purpose, then its use for personal trading is unlawful. An unlawful misappropriation triggers the "disclose or abstain" prohibition against insider trading.

REFERENCES

Aaron v. SEC, 446 U.S. 680 (1980).

American Bar Association; Section of Corporation, Business, and Banking Law; Conference on Codification of the Federal Securities Laws, 22 *Bus. Law.* 793, 922 (1967).

Bagby, "The Evolving Controversy Over Insider Trading," 24 *Am Bus. L.J.* 571 (Winter 1987).

Barry, "The Economics of Outside Information and Rule 10b-5," 129 *Univ. Pa. L. Rev.* 1307 (June 1981).

Carney, "Signalling and Causation in Insider Trading," 36 *Cath. Univ. L. Rev.* 863 (1987).

Carpenter v. United States, 484 U.S. 19 (1987).

Chiarella v. United States, 445 U.S. 222 (1980).

Garten, "Insider Trading in the Corporate Interest," 1987 *Wisc. L. Rev.* 573 (1987).

Haft, "The Effect of Insider Trading Rules on the Internal Efficiency of the Large Corporation," 80 *Mich. L. Rev.* 1051 (1982).

Hetherington, "Insider Trading and the Logic of the Law," 1967 *Wisc. L. Rev.* 720.

Manne, "In Defense of Insider Trading," *Harvard Business Review,* November–December 1966, pp. 113–122.

Manne, H., *Insider Trading and THE Stock Market,* 1966.

Note, "The Efficient Capital Market Hypothesis, Economic Theory and the Regulation of the Securities Industry," 29 *Stan. L. Rev.* 1031 (1977).

Note, "The Measure of Damages in Rule 10b-5 Cases Involving Actively Traded Securities," 26 *Stan. L. Rev.* 371 (January 1974).

Schotland, "Unsafe at Any Speed: A Reply to Manne 'Insider Trading and the Stock Market,'" 53 *Va. L. Rev.* 1425 (1967).

SEC v. Dirks, 463 U.S. 646 (1983).

SEC v. Materia, 745 F.2d 197 (2d Cir.) *cert. denied* 105 S. Ct. 211 (1985).

SEC v. Musella, 578 F. Supp. 425 (S.D.N.Y. 1984).

Strong v. Repide, 213 U.S. 419 (1909).

Tidwell and Aziz, "Insider Trading: How Well Do You Understand the Current Status of the Law?" 30 *Cal. Mgt. Rev.* 115 (Summer 1988).

TSC Indus. v. Northway, 426 U.S. 438 (1976).

United States v. Newman, 664 F.2d 12 (2d Cir. 1981).

DISCUSSION QUESTIONS

1 How might it be argued that the misappropriation theory would or would not apply in the following situations? Assume that the corporation's shares are traded by the person in question.

   a A clerk working for the law firm representing a takeover bidder deciphers the identity of the takeover target while assisting in the preparation of disclosure documents before the bid is announced. The law firm pledged confidentiality and coded the target's name in the draft documents to prevent employees from discovering its identity.

   b A layout artist worked for the financial printer that was hired by a takeover bidder to print the takeover disclosure documents. The artist discovers the target's identity before the bid is announced. The printing firm prohibited misuse of client confidences with numerous posted notices and a well known employee code of conduct.

   c A secretary working for the mergers and acquisitions department of an investment banking firm reads the boss's mail and discovers that a client firm is interested in a takeover of a target firm. Does it matter which entity the secretary trades based on the information: the target, the bidder, a competitor of the target, or the employing investment bank?

   d The clerk of a federal judge is given a draft of the judge's upcoming decision holding ABC Corp. liable to XYZ Corp. for $11 billion. Does it matter if the clerk purchases XYZ stock or sells ABC stock short?

   e At a public track meet, a famous football coach overhears a corporate president discussing confidential corporate business matters aloud with his spouse. Is the coach's investment in the corporate stock an illegal misappropriation?

2 Insiders have an incentive to time the public disclosure of material corporate information so that they can first trade in the corporation's stock. This permits the stock price to fully benefit from the information's impact. Does this practice violate the employee's fiduciary duty of loyalty to the corporation or its shareholders? By contrast, if insider trading is effectively prohibited, what impact will this have on management's incentive to disclose corporate news promptly? How will this affect the market for the corporation's stock?

SUGGESTED ANSWERS

1 **a** The takeover bidding firm owned the information about the takeover. Its communication to the law firm, a temporary insider, was in confidence with the expectation that the information would not be misused. There was a confidential *source* of the information, which had the *right* to maintain its confidentiality, the owner had the *intent* to maintain confidentiality until the takeover was announced publicly, and had undertaken *efforts* to maintain confidentiality. The clerk's misappropriation of the target's identity and subsequent trading is illegal insider trading under the misappropriation theory.

   b The financial printer is a temporary insider; its efforts to conceal the target's identity until after the bid is made render the information confidential. Therefore, the layout artist's trading is illegal misappropriation.

   c The secretary's trading in either the target or bidding firms is illegal misappropriation as discussed in *a* and *b*. The secretary's trading in the investment banking firm's shares is traditional insider trading although it may also constitute a misappropriation. The illegality of trading in a competitor's stock is less clear. The secretary must believe the takeover will affect the stock prices of the target's whole industry.

d The judge's clerk is guilty of illegal insider trading in either firm, based on the misappropriation theory, even though the court is not a consultant to the firms involved.

e There is no fiduciary relationship between the coach and the corporate president. Therefore, there can be no insider trading liability based on the misappropriation theory. However, it might be proved that the president intentionally spoke these corporate confidences aloud to give the coach an indirect benefit. In such a case, the president could be guilty of illegal tipping of inside information. Separately, the president could also be liable for breach of the fiduciary duty to the corporation by divulging such corporate confidences.

2 The corporate employee has an absolute duty to disclose information to shareholders as dictated by shareholder needs and/or the special duties imposed by the securities laws. Any manipulation of the timing of this disclosure violates the employee's fiduciary duty of loyalty to the corporation and the shareholders. A late disclosure causes damage to those shareholders who traded after the information should have been disclosed but before its actual disclosure. This may cause them to pay higher prices when buying stock that is later affected by the late disclosure of bad news. Alternatively, these shareholders may receive low prices when selling stock that is eventually affected by late disclosure of good news. Effective insider trading prohibitions removes much of management's incentive to manipulate the release of corporate news. Therefore, managers would have no insider trading opportunities to enhance by withholding disclosures, and the corporation's stock price will more accurately reflect the corporation's true condition, an "efficient market."

13

STANDARD OIL COMPANY OF NEW JERSEY V. UNITED STATES

Virginia G. Maurer
University of Florida

BACKGROUND TO THE SHERMAN ACT

The origins of U.S. antitrust law lie in our political tradition of viewing excessive concentrations of wealth, and the political power that is presumed to follow wealth, as inconsistent with democratic society and democratic government. In the 30-year period following the Civil War, this popular suspicion of concentrated wealth was fed by the growth of new and threatening forms of industrial organization. The revolution in manufacturing and transportation, made possible by expanding national markets, urbanization, technological advancement, and the availability of capital, introduced both production and competition on a scale the U.S. economy had not experienced.

Large business organizations emerged in production and manufacturing, transportation, and marketing. Often their growth involved vertical integration, forward or backward, to achieve economies, or horizontal mergers to meet expanding markets. In addition, in many industries, competitors sought relief from intensive competition. This relief could be achieved through horizontal combinations, ranging in form from horizontal price agreements to new organizations, called trusts, that formally controlled output and price of participating units and returned supracompetitive profits to the firms.

The trust was a successful strategy in several industries, including the railroad, oil, steel, and many consumer goods industries. The owners of stock in competing, or potentially competing, companies transferred their shares to a group of trustees, taking back shares in the trust. Using their power as owners of the participating companies, the trustees controlled output and prices and otherwise coordinated the activities of the firms so as to maximize the profit potential of the industry, insulated to a large extent from competition. There is some evidence that when faced with price competition in an area, the trust used the threat of slashing prices locally to effect a buyout of the competing firm.

From the standpoint of many political groups, the "trust"—and the forms of industrial organization associated with it in the popular mind—was a high-handed and unfair exercise of economic power, designed to maintain high prices for goods and transportation. Prices were maintained artificially at the expense of farmers, laborers, and small business owners, who were forced to bear the brunt of supracompetitive prices and were unable to exercise countervailing economic power.

Eventually, the political process operated to curb the economic power of the trusts. As early as 1876, in the case of *Munn v. Illinois*, 94 U.S. 113, the states successfully asserted their authority to regulate railroad rates and services, and, potentially, other industries. However, the limitation of state jurisdiction to intrastate railroads made these efforts ineffective. In 1887, therefore, Congress created the Interstate Commerce Commission (ICC), which eventually substituted direct regulation of railroad price and service terms for the discipline of competition. By 1888, political sentiment to curb the trusts was so great that the 1888 campaign platforms of both the Democratic and Republican parties included an antitrust plank.

THE SHERMAN ANTITRUST ACT

The Sherman Antitrust Act of 1890 was a broad-brush attempt to curb the trusts and to establish a new framework in the judiciary for addressing problems of monopoly and restraint of trade. In addition, the executive branch of the federal government, through the power of prosecution in the Department of Justice, was given a legal basis for forcing change in an industry. Economic and legal historians have debated whether Congress was motivated by the abusive behavior of the trusts, the cartelization of U.S. industry, or the economic concentration of U.S. industry. Although the intent of Congress in passing the legislation probably will never be clarified satisfactorily, most historians agree that in the Sherman Antitrust Act Congress expressed a faith in, and a preference for, free competition. In addition, Congress expected the courts to interpret the very broad language of the act to effect that preference in specific cases.

The two main provisions of the Sherman Act are:

Section 1. Every contract, combination in the form of trust or otherwise, or conspiracy, in restraint of trade or commerce among the several States, or with foreign nations, is hereby declared to be illegal.

Section 2. Every person who shall monopolize, or attempt to monopolize, or combine or conspire with any other person or persons, to monopolize any part of the trade or commerce among the several States, or with foreign nations, shall be deemed guilty.

Section 1 addresses agreements between or among firms to restrain trade in interstate commerce. A single firm, acting alone, cannot violate Section 1. Section 2 addresses monopolization of an industry, whether by a single firm or by a conspiracy. Violation of either section is punishable by fine or imprisonment.

The early problems of judicial interpretation of the Sherman Antitrust Act focused on the meaning of "commerce among the states," and on the scope of "restraint of trade". In an 1895 case, *United States v. E. C. Knight Co.,* 156 U.S. 1, the Court held that the act did not apply to a trust's monopoly of the sugar refining industry because the manufacturing process was not "commerce" and did not directly restrain interstate commerce. The rule would have restricted "commerce" to "transportation." Four years later, however, in *Addyston Pipe & Steel Co. v. United States,* 175 U.S. 211 (1899), and later in *Northern Securities Co. v. United States,* 193 U.S. 197 (1904), and *Swift & Co. v. United States,* 196 U.S. 375 (1905), the Court adopted a "flow of commerce" test that effectively put *E. C. Knight* to rest as a bar to Sherman Antitrust Act enforcement in manufacturing cases.

Interpreting the phrase "restraint of trade" proved a more formidable task for the Court. The phrase has antecedent roots in the common law; the legislative history is replete with evidence that the drafters of the act expected the courts to analyze purported restraints by common law rules. The common law cases involving agreements to restrain competition were not a well-developed or consistent body of law, however, and even the most restrictive line of cases permitted some direct restraints on competition. Nevertheless, in *United States v. Trans-Missouri Freight Association,* 166 U.S. 290 (1897), and again in *United States v. Joint Traffic Ass'n.,* 171 U.S. 505 (1897), Justice Peckham expressed the Court's view that the Sherman Antitrust Act overruled common law precedents when it declared *every* contract in restraint of trade to be illegal. Both cases involved the setting of freight rates by competing railroads, a restraint that the railroads argued to have been a permissible restraint of trade under applicable common law.

Finally, in *Northern Securities Company v. United States,* 193 U.S. 197 (1904), the Court upheld a decree dissolving a holding company under which two competing railroads running from the Midwest to the Pacific were controlled financially. The decision was 5 to 4, with Justice Harlan writing the majority opinion and Justice Holmes dissenting. Justice Harlan wrote, "The mere existence of such a combination and the power acquired by the holding company as its trustee constituted a menace to, and a restraint upon, that freedom of commerce which Congress intended to recognize and protect, and which the public is entitled to have protected." In dissent, Justice Holmes argued that the act did not address protection of consumers or of competition as a social goal of the act, but rather addressed the injury to a potential competitor of being precluded from a market and suffering from abuses of economic power. Because there were competitors along parts of the route, and there was no evidence of abusive or discriminatory practices toward competitors, there should be no violation of the Sherman Antitrust Act. Thus, the *Northern Securities* case exposed the Court's division on whether it should follow the literal language of the act or read the act against a common law background that permitted "reasonable" restraints of trade.

THE *STANDARD OIL* CASE

The Facts of the Case

In 1911, in *Standard Oil Company of New Jersey v. United States,* 221 U.S. 1 (1911), the Supreme Court once again applied the Sherman Antitrust Act. In 1906 the United States filed a complaint against 71 corporations and 7 individuals, alleging a conspiracy "to restrain the trade and commerce in petroleum, commonly called 'crude oil', in refined oil, and in the other products of petroleum among the several states...and to monopolize the said commerce." The facts of the government's case chronicle the efforts of John D. Rockefeller, William Rockefeller, Henry Flagler, and others to monopolize the petroleum industry. The Rockefellers and others were engaged in various partnerships in the business of refining crude oil and shipping crude oil products. In 1870 they organized the Standard Oil Company of Ohio along the model of the industrial trust. They transferred the business of their partnerships to the Standard Oil Company, and took back stock in the company. By 1872 the Standard Oil trust acquired all but three or four of the oil refineries in Cleveland, Ohio, as well as many others in Ohio, Pennsylvania, and New York. By 1882 the trust gained control of the oil pipelines from the eastern oilfields to the refineries. In 1882 a formal trust was formed, additional partnerships and previously independent firms were brought into the trust, and ownership of the various properties was transferred to the Standard Oil Companies of New York, New Jersey, Pennsylvania, and Ohio. Following state antitrust litigation in the state of Ohio, the trust device was replaced by a holding company—Standard Oil of New Jersey—which assumed financial control of all interests. Eventually, between 1882 and 1899, the group controlled almost 90 percent of the business of producing, shipping, refining, and selling petroleum and its products. It set the price and output levels of both crude and refined petroleum.

In addition to chronicling the use of the trust device to monopolize a major industry, the trial evidence chronicled the offensive business practices that the trust used to achieve and expand its economic power. By obtaining preferential rates, secret rebates, and discriminatory treatment from the railroads, the trust forced competitors either to join the trust or to go out of business. There was evidence of predatory practices such as local price cutting, coercion of competing pipelines' suppliers and customers, industrial espionage, and the operation of bogus independents to give the appearance of competition.

The Majority Opinion: Justice White's Analysis

The majority of the Court supported the lower court's decree that the combining of stock in the hands of the Standard Oil Company of New Jersey in 1889 constituted a combination in restraint of trade under Section 1 of the Sherman Antitrust Act and also an attempt to monopolize in violation of Section 2. The decree was against the 7 individual defendants and 38 corporate defendants found to have engaged in restraint or monopolization after the act was passed in 1890. The lower court enjoined the Standard Oil Company of New Jersey from exercising control over the other 37 corporations and also enjoined the corporations from paying dividends or otherwise acceding to the control of Standard Oil. The individuals were enjoined from taking any action to evade the decree.

Justice White's opinion is notable for craftsmanlike approach to the language of the act. White first found that the motivating purpose of the legislation was to address

> [T]he vast accumulation of wealth in the hands of corporations and individuals, the enormous development of corporate organization, the facility for combinations which such organizations afforded, the fact that the facility was being used, and that combinations known as trusts were being multiplied, and the widespread impression that their power had been and would be exerted to oppress individuals and injure the public generally.

In applying the language of the act, the Court asserted that Congress did not intend to restrain the right to make and enforce contracts, but to "protect ...commerce from being restrained by methods, whether old or new, which would constitute an interference—that is, an undue restraint." The standard for distinguishing ordinary contracts and combinations from those that unduly restrain trade was the standard of reason that had been applied at the common law. Courts were to determine whether a particular combination "had or had not brought about the wrong against which the statute provided." The Court had little difficulty concluding that the defendants' holding company arrangement was unreasonable because it interfered unduly with competition. Indeed, the creation of the Standard Oil trust probably was one of the specific "wrong[s] against which the statute provided."

With respect to the Section 2 claims of monopolization and attempt to monopolize, Justice White reasoned that construction of an organization of such seemingly abnormal size and capital, for the purpose of excluding others, gave rise to the *prima facie* presumption of intent to dominate the oil industry. The presumption was made conclusive by the Court's examination of the actions and practices of the trust in achieving domination of the industry. In particular, the Court drew upon evidence that the trust used its economic power to lower prices in selected areas to drive out competition or coerce competitors to join the trust. By inference, the Court ruled that merely achieving a monopoly position would not violate Section 2; proof of intent to monopolize would be required. This view has become a well-settled interpretation of Section 2 monopolization.

Justice Harlan's Opinion

Justice Harlan concurred generally in the holding of the case, although he disagreed with a modification made in the decree. He dissented on the reasoning of the majority opinion. Harlan reiterated his position in *Northern Securities,* that when Congress outlawed every contract, combination, or monopoly in restraint of trade, it did not intend for the courts to carve out exceptions based on the reasonableness of the restraint. In addition, his opinion foretold the difficulty of applying the rule of reason:

> [The Court has] now said: "You may *now restrain* such commerce, provided you are reasonable about it; only take care that the restraint is not undue."...[N]ow it is to be feared, we are to have, in cases without number, the constantly recurring inquiry—difficult to solve by proof—whether the particular contract, combination, or trust involved in each case is or is not an "unreasonable" or "undue" restraint of trade.

The Rule of Reason

Two weeks after the *Standard Oil* case, Justice White applied the new rule of reason in *United States v. American Tobacco Co.,* 221 U.S. 106 (1911). The defendant was created by a merger of five tobacco firms that accounted for almost 95 percent of cigarette production; as in *Standard Oil,* the Court found the combination and exclusion of others to be a restraint of trade. The defendant's intent to monopolize was inferred from its expansion into related tobacco products through price wars and acquisitions and its practice of buying up competitors and closing down their production.

Together, the pair of cases established the framework for Sherman Antitrust Act analysis used for many decades and still dominant today. A court must first find conduct—a contract, combination, or agreement. Then it must examine the effects of the conduct. If the conduct is inherently anticompetitive, with no likely beneficial effects (as was the conduct of the railroad in *Trans-Missouri Freight Association, Joint Traffic Association,* and *Northern Securities*), then the court can find a per se violation of the Sherman Antitrust Act without examining the reasonableness—the competitive and anticompetitive effects—of the conduct. If, however, the conduct is not inherently anticompetitive, if it does not fall within the line of cases in which the court has applied the per se rule, then the court may apply the rule of reason and undertake a detailed analysis of the nature and economic effects of the conduct. Under a rule of reason analysis, only those contracts, combinations, and agreements whose anticompetitive effects overshadow the procompetitive effects violate the Sherman Antitrust Act.

Reaction: The Federal Trade Commission Act and the Clayton Act

Justice White's opinions were greeted with horror by those who regarded them as an unwarranted cutting back on the antitrust laws and also by those who foresaw unbridled judicial discretion to scrutinize and criminally punish industry practices. Both groups favored more detailed statements of what commercial behavior was legal. In 1914 the Federal Trade Commission Act (FTC Act) and the Clayton Act were passed. The FTC Act established a federal administrative agency to provide expert assistance in sorting out acceptable and unacceptable trade practices. The Clayton Act addressed specific practices, such as price discrimination, exclusive dealing and tying arrangements, and the acquisition of competing companies "where the effect...may be to substantially lessen competition or to tend to create a monopoly." In addition, the Clayton Act gave a private right of action for treble damages to persons injured by violations of either the Clayton Act or the Sherman Antitrust Act.

Thus, Congress transferred to the FTC the authority to intervene in the economy at an administrative level, before cases rose to the level of Justice Department authority. In addition, Congress carved out of the rule of reason certain specific trade practices, and subjected them to a legislatively formulated "rule of reason"—the test of whether competition would be lessened or a monopoly created. In effect, Congress acceded to the reality that Justice White identified: that certain apparent restraints on trade were the product of new and economically beneficial forms of industrial organization and should be tolerated for the benefits they offered to a competitive economy.

THE RULE OF REASON AND THE PER SE RULE

Seven years after *Standard Oil*, in *Board of Trade of the City of Chicago v. United States,* 246 U.S. 231 (1918), the Court provided better guidance on how to apply the rule of reason of the *Standard Oil* case. In *Board of Trade,* the Court addressed the issue of whether an agreement for a fixed price for after-hours grain trading violated Section 1 of the Sherman Antitrust Act. In his opinion, Justice Brandeis identified the relevant factors in determining whether a restraint on competition was unreasonable.

> The court must ordinarily consider the facts peculiar to the business to which the restraint is applied; its condition before and after the restraint was imposed; the nature of the restraint and its effect, actual or probable. The history of the restraint, the evil believed to exist, the reason for adopting the particular remedy, the purpose or end sought to be obtained, are all relevant facts.[1]

The plaintiff, or the government, must prove that competition in a specific market has been restrained. The burden then shifts to the defendant to prove the economic justification of the restraint, which is the defendant's principal defense. This defense is lost if the plaintiff then proves that the economic benefit could be achieved through a less restrictive alternative. In addition, if the case is a private treble damages case, the plaintiff must show that it suffered the type of injury the antitrust laws were designed to prevent.

Sometimes the rule of reason can be applied almost summarily; some trade practices produce an injury so well understood, and so unlikely to be justified,

---

[1]246 U.S. at 238.

that the rule can be applied easily and the case settled. Actual rule of reason cases, however, often involve analysis that is complicated, prolonged, expensive, and frustrating, both to the litigants and to the judiciary. Section 2 cases brought by the government have been drawn out for well over 10 years. Each case requires detailed factual findings, guided and organized by an uncertain analytical framework, and relying on economic expertise and evidence that is conflicting, tentative, and invariably flawed. In short, courts do their best to do justice in each case; each case is unique and provides little guidance for subsequent parties.

Where judicial experience with a particular trade practice is sufficient, and the courts have found the practice repeatedly to have anticompetitive effects with no redeeming virtues, the courts may categorically apply a standard of per se illegality and thereby dispense with inquiry into the reasonableness of the practice. Trade practices which have been subjected to the per se rule include horizontal price-fixing, horizontal allocations of territory, customers, and other aspects of the market; group boycotts or collective refusals to deal; tying arrangements; and vertical price-fixing. If the government or the plaintiff proves that the contract, combination, or agreement existed and that the nature of the conduct impairs competition and holds little likelihood of redeeming beneficial effects, no evidence of reasonableness, purpose, market power, or actual competitive effect is examined. The per se conduct is conclusively presumed to be illegal.

The per se rule also is problematical. It is not always obvious which cases will be adjudicated under the rule of reason and which under the per se rule. The plaintiff usually argues that the defendant's conduct fits a per se category, and the defendant usually invokes the rule of reason. Although the per se rule offers the benefits of certainty and predictability, and eliminates vagueness in the antitrust laws, the rule is nevertheless inflexible and unaccommodating of developing economic understanding and analysis. In recent years, the economic scholars have influenced the Supreme Court to revisit the per se treatment of vertical distribution and tying restraints. There is substantial evidence that many nonprice vertical restraints such as tying arrangements are often, if not usually, procompetitive. In addition, many economists advance quite credibly the argument that vertical price fixing, or resale price maintenance, has procompetitive effects that should be examined under the rule of reason; the Supreme Court, however, has declined to adopt that posture. In short, while the rule of reason remains the basis for Sherman Antitrust Act analysis, the per se rule probably has a more precarious future.

PREDATORY PRICING

The *Standard Oil* case also is significant as an early precedent in the law of predatory pricing. The theory of predatory pricing is that a monopolist in one market can "extend" monopoly power by cutting prices below competitor's costs in a contested market until the competitor goes out of business or agrees to merge. The monopolist thereby expands the monopoly into a larger market. The predation constitutes an unreasonable restraint of trade and also evinces an intent to monopolize. For many years lawyers assumed that this theory explained the means by which the Standard Oil trust forced consolidation in the industry. Professor McGee's work in the 1950s, reanalyzing the voluminous record of the case in the light of better economic theory, suggests that the trust rarely, if ever, engaged in predatory pricing. Most expansion of the monopoly took place through relatively friendly mergers at satisfactory prices, reflecting a sharing of the anticipated profits (McGee). Thus, it was unnecessary to risk the potential deadweight losses of selling below costs.

This analysis of predatory pricing in the *Standard Oil* record has spawned substantial intellectual interest in the predatory pricing problem, fraught as it is with the prospect of firms reluctant to lower their prices to competitive levels for fear of predatory pricing accusations. In fact, recent legal and economic literature, as well as Supreme Court dictim, has suggested that "predatory pricing schemes are rarely tried, and even more rarely successful." *Matsushita Elec. Indus. v. Zenith Radio Corp.*, 106 S. Ct. 1348, 1358 (1986). In *Matsushita,* the Court laid down the requirement that plaintiffs in a predatory pricing case make a preliminary showing that it could have been reasonable of the defendant to seek to extend monopoly power through below-cost predatory pricing.

MANAGERIAL IMPLICATIONS

As a seminal case in the construction of the Sherman Antitrust Act, *Standard Oil* has shaped the basic contours of antitrust law. Antitrust law will be implicated whenever management decides to bring out a new product, define a product or territorial market, license patents or copyrights, alter the chain of distribution, price products, engage in trade organizations or industrial standard setting, train sales staff, or acquire a competitor or potential competitor. In fact, most decisions that affect the competitiveness of a firm also implicate antitrust law.

In seeking clear legal guidance on these decisions, either through a routine legal audit or when the firm initiates or responds to antitrust litigation, managers will encounter the odd dichotomy of the per se rule and the rule of reason. Although some trade practices can be identified readily as impermissible, others require analysis of such illusive concepts as "market power" and "lessening of competition"—concepts that require sustained and relatively sophisticated economic and legal analysis.

For example, franchisors, manufacturers, and even distributors will find cogent business reasons for trying to set the price the retailer charges to the consumer. They will be frustrated with retailers who charge more than the price that would maximize manufacturers' profits. Or they will have to address the concerns of retailers who complain about rival retailers who "free ride" on advertising and warranty services, and who want the errant retailers cut off from access to the product. Legal counsel will be quick, no doubt, to caution against entering into agreements on resale price, or threatening to cut off retailers who do not follow price suggestions. Agreements to fix the resale price of goods violate the per se rule against price fixing. Counsel ought also to be quick to offer alternative models of dealing with retailers and others in the chain of distribution that avoid the pitfall of per se illegality and are defensible under the alternative rule of reason.

If, however, the nature of the business decision involves structuring exclusive territorial agreements for distributors, retailers, or franchisees, counsel will not be so quick to evaluate the particular structure selected. Counsel will want to construct economic evidence that the particular restraint improves the ability of the firm to compete against rival brand products. Vertical nonprice restraints, such as exclusive territorial agreements, are subject to rule of reason analysis.

The meaning of the rule of reason becomes particularly significant in the litigation context. Rule of reason cases, particularly the monopolization cases brought by the government, usually involve protracted discovery and horrendous expense for lawyers and experts, and hold the potential for dramatic changes in the structure of an industry. Throughout the twentieth century, antitrust cases brought by the government under the Sherman Antitrust Act have provided business opportunities for new and rival firms of a dominant firm in an industry, as judgments and settlements force firms to divest themselves of assets and markets. Most recently, for example, the Justice Department's breakup of the telephone system in the early 1980s breathed competitive life into the entire telecommunications industry and provided a vast array of business opportunities in that industry. Thus, the implications of the rule of reason cases are important not only for potential defendants but also to opportunistic potential competitors.

CONCLUSION

The *Standard Oil* case is a landmark case in U.S. legal history. The importance of the case lies in Justice White's articulation of the rule of reason. Justice White read into the Sherman Antitrust Act Congress's intention that the Court develop, well into the future, a "common law" of antitrust, not simply read the language literally or treat the act as codifying the common law of trade restraint as of 1890. In *Standard Oil*, the Court recognized the relative permanence of a new industrial order in which the role of competition and competitive forces would continually change industrial structure. As a result, the federal judiciary has been able to respond to developing knowledge about the economic nature of business practices. In addition, the case established a basic framework for interpreting the Sherman Antitrust Act and analyzing restraints of trade and monopolization behavior. Finally, the case provided precedent for the Court's treatment of specific trade practices, and particularly predatory pricing.

REFERENCES

Addyston Pipe & Steel Co. v. United States, 175 U.S. 211 (1899).

Areeda, Phillip E., *Antitrust Analysis,* 3d ed. Little, Brown, Boston, 1981.

——*Antitrust Law: An Analysis of Antitrust Principles and Their Application,* vol. VII. Little, Brown and Company, Boston, 1988.

Breit, William, and Kenneth Elzinga, *The Antitrust Casebook: Milestones in Economic Regulation,* 2d ed. Dryden Press, Chicago, 1989.

Brodley and Hay, "Predatory Pricing: Competing Economic Theories and the Evolution of Legal Standards," 66 *Cornell L. Rev.,* 738 (1981).

Easterbrook, "Predatory Strategies and Counterstrategies," 48 *Univ. of Chi. L. Rev.* 263 (1981).

Einhorn, Henry A., and William Paul Smith, *Economic Aspects of Antitrust: Readings and Cases,* Random House, New York, 1968.

Fox and Sullivan, "Antitrust—Retrospective and Prospective: Where Are We Coming From? Where Are We Going?" 62 *N.Y.U. L. Rev.* 936 (1987).

Holmes, William C., *Antitrust Law Handbook.* Clark Boardman Company, Ltd., New York, 1988.

Hurwitz and Kovacic, "Judicial Analysis of Predation: The Emerging Trends," 35 *Vand. L. Rev.* 63 (1982).

Joskow and Klevorick, "A Framework for Analyzing Predatory Pricing Policy," 89 *Yale L. J.,* 213 (1979).

Koller, "The Myth of Predatory Pricing," 4 *Antitrust Law and Economics Review* 105 (1971).

Liebeler, "Whither Predatory Pricing? From Areeda and Turner to Matsushita," 61 *Notre Dame L. Rev.* 1052 (1986).

Marcus, Philip, *Antitrust Law and Practice.* West Publishing Co., St. Paul, Minn., 1980.

Matsushita Elec. Indus. v. Zenith Radio Corp., 106 S. Ct. 1348, 1357–58 (1986).

McGee, "Predatory Price Cutting: The *Standard Oil* (N.J.) Case," 1 *Journal of Law and Economics* 137 (1958).

Munn v. Illinois, 94 U.S. 113 (1876).

Neale, A. D., and D. G. Goyder, *The Antitrust Laws of the U.S.A.: A Study of Competition Enforced by Law,* 3d ed. Cambridge University Press, Cambridge, Mass., 1980.

Northern Securities Co. v. United States, 193 U.S. 197 (1904).

Oppenheim, "Federal Antitrust Legislation: Guideposts to a Revised National Antitrust Policy," 50 *Mich. L. Rev.* 1139–1244 (1952).

Pitofsky, "Antitrust in the Next 100 Years," 75 *Calif. L. Rev.* 817 (1987).

Standard Oil Company of New Jersey v. United States, 221 U.S. 1 (1911).

Sullivan, E. Thomas, and Herbert Hovenkamp, *Antitrust Law, Policy and Procedure,* The Michie Company, Charlottesville, Virginia, 1989.

Swift & Co. v. United States, 196 U.S. 375 (1905).

United States v. E. C. Knight Co., 156 U.S. 1 (1895).

United States v. Joint Traffic Assn., 171 U.S. 505 (1897).

United States v. Trans-Missouri Freight Assn., 166 U.S. 290 (1897).

DISCUSSION QUESTIONS

1 What alternatives did the U.S. Supreme Court have in formulating its approach to interpreting the Sherman Antitrust Act?

2 Why does the plaintiff usually argue for per se analysis while the defendant argues for rule of reason analysis?
3 How might Professor McGee's analysis of the evidence in the *Standard Oil* case have affected the Court's theory of monopolization?

SUGGESTED ANSWERS

1 The Court might have (a) applied the Sherman Antitrust Act in a literal manner and forced Congress to draft more specific legislation, or (b) looked to the nature of trade restraints permissible under the various strands of common law on restraint of trade; that is, used the common law in the narrow sense, as though Congress had codified the common law.
2 The plaintiff has a lesser requirement of proof under the per se rule; under the rule of reason the defendant has the opportunity to present more evidence in defense of its action. If the defendant has a "deeper pocket" than the plaintiff, it may have a superior ability to win the suit through attrition, through wearing down the opposition.
3 If the Court adopted McGee's analysis, it probably would not have established precedent in predatory pricing law; rather, it would have focused on the need to control "friendly" mergers in order to preserve competition in a market. Eventually, Congress took this approach in the Clayton Act.

14

WHITE-COLLAR CRIME:
Fundamental Causes and Possible Solutions

Paul E. Fiorelli
Xavier University

INTRODUCTION

White-collar crime has been defined as "[a]ll illegal acts committed by non-physical means and by concealment or guile, the purposes of which were to obtain money or property, to avoid payment for loss of money or property, or to obtain business or personal advantage inconsistent with law or public policy."[1] White-collar crime can be subdivided into either occupational or organizational crimes. Occupational crimes, such as fraud and embezzlement are committed by individuals for their own benefit. Organizational crimes, including price fixing and territorial limitations are committed by the corporation, its officers, or its employees to further the interests of the organization.

In the past, employees who broke laws in order to benefit their company, rather than themselves, received more support and probably lighter penalties if they were caught. "[I]t would be reasonable to hypothesize that executive criminals are treated far less harshly when their corporation is a *party* to the crime than when their corporation is the *victim* of the crime."[2] Judges were concerned about this type of sentencing discrepancy, and Congress has addressed the problem by passing the Federal Sentencing Reform Act of 1987.

This chapter is divided into two parts. Part 1 identifies motivations and different character traits exhibited by many white-collar criminals and offers em-

---

[1] Pollack and Smith, "White-Collar v. Street Crime Sentencing Disparity: How Judges See the Problem," 67 *Judicature* 175, 177 (October 1983).

[2] Orland, "Reflections on Corporate Crime: Law in Search of Theory and Scholarship," 17 *Am. Crim. L. Rev.* 501, 513 (1980).

ployers suggestions on how they can decrease the incidence of white-collar crime. Part 2 deals with congressional reaction to business's past failure to regulate white-collar crime. It analyzes the impact of the Federal Sentencing Reform Act of 1987 on white-collar criminals.

PART 1: Why Do Employees Commit White-Collar Crime?

MOTIVATION

Understanding what motivates white-collar criminals allows managers to evaluate whether their companies are likely targets for this type of crime. If management is aware of the causes of the problem—that is, unrealistic demands, misguided loyalty, employee greed, and so on—it can develop a strategy to minimize the occurrence of white-collar crime. Top management must do more than give directives and expect results. It needs to change the business environment in such a way that employees will be punished for illegal behavior and rewarded for ethical behavior.

Employees committing illegal acts are usually middle managers, and their motivations "range from altruistic loyalty to the corporate good to outright self-interest."[3] These motivations may be analyzed by looking at several different character traits that many white-collar criminals seem to exhibit. They include (1) altruism, (2) moral confusion based on unrealistic demands, (3) blind ambition, and (4) greed.

THE ALTRUIST

Altruists are team players. "Many employees...rationalize dishonest illegal behavior by seeing themselves as loyal corporate soldiers."[4] They carry out orders without question. Peter Drucker, one of the preeminent scholars in the field of management, stated, "Hence executive life not only breeds a parochialism of the imagination comparable to the 'military mind', but places a considerable premium on it."[5] Good soldiers are not mindless automatons. They have spent their entire lives developing their personal ethical standards. These standards are tested when they believe that they must commit illegal acts in order to benefit their company. All too often the individual's ethical standards become overshadowed by the perceived good of the corporation. What is it within the corporate environment that can change basically good people into

---

[3] Marshall B. Clinard and Peter C. Yeager, *Corporate Crime*, 1980, p. 66.

[4] Gregory Stricharchuk, "Business Crack Down on Workers Who Cheat to Help the Company," *The Wall Street Journal*, June 13, 1986, p. 25, col. 4.

[5] Peter Drucker, *The Concept of the Corporation*, 1972, p. 81; M. Clinard and P. Yeager, *Corporate Crime*, 1980, p. 63.

white-collar criminals? The answer may lie in the process of becoming a middle manager.

Top management normally promotes people like themselves. "In every large-scale organization there is a natural tendency to discourage initiative and to put a premium on conformity."[6] This conformity is nurtured through the process of industrial initiation:

> Through both the tribal and the industrial initiation new members are indoctrinated into their social roles: they learn new languages; they share new values with other group members; they assume new identities; they develop new associates and new loyalties; and they internalize new emotional responses. Thus, through initiation, social institutions shape new members into the institutional mold. Cloning not being possible, initiations are the way older members and leaders can replicate themselves.[7]

During this initiation process, the corporation becomes a surrogate family for employees. They may have difficulty establishing contacts with the outside community owing to frequent transfers. Their family life may suffer because of the long hours demanded by the job. Many, if not most, of their social contacts are with fellow employees. Given this scenario, it is not surprising that employees develop a deep sense of loyalty to their company. This loyalty could be so great that employees may have difficulty refusing either explicit or implicit requests to break the law.

Altruists' motives may not always be as pure as they appear. The motives may be a combination of company and self-interest. Violators may own stock or stock options or receive performance-based bonuses. As long as the illegal activity remains undetected, they receive the indirect benefits of continued employment and an increase in net worth, vis-à-vis the increase in the value of their stock. This constant push towards profit may be either self-motivated or demanded by top management.

THE PRESSURE COOKER

When top management sets unrealistic goals, middle managers only have a few choices. They can seem to be inadequate by not accomplishing goals, or perhaps even "corporate whiners" by complaining that the goals are too high. It is unlikely that corporate "nay-sayers" will advance as quickly as counterparts with a "can-do" attitude. Unfortunately, sometimes managers believe that the only way to meet their targets is to cut corners and break the law.

Employees' acquiescence to act illegally can be accelerated by their pessimistic view of the business world. Many middle managers rationalize their actions by believing that violations are common practice. Employees ask themselves the question, "As long as everyone else is doing it, why shouldn't I?"

---

[6] Peter Drucker, *The Concept of the Corporation*, 1972, p. 40.
[7] Diane R. Margolis, *The Managers*, 1979, pp. 45–46.

In fact they may even feel that their careers and companies are being placed at a competitive disadvantage for acting too ethically. Some employees may fear that they will be branded as troublemakers and lose their job for being too conservative.

Some middle managers assume that their superiors at least tacitly approve their illegal acts. They believe that upper management know that the only way to make the target is for the middle managers to compromise their personal ethics or even break the law. "They had to know that we were speeding up the line,...but they never asked questions, so while we knew what we were doing was wrong ethically, we figured it must have been okay in the eyes of the company."[8] Most companies' management do not want to know about illegal activity; they merely want results. This tacit approval is reinforced when violators are rewarded for achieving the goals. This "winking through the blindfold," creates an atmosphere of "Do whatever it takes, just don't tell me about it!"

Middle managers who "do whatever it takes," without telling their superiors are one reason why upper management is rarely convicted for white-collar crimes. Typically, top executives plan policy and middle managers translate this into corporate action. This creates a decentralized, almost bureaucratic structure. The organizational structure makes it difficult to assign guilt to one decision maker:

> [W]ho is responsible? "The low level engineer who designs the unsafe gas tank, the chief engineer who approves it, or the president who never heard of the problem but who insisted from afar that underlings who wished to advance within the corporate hierarchy demonstrate an ability to cut costs dramatically?"[9]

Because intent is a necessary element in most white-collar crimes, many top managers have been able to escape criminal conviction by hiding behind layers of middle managers. Prosecutors have a difficult time establishing that the specific intent to commit the crime should be transferred from the employees to the CEOs.

Middle managers are caught between the proverbial rock and a hard place. They can appease management by meeting the targets, regardless of laws, or refuse and appear incompetent. They are not afforded the same protection against firing that unionized production workers have and probably were not involved in the decision-making process that established the unrealistic goals.

> Gerald C. McDonough, Chairman and chief executive of Leaseway Transportation Corp., says one key to minimizing cheating is setting goals that employees can meet without having to "resort to less than ethical standards." He says Leaseway, a Cleveland-based trucking concern has annual reviews to make sure managers don't

---

[8] George Getschow, "Overdriven Execs, Some Middle Managers Cut Corners to Achieve High Corporate Goals," *The Wall Street Journal,* November 8, 1979, p. 34, col. 4.

[9] John C. Coffee, Jr. "Making the Punishment Fit the Corporation," 1 *N. Ill. U. L. Rev.* 3, 13 (1980).

set goals that are out of line. Mr. McDonough adds that Leaseway's policies are made known to suppliers and customers, who are encouraged to report suspected cheating.[10]

Middle managers responsible for implementing policy should have more input into establishing that policy. They are in the best position to know whether the goals are reasonable and can be obtained through legitimate business efforts.

Organizational crime, which arguably benefits the company in the short run, is difficult to detect. With its established internal controls, the corporation is in the best position to discover these violations. But, "[b]ecause organizational crimes are committed to further corporate goals of accumulation of power and wealth, they are seldom reported by those most likely to be aware of their occurrence."[11] Absent effective deterrents, there was no internal economic incentive for a business to punish an employee who was directly benefitting the corporation. By enacting the Federal Sentencing Reform Act of 1987, Congress has attempted to improve deterrence of white-collar crime by significantly increasing the certainty of imprisonment, increasing fines, requiring restitution, and calling for forfeiture in appropriate cases.

BLIND AMBITION

Occasionally managers are more concerned with their immediate career path than with the company's long-term well-being. In fact, they may act in a way that is contrary to the company's best interest.

> Hence a scientist in a pharmaceutical company might unlawfully conceal rat studies showing lack of safety for a product which he or she has discovered...[t]he revelation that his or her discovery is a failure would certainly cost a promotion. Hence, the rational cost-benefit assessment for the individual is to perpetrate the illegality, while the rational choice for the corporation is to be honest.[12]

Within a given company, it might be silently understood that only people who significantly increase profits or decrease costs are promoted or receive the highest merit raises. These cutthroats may take shortcuts to enhance their careers, but at the same time expose their companies to unnecessary risks. Of course, if the idea that the "wunderkind" developed backfires, the manager may be disciplined or even fired. Irrespective of the threat of discipline, the temptation to cut corners is great. Prior to the passage of the Sentencing Reform Act of 1987, the inherent rewards seemed vast compared to the relatively low risk of detection and ultimate discipline.

---

[10] Gregory Stricharchuk, *supra* n. 4, at 25, col. 4.

[11] Comment, "Occupational Disqualification of Corporate Executive: An Innovative Condition of Probation," 73 *J. Crim. L. & Criminology* 604, 605–606 (1982).

[12] John Braithwaite, "*Challenging Just Desserts*," 73 *J. Crim. L. & Criminology* 723, 728 (1982).

But for the middle level official, the question is not whether the behavior is too risky to be in the interest of the corporation from a cost-benefit standpoint. Rather, it is which risk is greater—the criminal conviction of the company, or the dismissal for failure to meet targets set by an unsympathetically demanding senior management. Because the conviction of the corporation effects him only indirectly, it can seldom exceed the penalty that dismissal or demotion means to the career-minded middle manager. Caught between "the devil and the deep blue sea," the middle level manager then faces a very different opportunity set of potential costs and benefits than does the corporate entity itself.[13]

Corporations may help protect against this situation by establishing a strong company code of ethics. One advantage to a standardized code of ethics is that if managers object to questionable activities, it may be easier for them to cite how the action violates the code, rather than refuse outright. Some have challenged codes of ethics, calling them ineffective. These codes may look good on paper, but they must be backed by the deeds of top management. Employees will only follow the code of ethics if they see top management living by its credo, and violators being swiftly and effectively punished. Companies that have unenforced codes of ethics and continue to "wink through the blind-folds" by rewarding unethical behavior, will promote cynicism in their employees and cannot expect them to act ethically and legally.

THE HEDONIST

"The Wall Street scandals produce a new definition of Yippies—'young, indictable professionals.'"[14] These corporate hedonists are occupational criminals who commit crimes against the company. Typically, these crimes involve embezzlement or fraud, whereby employees steal money from companies with lax internal controls. Sometimes this can only be discovered by a formal audit, and even that does not guarantee detection.

If occupational crimes are detected, companies will probably act swiftly to discipline the guilty employees. Swift action does not necessarily mean prosecution. Companies are often too embarrassed and do not want shareholders, customers, and creditors to know about their lack of control. Publicity could cause them to lose goodwill, or even expose them to a shareholder's derivative action for negligence.

Many times the company merely wants to get rid of the problem by firing the employee. The *Wall Street Journal* reported about David L. Miller, a manager who had been fired for embezzling from six different companies. Each time his employer discovered the embezzlement it failed to prosecute him. The embezzler promised to repay the stolen money, and each employer seemed satisfied with Mr. Miller's contrition. The problem was compounded by the fact that some hiring employers failed to check references and some firing em-

---

[13] John C. Coffee, Jr. *supra* n. 9, at 11.
[14] *The Wall Street Journal,* November 28, 1986, p. 1, col. 5.

ployers allegedly did not fully disclose information about the employee's termination. Employers must be more diligent in the hiring process and should seek prosecution of both occupational and organizational criminals. Refusing to prosecute after a promise of restitution merely shuffles the problem from one employer to another.

PART 2: The Sentencing Reform Act of 1987

Because corporations were unable to effectively police themselves, Congress enacted the Federal Sentencing Reform Act of 1987. The goal was to deter white-collar crime by increasing the certainty that violators would spend time in jail. This part of the chapter will discuss (1) the conditions which led to the passage of the Sentencing Reform Act of 1987, (2) its impact on white-collar criminals, (3) how to apply the new federal sentencing guidelines, and (4) constitutional challenges that the Supreme Court has overruled in *Mistretta v. United States,* 109 S. Ct. 649 (1989).

HISTORY

In 1984 Congress enacted the Comprehensive Crime Control Act. Included within this legislation was a plan to drastically reform the existing federal sentencing practices. Congress was concerned about the lack of uniformity in sentencing. "The shameful disparity in criminal sentences is a major flaw in the existing criminal justice system, and makes it clear that the system is ripe for reform."[15] Under similar circumstances, some judges were giving convicted offenders probation, whereas others were imposing maximum prison terms. Congress feared that this lack of uniformity bred contempt and was not an effective deterrent.

To attempt to remedy this situation, Congress created the Sentencing Commission (hereafter referred to as the "Commission"), composed of seven voting and two ex-officio members. Out of the seven voting members, three are sitting federal judges, and not more than four members can be from the same political party. The president has the power to appoint or remove commissioners, and Congress can amend or revoke any of the guidelines. Congress instructed the Commission to create sentencing guidelines that all federal judges would follow, unless they stated in open court the reasons for their departure.

IMPLICATIONS FOR WHITE-COLLAR CRIMINALS

Congress and the Commission acknowledged that the four purposes of criminal punishment are (1) retribution (act as "just desserts" for the crime), (2)

---

[15] S. Rep. No. 225, 98th Cong., 2d Sess. 37,—, reprinted in 1984 U.S. Code Cong. & Admin. News 3220, 3248.

deterrence, (3) incapacitation of the offender, and (4) rehabilitation. Congress instructed the Commission to consider these factors in determining their sentencing guidelines. The Commission considered the factors, but did not specifically adopt one over the other.

Even though the Commission did not explicitly adopt a sentencing philosophy for all federal crimes, it was clear that the major reason for punishing white-collar criminals was deterrence. Congress believed that too many white-collar criminals were receiving little, if any punishment.

> Under present sentencing practice, courts sentence to probation an inappropriately high percentage of offenders guilty of certain economic crimes, such as theft, tax evasion, antitrust offenses, insider trading, fraud, and embezzlement, that in the Commission's view are "serious". If the guidelines were to permit courts to impose probation instead of prison in many or all such cases, the present sentences would continue to be ineffective.[16]

The Commission stated that an increased certainty of prison sentences was the most effective way to deter white-collar crime.

The sentences would not have to be long in order to be effective. Once a white-collar criminal is imprisoned for more than a nominal time, it is questionable what marginal effect a lengthier sentence will have. Short but certain sentences should provide the necessary deterrence while not overburdening an already overcrowded prison system. White-collar criminals will also be expected to pay for the cost of probation, supervised release, and imprisonment. This amount will be in addition to any fines or restitution that the defendant pays.

APPLICATION OF THE SENTENCING GUIDELINES

In order to decrease sentencing discrepancies for white-collar and other crimes, the Commission established a sentencing table (see Appendix A) that federal judges are now obligated to follow, unless they give reasons for their departure. The Commission created a matrix of 258 sentencing ranges. The rows of the grid are composed of 43 offense levels. Each increased level carries with it a correspondingly higher sentencing range; for example, a level 10 offense has a range of 6 to 12 months, and a level 11 offense has a range of 8 to 14 months.

The columns are six categories based on the defendant's criminal history. This is a function of the number and the severity of each prior conviction. Career offenders and repeat drug offenders will automatically be placed at the highest grade, category VI. As was true in the offense level analysis, each increased category carries with it a higher sentencing range. When the relevant criminal history column is matched with the total offense level, the sentencing table will produce one sentencing range.

---

[16] *United States Sentencing Comm'n, Federal Sentencing Guidelines Manual,* 1988, p. 8.

Although this appears to be a dispassionate application of a mathematical formula, Congress and the Commission did not want judges to lose all their discretionary power.

> The Committee does not intend that the guidelines be imposed in a mechanistic fashion. It believes that the sentencing judge has an obligation to consider all the relevant factors in a case and to impose a sentence outside the guidelines in an appropriate case. The purpose of the sentencing guideline is to provide a structure for evaluating the fairness and appropriateness of the sentence for an individual offender, not to eliminate the thoughtful imposition of individualized sentences.[17]

If a judge believes that the sentencing range is inappropriate as either being too harsh or too lenient, he or she may depart from the guideline, but must declare his or her reasons in open court. The guidelines only apply to violations that have occurred after November 1, 1987. They have not met with universal acceptance.

CONSTITUTIONAL CHALLENGES

In *Mistretta v. U.S.,* the Supreme Court granted *certiorari* to determine the constitutionality of the Sentencing Reform Act of 1987. The defendant in *Mistretta* was indicted on December 10, 1987, for three counts dealing with the sale of cocaine. He challenged the sentencing guideline's constitutionality as being contrary to the established doctrine of separation of powers, and an excessive delegation of authority by Congress to the Judiciary. The district court rejected his challenges. The defendant pleaded guilty to the first count of his indictment (conspiracy and agreement to distribute cocaine), and the government dismissed the remaining charges. Under the sentencing guidelines, he received an 18-month prison sentence, followed by 3 years of supervised release, and a $1000 fine.

In a 8-1 decision (Justice Scalia dissenting), the Supreme Court affirmed the district court's decision. The petitioner argued that:

> Congress, in constituting the Commission as it did, effected an unconstitutional accumulation of power within the Judicial Branch while at the same time undermining the Judiciary's independence and integrity. Specifically, petitioner claims that in delegating to an independent agency within the Judicial Branch the power to promulgate sentencing guidelines, Congress unconstitutionally has required the Branch, and individual Article III [Federal] judges, to exercise not only their judicial authority, but legislative authority—the making of sentencing policy—as well. Such rulemaking authority, petitioner contends, may be exercised by Congress, or delegated by Congress to the Executive, but may not be delegated to or exercised by the Judiciary.[18]

---

[17] S. Rep. No. 225, *supra* n. 15, at 3235.
[18] 109 S. Ct. 647 (1989).

The Supreme Court disagreed with the petitioner's challenge and analogized the fact that Article III judges were performing a quasi-legislative function from the time that the Supreme Court established the Federal Rules of Criminal and Civil Procedure. "Just as the rules of procedure bind judges and courts in the proper management of the cases before them, so the Guidelines bind judges and courts in the exercise of their uncontested responsibility to pass sentence in criminal cases."[19] Because both the rules of procedure and sentencing are part of the judicial process, it was not inappropriate to have judicial involvement in either one's enactment.

The petitioner also argued that Congress transferred excessive power to the Sentencing Commission. He believed this was a violation of the Constitution's nondelegation doctrine. The Supreme Court disagreed with this contention holding that "[t]he Commission is fully accountable to Congress, which can revoke or amend any or all of the Guidelines as it sees fit either within the 180-day waiting period of the Act, or at any time."[20] In his dissent, Justice Scalia was concerned that the creation of the Commission was an excessive delegation of power, and that future Congresses would pass off politically unpopular causes to similar commissions.

MANAGERIAL IMPLICATIONS

White-collar criminals commit crimes for many different reasons. Their motivations include trying to benefit the company, succumbing to pressures to perform, immediate career advancement, and greed. Once management becomes more aware of why employees commit white-collar crimes, they can implement corrective actions.

Employers can decrease white-collar crime by (1) establishing a formal code of ethics and having all employees follow it strictly, (2) involving middle managers in the decision-making process in order to establish realistic goals that are obtainable without violating laws, (3) having top management ask how goals are met, not merely accepting the results, and (4) terminating and cooperating in the prosecution of employees who are breaking the law and not looking after the company's best interest, either because they are more concerned with their own immediate career advancement or merely satisfying their own greed.

Congress responded to business's inability to deter white-collar crime by adopting the Federal Sentencing Reform Act of 1987. Because the Supreme Court failed to declare the act unconstitutional, managers must set realistic goals for their employees and demand that they are accomplished legally, or risk imprisonment and meaningful fines. Violators who are convicted can no longer rely on their good standing in the community to keep them out of jail.

---

[19] *Id.* at 664.
[20] *Id.* at 666.

CONCLUSION

Top management have several alternatives in dealing with white-collar crime. They can ignore it and be subjected to the strict guidelines of the Sentencing Reform Act of 1987, or they can limit this type of activity by modifying the business environment. If corporations choose to address the problem, they can no longer accept the benefits of the illegal activity and "wink through the blindfolds" until the employee is caught. The business environment can be changed if employers place a premium on ethical and legal activity by their employees. If corporations refuse, more white-collar criminals will be spending time in prison.

REFERENCES

Braithwaite, John, "Challenging Just Desserts," 73 *J. Crim. L. & Criminology* 723, 725–726, n.17 (1982).

Burrough, Brian, "The Embezzler, David L. Miller Stole from His Employers and Isn't in Prison, *The Wall Street Journal,* September 19, 1986, p. 1, col. 1.

Clinard, Marshall, and Peter C. Yeager, *Corporate Crime,* Free Press, New York, 1980, p. 66.

Coffee, John C., Jr., "Corporate Crime and Punishment: A Non-Chicago View of the Economics of Criminal Sanctions," 17 *Am. Crim. L. Rev.* 419 (1980).

———, "Making the Punishment Fit the Corporation," 3 *N. Ill. U. L. Rev.* 3, 13 (1980).

Comisky, Ian M., "New Guidelines Impose Harsher Terms for Criminal Tax Offense, *J. Tax'n,* 78, 80 (February 1988).

Comment, "Occupational Disqualification of Corporate Executive: An Innovative Condition of Probation, 73 *J. Crim. L. & Criminology* 604, 606–607 (1982).

Crane, Mark, "Commentary: The Due Process Consideration in the Imposition of Corporate Liability, 3 *N. Ill. U. L. Rev.* 39 (1980).

Drucker, Peter, *The Concept of the Corporation,* The John Day Company, New York, 1972.

Fiorelli, Paul E., "Winking through the Blindfold: What Motivates the White Collar Criminal?," 21 *Akron L. Rev.* 327 (Winter 1988).

Fisse, Brent, "The Use of Publicity as a Criminal Sanction against Business Corporations," 8 *Melb. U. L. Rev.* 107 (June 1971).

Getschow, George, "Overdriven Execs, Some Middle Managers Cut Corners to Achieve High Corporate Goals," *The Wall Street Journal,* November 8, 1979, p. 34, col. 4.

Margolis, Diane R., *The Managers,* Morrow, New York, 1979, pp. 45–46.

Ogletree, Charles J., Jr., "The Death of Discretion? Reflections on the Federal Sentencing Guidelines," 101 *Harv. L. Rev.* 1938, 1948 (1988).

Orland, "Reflections on Corporate Crime: Law in Search of Theory and Scholarship," 17 *Am. Crim. L. Rev.* 501, 513 (1980).

Pollack and Smith, "White-Collar v. Street Crime Sentencing Disparity: How Judges See the Problem," 67 *Judicature* 175 (October 1983).

Posner, Richard A., "Optimal Sentences for White-Collar Criminals," 17 *Am. Crim. L. Rev.* 409 (1980).

Pub. L. No. 98-473, tit. 2, 98 Stat. 1837, 1976 (1984).

S. Rep. No. 225, 98th Cong., 2d Sess. 37,—, *reprinted in* 1984 U.S. Code Cong. & Admin. News 3220, 3248.

Stricharchuk, Gregory, "Business Crack Down on Workers Who Cheat to Help the Company," *The Wall Street Journal,* June 13, 1986, p. 25, col. 4.

United States Sentencing Comm'n, Federal Sentencing Guidelines Manual, West Publishing Co., St. Paul, Minn., 1988.

The Wall Street Journal, November 28, 1986, p. 1, col. 5.

The Wall Street Journal, December 11, 1986, p. 1, col. 5.

Werden, Gregory J., and Marilyn J. Simon, "Why Price Fixers Should Go to Prison," *Antitrust Bulletin,* Winter 1987, pp. 917–937.

DISCUSSION QUESTIONS

1 How would you go about creating a company code of ethics?
2 What impact will the Federal Sentencing Reform Act of 1987 have on white-collar crime?

SUGGESTED ANSWERS

1 Establish that top management are committed to the ethics program. This commitment must be more than lip service to a written document. The code of ethics should be given to all employees, and appropriate training should follow.

Management must consistently discipline executives and staff alike. It may also be helpful to establish a whistleblowing mechanism (that is, a company hotline, ethics committee, or ombudsperson). The company must treat the whistleblower with as much anonymity as possible and make sure that the violator, and not the whistleblower, is disciplined. It may be helpful to have an annual review process whereby employees certify that they have not violated the code of ethics. The company could also include an ethics component in the performance review process.

2 Assuming that there are adequate resources to detect and prosecute white-collar criminals, there should be a strong deterrent effect. If managers see their colleagues consistently being prosecuted and going to prison, in theory they will change their illegal behavior.

One interesting question is, Does this increase in incarceration overburden an already overcrowded criminal justice system? Congress believed that the additional revenues generated by corporations acting legally (that is, paying tax dollars on all income) would generate enough money to pay for new prisons. This may seem to be an oversimplified answer, but in the legislative history, Congress did not address the question further.

Appendix A

GUIDELINES

SENTENCING TABLE
Criminal History Category

Offense Level	I 0 or 1	II 2 or 3	III 4, 5, 6	IV 7,8,9	V 10, 11, 12	VI 13 or more
1	0– 1	0– 2	0– 3	0– 4	0– 5	0– 6
2	0– 2	0– 3	0– 4	0– 5	0– 6	1– 7
3	0– 3	0– 4	0– 5	0– 6	2– 8	3– 9
4	0– 4	0– 5	0– 6	2– 8	4– 10	6– 12
5	0– 5	0– 6	1– 7	4– 10	6– 12	9– 15
6	0– 6	1– 7	2– 8	6– 12	9– 15	12– 18
7	1– 7	2– 8	4– 10	8– 14	12– 18	15– 21
8	2– 8	4– 10	6– 12	10– 16	15– 21	18– 24
9	4– 10	6– 12	8– 14	12– 18	18– 24	21– 27
10	6– 12	8– 14	10– 16	15– 21	21– 27	24– 30
11	8– 14	10– 16	12– 18	18– 24	24– 30	27– 33
12	10– 16	12– 18	15– 21	21– 27	27– 33	30– 37
13	12– 18	15– 21	18– 24	24– 30	30– 37	33– 41
14	15– 21	18– 24	21– 27	27– 33	33– 41	37– 46
15	18– 24	21– 27	24– 30	30– 37	37– 46	41– 51
16	21– 27	24– 30	27– 33	33– 41	41– 51	46– 57
17	24– 30	27– 33	30– 37	37– 46	46– 57	51– 63
18	27– 33	30– 37	33– 41	41– 51	51– 63	57– 71
19	30– 37	33– 41	37– 46	46– 57	57– 71	63– 78
20	33– 41	37– 46	41– 51	51– 63	63– 78	70– 87
21	37– 46	41– 51	46– 57	57– 71	70– 87	77– 96
22	41– 51	46– 57	51– 63	63– 78	77– 96	84–105
23	46– 57	51– 63	57– 71	70– 87	84–105	92–115
24	51– 63	57– 71	63– 78	77– 96	92–115	100–125
25	57– 71	63– 78	70– 87	84–105	100–125	110–137
26	63– 78	70– 87	78– 97	92–115	110–137	120–150
27	70– 87	78– 97	87–108	100–125	120–150	130–162
28	78– 97	87–108	97–121	110–137	130–162	140–175
29	87–108	97–121	108–135	121–151	140–175	151–188
30	97–121	108–135	121–151	135–168	151–188	168–210
31	108–135	121–151	135–168	151–188	168–210	188–235
32	121–151	135–168	151–188	168–210	188–235	210–262
33	135–168	151–188	168–210	188–235	210–262	235–293
34	151–188	168–210	188–235	210–262	235–293	262–327
35	168–210	188–235	210–262	235–293	262–327	292–365
36	188–235	210–262	235–293	262–327	292–365	324–405
37	210–262	235–293	262–327	292–365	324–405	360–life
38	235–293	262–327	292–365	324–405	360–life	360–life
39	262–327	292–365	324–405	360–life	360–life	360–life
40	292–365	324–405	360–life	360–life	360–life	360–life
41	324–405	360–life	360–life	360–life	360–life	360–life
42	360–life	360–life	360–life	360–life	360–life	360–life
43	life	life	life	life	life	life

PART SIX

REGULATION OF
BUSINESS ACTIVITY

15

UNCONSCIONABILITY:
Contract Abrogation by the Courts Protects the Consumer

Tracy Dobson
Michigan State University

INTRODUCTION

Until the twentieth century, the Latin maxim *caveat emptor*[1] ("buyer beware") operated as a working principle that guided courts in deciding consumer suits against business. In the consumer-business contract for goods or services, it was presumed that the consumer had a fair opportunity to examine and test a variety of reasonably diverse alternatives and to understand the advantages and disadvantages of a given good or service based on personal knowledge. In other words, the courts made decisions based on a firm belief that the economic free-enterprise principle of perfect information in a competitive marketplace was operating. This judicial approach, along with other legal doctrines such as privity of contract, insulated business from consumer suits. Further enhancing this judicial bent was economic conservatism. Some commentators suggest that most U.S. judges in the eighteenth, nineteenth, and early twentieth centuries were politically conservative. Protectors of a new nation's growing economy, they rendered decisions that would stimulate economic growth by shielding businesses from liability to customers.[2]

Rendering judgments based on the principle of *caveat emptor* in a market

[1] According to *Black's Law Dictionary:* "This maxim summarizes the rule that a purchaser must examine, judge, and test for himself; Miller v. Tiffany, 1 Wall 309, 17 L.Ed. 540; Hargous v. Stone, 5 N.Y. 82; Humphrey v. Baker, 71 Okl. 272, 176 P. 896; the purchaser takes risk of quality and condition unless he protects himself by a warranty or there has been a false representation, State ex rel. Jones Store Co. v. Shain, Mo., 179 S.W.2d 19, 20."

[2] M. Horowitz, *The Transformation of American Law, 1760–1860,* pp. 63–108 and 253–66 (1977).

183

conclusively presumed competitive may have been reasonable and appropriate in the early days of our country, when products were relatively simple and consumer buyers often dealt with small sellers, putting them in a more or less equal bargaining position. As we moved deeper into the twentieth century, however, these principles and assumptions increasingly conflicted with the dramatically changed realities of the typical consumer transaction. These realities are explored herein.

As a result of technological advances, consumer products became far more numerous and complex. In the face of hundreds and then thousands of new products and services of often vastly greater degrees of complexity, consumers were overwhelmed by the available alternatives. Furthermore, these sellers spent larger and larger sums on mass advertising to build markets for their products, inducing consumers to buy.

Concomitant to these alterations to the market came a narrowing of the individual consumer's expertise. The consumer who had been a jack of all trades in simpler times became a specialist knowing more and more about less and less, weakening his or her evaluative capability. Thus, we find the consumer specialist induced to buy many products and forced to rely on biased seller-provided information in decision making.

In addition, transactions increasingly involved individual consumer buyers and corporate sellers. This transformation of the market meant that buyers had little or, more likely, no bargaining power. Related to the increased concentration of market power in sellers, buyers often had virtually no alternative sales contract terms from which to choose, making matters worse from the consumer perspective. Owing to the oligopolistic structure of some industries and the anticompetitive approach to business practices used in other major industries, buyers found it impossible to find a more advantageous contract with a competing brand because all companies used a substantially similar, one-sided contract.[3]

In fact, most sellers came to rely on printed, standardized sales contracts, narrowing the "bargaining" phase of the contract negotiation process to a simple "yes" or "no" decision. Indeed, today it is fair to say that customized consumer contracts do not exist. In addition to standardized forms whose provisions could not be altered by the consumer, sellers frequently added "boilerplate" clauses that benefited sellers to the detriment of buyers. Such clauses eliminated or significantly reduced the buyers' rights.

The law literature and cases are replete with examples of the diversity of abusive contract clauses. Some forms included "confession of judgment" provisions that in essence dictate that, in the event of a dispute between buyer and seller, the buyer admits in advance to being wrong. Another such provision typically found in form sales contracts is one that limits damage recovery

---

[3] In *Henningsen v. Bloomfield Motors, Inc.*, the court discusses the oligopolistic nature of the automobile industry and the resultant lack of choice for auto buyers. *Id.* at 32 N.J. 358, 161 A.2d 69 (1960).

to replacement of defective parts, prohibiting recovery of consequential damages.[4] This limitation guarantees replacement of, for example, a defective smoke detector, but precludes recovery for fire damage. A low water mark is established by the "exculpatory clause" that excuses damage caused by the seller's own negligence.[5]

As the information and bargaining power gulf widened between consumers and business, some courts, in effect, responded by rewriting the sales contract. These courts declared that onerous, one-sided contract provisions were unconscionable under the circumstances and would therefore not be enforced against consumers. Unconscionability thus became a defense to contract enforcement. In such contracts, there is no true "meeting of the minds" or mutual assent, required for a contract to be binding.

Unconscionability as a principle of judicial decision making was not derived initially to protect consumers, however. Rather, it has its roots in court opinions protecting government and businesspersons from contracts rendered unfair by an inability to comprehend contract terms,[6] unanticipated circumstances,[7] or circumstances bordering on duress.[8] In fact, early attempts to use the unconscionability defense and related arguments in the consumer context usually were rejected on the basis of notions of freedom of contract.[9] In these cases, courts took a hard line, holding that because the consumer had the opportunity to read and reject the contract, it could not be voided for one-sidedness. In their view, any other result would violate U.S. policies on freedom of contract, fundamental to the U.S. economic and political system.

The consumer protection movement, stalled during the 1940s and 1950s, was revitalized in the late 1950s and early 1960s. In the context of this growing demand for consumer protection, the 1960s produced a number of court decisions relieving consumers of unfair contract provisions such as those previously discussed. A detailed review of one of the more significant of these cases, *Williams v. Walker-Thomas Furniture Co.*, 121 U.S. App. D.C. 315, 350 F.2d 445 (1965), will provide insight into the factors that might lead a modern

---

[4] As an example, note the language on the package of a Sears "Early One" Smoke and Fire Detector: "FULL ONE YEAR WARRANTY ON SMOKE DETECTOR. For one year from the date of purchase, Sears will repair or replace this smoke detector free of charge, if defective in material or workmanship. This warranty shall not apply to the batteries, which are expendable. To obtain warranty service, simply return the smoke detector to your nearest Sears store throughout the United States. LIMITATION ON LIABILITY. Sears will not be liable for loss or damage to property or any incidental or consequential loss or expense from property damage detector is designed to detect."

[5] See, e.g., *O'Callaghan v. Waller & Beckwith Realty Co.*, 15 Ill. 2d 436, 155 N.E.2d 545 (1959) (tenant barred from recovery owing to exculpatory clause in lease).

[6] *Earl of Chesterfield v. Janssen*, 2 Ves. Sr. 125 (1750).

[7] See, e.g., *Hume v. United States*, 132 U.S. 406 (1889).

[8] *Post v. Jones*, 60 U.S. (19 How.) 150 (1856).

[9] See, e.g., *Swinton v. Whitinsville Sav. Bank*, 42 N.W.2d 809 (1942) (fraud not committed by concealment of termites); *O'Callaghan v. Waller & Beckwith Realty Co.*, 15 Ill. 2d 436, 155 N.E.2d 545 (1958) (tenant precluded from suing for damage caused by landlord's negligence because her lease contained an exculpatory clause).

court to step into the contract between business and consumer, altering it in ways that benefit the consumer.

A person of limited education, Ora Lee Williams was separated from her spouse and raising seven children by herself on a small monthly stipend of $218 from a public assistance agency. The record reveals that between 1957 and 1962, Ms. Williams purchased a number of household articles from Walker-Thomas Furniture Co., signing 14 contracts with the furniture company. Shortly after she signed a contract to purchase a stereo for $514.95, she defaulted. Prior to her default, she had paid over $1400 to the company. Walker-Thomas repossessed the stereo, a washing machine, a bed, and a chest of drawers using a writ of replevin. Shortly thereafter, in 1963, a hearing was held in which Ms. Williams urged that the contract be held enforceable, alleging fraud and violation of public policy.[10]

All the household goods contracts she signed were identical and contained a clause providing that in the event of default, Walker-Thomas could repossess all items purchased from them. Specifically, the contracts provided that:

> the amount of each periodical installment payment to be made by [purchaser] to the Company under this present lease shall be inclusive of and not in addition to the amount of each installment payment to be made by [purchaser] under such prior leases, bills or accounts; *and all payments now and hereafter made by [purchaser] shall be credited pro rata on all outstanding leases, bills and accounts* due the Company by [purchaser] at the time each such payment is made. [Emphasis added.][11]

At trial, Ms. Williams testified that she believed that when she had paid a sufficient amount to cover the cost of an item, it became hers. In other words, she did not understand the contract language by which the furniture company retained ownership of all items until the entire balance was paid. It was further adduced at trial that the company was fully aware of her reduced financial and educational circumstances and had made most of the sales to Ms. Williams in her home.

In the District of Columbia Court of General Sessions, Ms. Williams lost her bid to regain possession of her goods. She appealed to the District of Columbia Court of Appeals where she lost again, on March 30, 1964.[12] In its opinion, the appellate court expressed concern about the "sharp practices" of the furniture company. Much as it deplored Walker-Thomas's actions, however, it felt constrained to hold for the company owing to the lack of District of Columbia law on the point. In his opinion, Judge Quinn went on to urge that Congress take action to correct a potentially abusive situation.

Joined with another disappointed buyer in a similar case involving a Walker-Thomas repossession, Ms. Walker appealed her case again, to the United States Court of Appeals, District of Columbia Circuit. This time the

[10] *Williams v. Walker-Thomas Furniture Co.*, 198 A.2d 914, 915 (1964).
[11] *Williams v. Walker-Thomas Furniture Co.*, 121 U.S. App. D.C., 350 F.2d 445, 447 (1965).
[12] *Williams v. Walker-Thomas Furniture Co.*, 198 A.2d 914 (1964).

court did more than express concern and offer sympathy. On August 11, 1965, Circuit Judge Skelly Wright declared that the contract provision permitting the furniture company to retain an interest in all items purchased might be unconscionable as a matter of law, and, hence, unenforceable.[13] Thus, he remanded both cases for findings on this issue.

To understand the circumstances in which a finding of unconscionability might be made, culminating in a refusal to enforce contract provisions, Judge Skelly Wright's reasoning merits careful analysis. In a brief but succinct opinion, he sets out criteria that are representative of those generally relied on by courts assessing similar fact situations. His analysis began with a review of the state of the District of Columbia common law. Because the Uniform Commercial Code (UCC) was not adopted in the District of Columbia until after the actions on these contracts were filed, the decision had to be based on common law. Noting that no common law District of Columbia precedents directly addressed cases of this nature, the judge declared that reliance on unconscionability to void contracts was nonetheless not "novel." He pointed to a U.S. Supreme Court opinion and appellate opinions in other jurisdictions as supporting his approach.[14]

Interestingly, Judge Skelly Wright also relied on the UCC's unconscionability provision, Section 2-302, to support his position. Section 2-302 provides:

> (1) If the court as a matter of law finds the contract of any clause of the contract to have been unconscionable at the time it was made the court may refuse to enforce the contract, or it may enforce the remainder of the contract without the unconscionable clause, or it may so limit the application of any unconscionable clause as to avoid any unconscionable result.

Recognizing that the UCC had not been enacted in time to apply to Ms. Williams' case, he nevertheless declared that its subsequent adoption indicated what might all along have been the public policy of the District of Columbia. Because that contention was debatable, however, he observed that the court could adopt a similar rule in developing the common law of the District. Thus, under these alternative analyses, Judge Skelly Wright found authority to establish what he believed to be the correct rule of law.

Once the rule was in place, it remained for the court to develop and explain the criteria that would be used and how they would be used in determining whether a case was a proper one for a finding of unconscionability. As with many legal rules, in this case one may not refer to a simple checklist to ascertain under which circumstances an unconscionable contract or contract clause exists. A detailed factual analysis is required.

---

[13] *Williams v. Walker-Thomas Furniture Co.,* 121 U.S. App. D.C. 315, 350 F.2d 445 (1965).

[14] *Scott v. United States,* 79 U.S. (12 Wall.) 443, 20 L. Ed. 438 (1870); *Campbell Soup Co. v. Wentz,* 3 Cir., 172 F.2d 80 (1948); *Indianapolis Morris Plan Corp. v. Sparks,* 132 Ind. App. 145, 172 N.E.2d 899 (1961); *Henningsen v. Bloomfield Motors, Ind.,* 32 N.J. 358, 161 A.2d 69 (1960).

When a contract whose terms unreasonably favor one party over the other, the court, Judge Skelly Wright tells us, must determine whether the weaker party lacked meaningful choice. To make that determination, the court must review the totality of the circumstances and in that context assess the bargaining positions of the parties. Where there is gross inequality of bargaining strength, meaningful choice is negated in the view of the *Williams* court. Generally, in a transaction between a consumer and a medium- to large-sized business, the court will find such inequality.

Also crucial to ascertaining the presence or absence of unconscionable contract terms is the extent of the parties' knowledge. In its analysis, the court must determine and consider the difference in their educational backgrounds. When the weaker party, as was true of Ms. Williams, is not well educated, and the stronger party is aware of this fact, the difference in bargaining power becomes magnified and the weaker party's ability to choose well for his or her own protection is lessened in the court's view.

In furthering its assessment of the parties' knowledge and to develop as complete a factual picture of the circumstances of the case as possible, the court must ascertain whether the consumer had the opportunity to review the contract and to ask questions about its terms and whether the consumer understood the contract when he or she signed it. The facts as found in *Williams* indicated that the consumer has such an opportunity and had not asked questions. As the courts' opinions in the case make clear, however, Ms. Williams mistakenly thought she understood the contract terms and the company took no steps to explain its legal wording.

In evaluating the fairness of the contract, the court must also determine whether material terms are hidden in the document. Such terms could be hidden because they are buried in lengthy text presented in fine print. The complexity of the language used must also be scrutinized to determine whether the buyer had fair warning of the nature and content of its terms. The contract Ms. Williams signed was short, only 6 inches long, but it was written in legal terms easily susceptible to misinterpretation, especially by a person of limited education. Implicit in Judge Skelly Wright's reasoning on this point is an underlying fundamental question of contract interpretation: Was there a meeting of the minds? In *Williams,* that question was answered in the negative.

Also embedded within Judge Skelly Wright's analysis is the issue of contractual bargaining. Under the common law, the parties are presumed to have dickered and negotiated to arrive at a final contract. When a court is asked to deny enforcement of consumer contracts, it is appropriate for the court to ask: To what degree did true contractual bargaining take place in the contract formation process? Readily apparent in this case was a total absence of bargaining, typical of modern consumer contracts. Ms. Williams was presented with a printed, standardized form to which her assent was required to obtain the goods.

In summing up his view that, despite its inherent complexity in application, an unconscionability doctrine is necessary to protect consumers against unfair business practices, Judge Skelly Wright emphatically stated:

But when a party of little bargaining power, and hence little real choice, signs a commercially unreasonable contract with little or no knowledge of its terms, it is hardly likely that his consent, or even an objective manifestation of his consent, was ever given to all the terms. In such a case the usual rule that the terms of the agreement are not to be questioned should be abandoned and the court should consider whether the terms of the contract are so unfair that enforcement should be withheld.[15]

Thus, under the facts of the *Williams* case, application of the court's stated criteria dictated a remand for further fact-finding.

The holding in *Williams* was not unanimous, however. Judge Danaher dissented, disagreeing with the remedy created in the majority opinion. He argued that if undesirable business practices needed reforming or correction, the better remedies lie elsewhere. He agreed with the trial court that Congress was the proper body to make an exception to the general rule regarding freedom of contract. He also pointed to a District of Columbia loan-sharking statute that might afford relief. The dissenter further reasoned that the majority's rule might harm consumers by diminishing alternatives for persons on public assistance through creation of a disincentive to loan to such persons.[16]

The unconscionability doctrine articulated in *Williams v. Walker-Thomas Furniture Co.* and other cases gives notice to the business community that unfair practices preying on disadvantaged consumers may not be tolerated. It is one of many avenues of potential relief open to modern-day consumers that include federal consumer credit protection statutes,[17] state consumer protection acts,[18] and Federal Trade Commission consumer protection rules.[19] Owing to the discretionary nature of its application, however, the doctrine may be helpful more for its symbolic value than the actual relief it provides to consumers.

MANAGERIAL IMPLICATIONS

The equitable principle of unconscionability is widely acknowledged across the United States in statutes and court decisions. Consequently, successful managers will take this principle into account when dealing with customers and training staff. As a matter of limiting an enterprise's liability exposure and

---

[15] *Williams v. Walker-Thomas Furniture Co.*, 121 U.S. App. D.C. 315, 350 F.2d 445, 450 (1965).

[16] *Williams v. Walker-Thomas Furniture Co.*, 121 U.S. App. D.C. *315*, 350 F.2d 445, 450–451 (1965).

[17] Equal Credit Opportunity Act, 15 U.S.C. § 1691 (1983); Truth in Lending, 15 U.S.C. § 1631–32 (1983); Fair Credit Billing Act 15 U.S.C. § 1666; Fair Credit Reporting Act, 15 U.S.C. § 1681; Fair Debt Collection Practices Act, 15 U.S.C. § 1692 (1983).

[18] See, e.g., Michigan Consumer Protection Act., Mic. Comp. Laws Ann. § 445.901–922 (West 1988–89 cum. ann. pocket part).

[19] For example, the FTC promulgated a rule that eliminates the holder-in-due-course defense to consumer contract claims. 16 CFR 433.1–433.3 (1975). It also eliminated by rule enforceability of savior of defense clauses in consumer contracts. 16 CFR 444.2 (1984). The FTC strictly regulates consumer mail order sales. 16 CFR 435.1 and 435.2 (1975).

damage to its public image, creating situations such as that portrayed in *Williams v. Walker-Thomas Furniture* is to be avoided.

Managers and other employees ought to be aware that high-pressure sales tactics may come back to haunt them. A few simple rules of thumb will be helpful in achieving appropriate behavior. Sales personnel must fairly convey pertinent facts to customers in an understandable manner. As a corollary to this rule, sales personnel need to gauge and be sensitive to customers' educational background to develop an understandable presentation. Sales personnel also need to exercise caution in creating what might be perceived as undue pressure through coercive circumstances, such as selling in the customer's home.

Finally, in developing agreements, especially form agreements, managers should protect themselves by seeking legal advice to minimize the possibility of forms or form clauses being determined to be illegal.

REFERENCES

Hurd and Bush, "Unconscionability: A Matter of Conscience for California Consumers," 25 *Hastings L.J.* 1 (1973).

K. Llewellyn, *The Common Law Tradition* (discussion of "boilerplate agreements") pp. 362–71 (1960).

Ellinghaus, "In Defense of Unconscionability," 78 *Yale L.J.* 757 (1969).

Leff, "Unconscionability and the Code—The Emperor's New Clause," 115 *U. Pa. L. Rev.* 485 (1967).

———, "Unconscionability and the Crowd—Consumers and the Common Law Tradition," 31 *U. Pitt. L. Rev.* 349 (1970).

D. B. Dobbs, *Handbook on the Law of Remedies*, § 10.7, Unconscionable Conduct and the UCC (1973).

DISCUSSION QUESTIONS

1 Ms. Williams admitted signing the agreement with the furniture company. Thus, she had an opportunity to read and ask questions about the sales agreement. Why didn't the court follow the general rule of holding a party to an agreement freely signed?

2 The *Williams* case provides important information for businesses wishing to avoid such lawsuits. By what criteria can one evaluate circumstances giving rise to a holding of unconscionability?

3 What is the public policy basis for creating unconscionability protection for consumers?

SUGGESTED ANSWERS

1 Because of exceptional circumstances, the court felt it might be unfair to hold Ms. Williams to the contract. From her testimony, it was clear that she was a person of limited education and didn't understand the agreement. The furniture company knew of her background and circumstances and pressured her into buying the goods. Because it was a coercive situation involving a weaker and a much stronger and more

knowledgeable party, and because Ms. Williams was unaware of the consequences of her failure to pay, the court concluded that it would be unfair to hold her to the agreement.

2 Judge Skelly Wright stated that all of the circumstances surrounding the transaction must be evaluated. In particular, the following factors should be considered:

a Equality/inequality of bargaining power.

b The manner in which the contract was entered.

c Each party's ability and opportunity to understand the terms of the contract.

d The degree to which the contract is one-sided.

3 The change in market conditions was the driving force behind expansion of this principle. Today's market differs dramatically from that at the turn of the century. Consumers then more frequently dealt one-on-one with sellers, and products were relatively simple to evaluate. Today's consumers are besieged by thousands of technically complex products that they do not have the expertise to evaluate. In addition, vastly increased concentration of economic power (large corporations have replaced the individual seller) puts the consumer in a very weak bargaining position where most transactions are handled on a take-it-or-leave-it basis.

16

MANAGING LABOR RELATIONS IN A CHANGING LEGAL AND SOCIAL ENVIRONMENT:
The Lesson of *Flood v. Kuhn*

David Silverstein
Suffolk University

INTRODUCTION

In a seminal article entitled "The Litigation Audit: Preventive Legal Mainte-nance for Management," this author advocated implementation of a "litigation audit" as part of a proactive management strategy designed to target emerging legal problems before they become the subject of legislation, lawsuits, or other social action. Through early identification of emerging legal problems, manage-ment may be able to take steps to head off legal or social intervention or, at least, help to shape the final result. This chapter illustrates an application of these general management principles to the field of labor relations.

LABOR RELATIONS IN THE TWENTIETH CENTURY

Labor relations have undergone dramatic and far-reaching legal changes dur-ing the twentieth century. Contemporary labor relations demonstrate the ex-tent to which late nineteenth century *laissez-faire* policies and "freedom of contract" doctrines have given way to growing government intervention. To-day, for example, managers are faced with a wide array of federal and state laws (minimum wage, workers' compensation, social security, affirmative ac-tion, regulation of employment of children, and laws mandating a safe work environment, to name a few) that restrict managers' freedom of choice and su-persede the freedom of contract principles that dominated employer-employee relations well into the twentieth century. Public reaction to widely publicized abuses has also led to new legislation giving some employees the right to know about hazardous chemicals in the workplace and 60 days' notice of layoffs in large industries.

Important changes in labor relations have also come about through judicial intervention. Recent court decisions have held businesses liable for millions of dollars in damages in lawsuits based on unsafe working conditions, breach of contract, wrongful dismissal, employment discrimination, and sexual harassment. In the 1985 case of *Woolley v. Hoffman-La Roche. Inc.,* 99 N.J. 284, 491 A.2d 1257, *modified,* 101 N.J. 10, 499 A.2d 515 (1985), the New Jersey Supreme Court explained its surprising departure from traditional employment-at-will principles in part by observing that the laissez-faire climate and freedom of contract doctrine that had encouraged industrial growth in an earlier era were not well suited to the twentieth century where the typical employer is a corporation with greatly superior bargaining power over its employees.

The legalization and institutionalization of labor organizations has also had a profound impact on the workplace during the twentieth century. The National Labor Relations Act of 1935 guaranteed employees the right to unionize and bargain collectively. The landmark 1937 U.S. Supreme Court decision in *NLRB v. Jones & Laughlin Steel Corp.,* 301 U.S. 1 (1937), upheld the constitutionality of the National Labor Relations Act and recognized the need for unions as a counterweight to the unequal bargaining power of employees in the typical employment contract. Even in nonunion shops where managements' hands are not already tied by a collective bargaining agreement, the ever-present threat of unionization requires that greater deference be given to the needs and demands of employees.

These changes in the legal environment of labor relations, however, did not occur suddenly or without warning. Rather, they were the outcome of a gradual evolution of legal and social factors. Managers who do not appreciate the dynamic and evolutionary nature of the U.S. legal system and the interaction among legislation, judicial decisions, and collective bargaining—the three ''tools'' of modern labor relations—are likely to be caught off guard by such legal developments, leaving their companies unprepared to deal with the consequences. One commentator, surprised by the continuing inertia of management's practicing enlightened labor relations, recently observed: ''Many business people cannot seem to surrender the illusion that they are still absolute masters of their work force, even though the discharge of any black (or white), or female (or male), or person between 40 and 70, and so on, already may subject them to proceedings before some federal or state tribunal (and often several).[1]

At least in the United States, legal change occurs through an orderly and largely predictable incremental process. Managers who were sensitive to the changing legal and social environment of labor relations during the twentieth century could have timely forecast many of the key legal changes and taken

---

[1] Jack Stieber, ''Recent Developments in Employment-at-Will,'' *Labor Law Journal* (Aug. 1985) 557, 567.

steps to minimize the impact of those changes on their firms. By viewing the dominant environmental forces at work in the marketplace today from a dynamic perspective, astute managers can make highly reliable predictions about the changing legal environment and thereby better position their firms to meet future legal challenges.

LAW AS A RESPONSE TO PUBLIC OPINION

The legal environment is only part of a broader social context within which business must operate, but the two are closely connected. At the turn of the century, English legal scholar A. V. Dicey in *Law and Public Opinion in England* argued that, because of the nature of a modern democratic society, the law is invariably responsive to public opinion. According to Dicey, "[T]he law of a country may fail, for a time, to represent public opinion owing to the lack of any legislative [or judicial] organ which adequately responds to the sentiment of the age." But, in general, he believed the legal system would eventually be responsive to genuine and persistent social demands. "Nowhere," he observed, "have changes in popular convictions or wishes found anything like such rapid and immediate expression in alterations of the law as they have in Great Britain during the nineteenth century.... [I]t is at bottom opinion which controls legislation."

Other legal scholars have noted a corresponding responsiveness of the U.S. legal system to social needs. Wallace Mendelson presented a development model for the United States based on three distinct periods of evolution of the business-government interface, each dictated by changing social priorities: Stage 1 is the "era of nationalism," when Supreme Court decisions subordinated states' rights to federalism in the interest of achieving national unity; stage 2 is the "era of industrialization," when a spirit of laissez-faire freed business from most of the social costs of industrialization, thereby facilitating capital accumulation and unbridled growth; and stage 3 is the "era of the welfare state," when plentiful resources and the establishment of industry led to growing sentiment for a redistribution of wealth through government intervention.[2]

Historically, the business-government interface in this country has, with some lag time, been quite responsive to public opinion, and there is no reason to believe that this lagged relationship will not continue to operate in the future.

THE CHANGING LEGAL AND SOCIAL ENVIRONMENT OF LABOR RELATIONS

Mendelson's development model is useful in understanding the different social contexts for labor relations in the United States during the nineteenth and

---

[2] Mendelson, "Law and the Development of Nations," 32 *Journal of Politics* 223 (1970).

twentieth centuries. Mendelson observed that the *laissez-faire* spirit during stage 2 in his model found expression in such specific legal rules as *caveat emptor* (let the buyer beware) and privity of contract, which "protected manufacturers of defective goods from liability to third-party consumers, and in...[the fellow servant rule] that all but freed employers from the cost of industrial accidents."[3] The objective of these legal rules, according to Mendelson, was to promote the accumulation of capital, without which the Industrial Revolution never could have succeeded. If the legal system had immediately placed on the United States' newly emerging infant industries the full burden of the social costs of industrialization, it might have squelched these businesses before they ever got off the ground. "Decisions that block the claims of labor and consumer," said Mendelson, "promote the growth of investment capital. And if a 'traditional' society wants mass production, its first economic task is to accumulate capital." In order to accumulate capital, Mendelson argued:

> [A] society must refrain using all its current energies and materials to satisfy its current wants, no matter how urgent these may be. Saving is the act by which a...[nation] releases some portion of its labor and material resources from the task of providing for the present so that both can be applied to building for the future. When the Supreme Court suppressed worker and consumer claims and taught us the blessings of laissez faire and the Gospel of Wealth, it fostered capital accumulation.

Another legal scholar, Carl Auerbach, described this critical development period in comparable terms:

> The achievements of the 19th century American capitalism were great. But its social costs were very high. The law did little to curb the extravagant exploitation of our natural resources....Human resources were also cruelly used. The public health was nobody's concern. The workday and work week were very long and earnings very low, though conditions of the American worker in the 19th century were probably better than the conditions of the worker anywhere else. Workers and their families bore the staggering costs of industrial accidents. The business cycle which recurred throughout the 19th century, victimized farmers and workers.[4]

The excesses of big business began to provoke public reaction and calls for change. Auerbach noted that the latter part of the nineteenth century was a period of growing social unrest in the United States.

> Social unrest grew and found expression in the protest movements of the farmers; the railroad strikes of 1877 and 1894; the Haymarket bomb throwing in 1886; the Homestead strike riot of 1892 and Coxey's army of the unemployed in 1894. This unrest found political expression in the bitter Presidential campaigns of the 1890's. Before the close of the 19th century, the law began to do something about these unintended consequences of rapid industrialization based upon private economic decision-making in order to allocate, in a more just and humane fashion, the material

---

[3] Mendelson, *supra,* at 226.
[4] Auerbach, "Law and Social Change in the United States," 6 *UCLA L. Rev.* 516, 524 (1959).

and human costs which did not show up in the accounts of any private firm.[5]

This marked the transition of the United States from Mendelson's stage 2 into stage 3, the era of the welfare state. By this time, the industrialization of the United States was well underway and the position of big business secure. According to Mendelson:

> Having achieved mass production, the United States entered stage three—the era of the welfare state. The problem now was not production, but distribution. Consumer goods were so potentially plentiful and so near at hand that there was less need to restrain consumption. We could afford Social Security, collective bargaining, minimum wages, the forty-hour week, Medicare, and similar measures. The common element in these programs is a redistribution of wealth. Income that earlier might have been channeled toward capital formation was now diverted to provide goods and services for the common man. His fathers' unwilling investment in American plant capacity began at last to pay him dividends.[6]

THE LEGACY OF LAISSEZ-FAIRE IN LABOR RELATIONS

Robert Ackerman,[7] a management scholar, observed the tendency of managers to see legal issues in black-and-white terms instead of as a spectrum of varying shades of gray. Ackerman argued that managers tend to a static view of legal issues as being relatively permanently fixed either at one end of the spectrum, where there is legal regulation and little or no managerial discretion, or else at the opposite end where there is no legal regulation and, correspondingly, almost complete managerial discretion. By treating a legal environment issue as static, however, a manager may be forfeiting the opportunity to exercise influence during the most critical time period—that transitional period when evolving legal issues are neither black nor white, which Ackerman called the "Zone of Discretion."

The 1972, U.S. Supreme Court decision in *Flood v. Kuhn*, 407 U.S. 258, 32 L. Ed. 728, serves as a nonfiction parable of what can happen when managers stubbornly cling to the past in reliance on the status quo rather than seize the opportunity suggested by Ackerman's "Zone of Discretion" to timely adapt to new social priorities. This case also vividly demonstrates why it is shortsighted for managers to focus on legislative and judicial developments in labor law while ignoring the potential impact of collective bargaining. On its face, *Flood v. Kuhn* was not a labor law case but an antitrust case. Curt Flood, a popular and extremely successful baseball player during the 1960s, sued Bowie Kuhn, then commissioner of baseball, to have the so-called reserve clause in baseball players' contracts declared unenforceable as an illegal restraint on trade. In what at the time appeared to be a stunning victory for

---

[5] Auerbach, *supra,* at 226.
[6] Mendelson, *supra,* at 228.
[7] Ackerman, "How Companies Respond to Social Demand," 51 *Harvard Business Review* 88 (1973).

management over employees, the Supreme Court for the third time in 50 years reaffirmed a judicially created antitrust exemption for baseball. As later discussed, however, the jubilation of baseball management over this legal victory was short-lived.

The Enforceability of Negative Covenants

The seeds of *Flood v. Kuhn* were sown more than a century earlier in the 1852 English legal classic of *Lumley v. Wagner,* 1 DeG.M. & G. 604, 42 Eng. Rep. 687. World-famous opera star, Johanna Wagner, had signed a contract for an exclusive engagement at Lumley's theater in London. The contract contained provisions that the Court of Chancery interpreted as amounting to a "negative covenant," that is, an agreement by Wagner that during her engagement at Lumley's theater she would not perform elsewhere. When the arrangements between Lumley and Wagner broke down, Lumley sought an injunction to prevent Wagner from singing at another theater. The key legal issue in this case was whether the court had the power to enforce a "negative covenant" through its injunctive powers.

The Lord Chancellor readily acknowledged that Chancery had no power to enforce a "positive" covenant to perform a personal services contract; that is, the Chancellor could *not* order Wagner to sing at Lumley's theater even though that is what she had agreed to do. Such an order was repugnant as a form of involuntary servitude; furthermore, Chancery was loath to issue an order it could not properly enforce. It might compel Wagner to sing at Lumley's, but it had no means to ensure that she would perform at her best. For example, who would want brain surgery performed by a recalcitrant neurosurgeon acting under court order?

Wagner argued, however, that by enforcing the "negative covenant," the court would, in effect, be compelling her to perform at Lumley's theater against her will. After all, how was this world-famous opera singer supposed to support herself during the duration of her engagement at Lumley's if she was enjoined from singing elsewhere?

Lumley v. Wagner was decided in 1852, almost 30 years before the English Judicature Acts that merged Chancery and the Common Law courts. Under this bifurcated court system, Chancery could award injunctive relief but had no power to award money damages. As discussed, Chancery also could not compel performance of Wagner's personal service contract. Thus, unless the Lord Chancellor had power to enforce the "negative covenant," he would be powerless to help Lumley. The centuries-old rivalry between Chancery and the Common Law courts and the Chancellor's unwillingness to appear impotent in this case were evident in his gratuitous remark that: "[Chancery] will not suffer them to depart from their contracts at their pleasure, leaving the party with whom they have contracted to the mere chance of any damages which a [common law court] jury may give." With the seemingly tongue-in-cheek declaration that "I disclaim doing indirectly what I cannot do directly," the Lord Chancellor ruled that he could indeed enforce the negative covenant against Wagner *even* if it had the effect of compelling her to perform at Lumley's theater.

The Freedom of Contract Fiction

To be sure, it is difficult to muster much sympathy for Johanna Wagner under the circumstances of this case. Even assuming that the practical result of the Lord Chancellor's ruling was to compel Wagner to sing at Lumley's theater, she would be doing no more than what she had freely bargained for.

Freedom of contract doctrine was based on the legal fiction that the parties to a contract were of substantially equal bargaining power, that they were fully appraised of their legal rights and the terms of the obligations they were undertaking, and that with full understanding they voluntarily entered into the agreement. Even in the heyday of laissez-faire during the nineteenth century in the United States, however, it was clear that most employer-employee contracts were simple take-it-or-leave-it affairs. There was typically little or no negotiation over salary, working conditions, hours, or other terms. During this "era of industrialization," employees had no more power to bargain for an exemption to the fellow-servant doctrine or other abusive legal rules than to demand million-dollar salaries. Even today among educated white-collar workers, how many ambitious young managers would risk demanding modifications in their companies' basic employment contracts?

But Johanna Wagner was not an unsophisticated, unskilled laborer, interchangeable with hundreds of others. As a world-renowned opera star in great demand, it is likely that her bargaining power equalled or exceeded that of Mr. Lumley. We can also surmise that, in negotiating her contract with Lumley, she was literate, knowledgeable in the ways of commerce, and, in all probability, had legal representation. Thus, this situation probably came about as close to true "freedom of contract" as one is likely to encounter in the employment realm. Under these circumstances, it hardly seemed unjust for the court to hold Wagner to her freely bargained agreement. The decision in *Lumley v. Wagner* affirming the enforceability of "negative covenants" in personal service contracts was not, however, expressly limited to such "ideal" freedom of contract cases. The case of *Flood v. Kuhn* dramatically illustrated the potential for abuse when the precedent of *Lumley* was applied to a situation involving a gross inequality of bargaining power.

TEMPORARILY PRESERVING THE STATUS QUO IN A CHANGING LEGAL AND SOCIAL ENVIRONMENT

The Facts of *Flood v. Kuhn*

In 1969, following 14 extremely successful seasons of playing first with the Cincinnati Reds and later with the St. Louis Cardinals baseball clubs, Curt

Flood was involuntarily traded to the Philadelphia Phillies. Curt Flood rose to fame as a center fielder with the Cardinals between 1958 and 1969, compiling a batting average of .293 and ranking among the top 10 major league outfielders. His salary with St. Louis rose steadily from $16,000 in 1958 to $90,000 in 1969. Indeed, the trade to Philadelphia involved a further increase in Flood's salary from $90,000 to 100,000 (a pittance, perhaps, by today's standards, but at the time, one of the top salaries in baseball). For whatever reasons, however, Flood objected to the trade and refused to play for Philadelphia.

Flood's contract with St. Louis required him to play ball for St. Louis or any other club to which he might be traded. But the same considerations that prevented the English Court of Chancery from ordering Wagner to sing at Lumley's theater also precluded any possibility that a court would order Flood to play ball for Philadelphia against his will.

The problem for Curt Flood was that his contract with St. Louis *also* included the so-called reserve clause—in effect, a "negative covenant" that prohibited Flood from playing for any other baseball club while he was under contract to St. Louis. Following the precedent of *Lumley v. Wagner,* there was little doubt that a U.S. court, exercising its equitable jurisdiction, had the power to restrain Curt Flood from playing ball for any other baseball club.

The Involuntary Servitude Argument

Curt Flood launched a two-pronged legal attack against this contractual restriction. First, following Johanna Wagner's unsuccessful strategy, Curt Flood argued that by enforcing the "reserve clause" the court would, in effect, be compelling him to play against his will for Philadelphia in violation of the Thirteenth Amendment to the U.S. Constitution. With no education, skills, or training apart from playing baseball, what realistic employment alternatives did Curt Flood have at comparable pay?

But the U.S. Supreme Court was not moved by such arguments anymore than was the Lord Chancellor in *Lumley v. Wagner.* Instead, the Supreme Court held that enforcement of the "reserve clause" did *not* involve any involuntary compulsion; it merely forced Curt Flood to choose between playing baseball or not playing baseball. Moreover, the Court held that the "reserve clause" was part of a freely bargained contract, so there was no injustice in enforcing the terms of that agreement.

Was this, then, just another case of a prima donna who grew disenchanted with the terms of his or her contract and tried to back out? Didn't Curt Flood, as a nationally acclaimed baseball star, just as Wagner the renowned opera singer, have bargaining power substantially equal to that of his employer? Upon closer examination of the facts in this case, however, any illusion of "freedom of contract" is quickly dispelled.

The Antitrust Argument

Curt Flood signed his first baseball contract in 1956 to play for the Cincinnati Reds for a modest $4000 a year. He was 18 years old at the time—a poor black kid from an urban ghetto being offered the opportunity of a lifetime, a chance to break into major league baseball. Lured by the glamour and the promise of fame and fortune, Curt Flood signed that first fateful contract without lawyer, agent, or professional advice of any kind. It is doubtful that he even bothered to read that long and technical document, much less to have understood it. That first contract with Cincinnati was fateful for Curt Flood because, buried in the text of that document, was the so-called reserve clause. The reserve clause prohibited Curt Flood from playing baseball for any club other than Cincinnati, or such other club as Cincinnati might trade him to, for the duration of his contract. *And,* the contract was automatically renewable each year, *at the option of the ball club.*

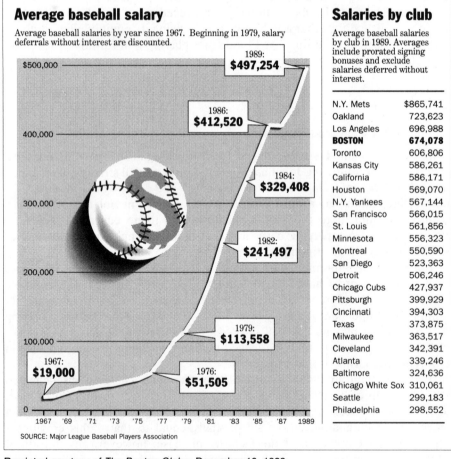

Average baseball salary

Average baseball salaries by year since 1967. Beginning in 1979, salary deferrals without interest are discounted.

1989:	**$497,254**
1986:	**$412,520**
1984:	**$329,408**
1982:	**$241,497**
1979:	**$113,558**
1976:	**$51,505**
1967:	**$19,000**

SOURCE: Major League Baseball Players Association

Salaries by club

Average baseball salaries by club in 1989. Averages include prorated signing bonuses and exclude salaries deferred without interest.

N.Y. Mets	$865,741
Oakland	723,623
Los Angeles	696,988
BOSTON	**674,078**
Toronto	606,806
Kansas City	586,261
California	586,171
Houston	569,070
N.Y. Yankees	567,144
San Francisco	566,015
St. Louis	561,856
Minnesota	556,323
Montreal	550,590
San Diego	523,363
Detroit	506,246
Chicago Cubs	427,937
Pittsburgh	399,929
Cincinnati	394,303
Texas	373,875
Milwaukee	363,517
Cleveland	342,391
Atlanta	339,246
Baltimore	324,636
Chicago White Sox	310,061
Seattle	299,183
Philadelphia	298,552

Reprinted courtesy of *The Boston Globe*; December 10, 1989.

How much bargaining power did Curt Flood actually have when he signed that 1956 contract? Would negotiations have proceeded any differently if Curt Flood had been represented by an attorney? If Curt Flood, with the benefit of legal advice, had quibbled with Cincinnati over the reserve clause, how many other poor, ghetto kids with some athletic ability were waiting in the wings, ready to take Flood's place, and happy to sign *anything* for the chance to play major league baseball?

But let's go a step further. Assume that Curt Flood had had a lawyer. Assume, too, that Curt Flood was not just an above-average, untested athlete but a high school superstar who had baseball teams from all over the country competing for his talents. Now, would Curt Flood have had the bargaining power to negotiate the reserve clause out of his contract?

The astonishing answer is no! Cincinnati might have offered Flood triple the normal salary for new recruits and numerous other embellishments to sign him, but the one thing Cincinnati had no power to offer Flood was dropping the reserve clause from his contract. The reason was that, as part and parcel of the major league baseball contract signed by Cincinnati, there was a provision that prohibited any major league club from signing a player contract that did not contain a reserve clause. No matter how badly Cincinnati wanted to sign Curt Flood, and no matter how much bargaining power Flood had, Cincinnati could delete the reserve clause from his contract only at the risk of being sanctioned by or even ejected from the National League. Every major league baseball club in the country was bound by the same league contract requiring uniform player contracts.

This was the basis for Curt Flood's second line of argument before the U.S. Supreme Court. Flood contended that the agreement of the major league baseball clubs to adhere to uniform player contracts containing the reserve clause was an illegal restraint of trade in violation of the federal antitrust laws. This was certainly not the first time that the reserve clause in baseball player contracts, as well as in contracts in other professional sports, had been challenged on this basis. In two earlier cases, however, the Supreme Court had exempted baseball from the antitrust laws.

Adhering to an Anamolous Precedent

When this issue was first raised in the 1922 case of *Federal Baseball Club v. National League,* 259 U.S. 200, 66 L. Ed. 898, the Supreme Court, in a unanimous opinion by Justice Oliver Wendell Holmes, held that baseball did not involve "interstate commerce" and, therefore, was not covered by the antitrust laws. When this issue was next raised in the 1953 case of *Toolson v. New York Yankees, Inc.,* 346 U.S. 356, 98 L. Ed. 64, the advent of radio and television and the proliferation of professional baseball clubs made it clear that baseball was no longer just a friendly game played on neighborhood sandlots; it was an international, multimillion-dollar-a-year business. Such arguments notwithstanding, the Supreme Court in *Toolson* stubbornly stuck to its precedent in *Federal Baseball* observing:

> Congress has had the ruling under consideration but has not seen fit to bring such business under these laws by legislation having prospective effect....The present cases ask us to overrule the prior decision and, with retrospective effect, hold the legislation applicable. We think that if there are evils in this field which now warrant application to it of the antitrust laws it should be by legislation.

By the time the *Flood* case came before the Supreme Court, many observers believed that the Court could no longer ignore this glaring legal anomaly. In every other professional sport in which the reserve clause issue had arisen, the Supreme Court had ruled that it was a violation of the antitrust laws. But, to the chagrin of major league ball players across the country, the Supreme Court held firm by a divided 5-3 vote with the majority observing that a precedent of such long standing as *Federal Baseball,* if it was going to be changed, should be changed by Congress (even though it was the Supreme Court that carved out this exemption in the first place!). In concluding his majority opinion, Justice Blackmun observed: "If there is any inconsistency or illogic in all this, it is an inconsistency and illogic of long standing that is to be remedied by the Congress and not by this Court.... Under these circumstances, there is merit in consistency even though some might claim that beneath that consistency is a layer of inconsistency."

Baseball management had stubbornly clung to an antiquated mandatory reserve clause system even though that system was under widespread attack and rested uneasily on the nineteenth century freedom-of-contract fiction, the questionable precedent of *Lumley v. Wagner,* and the historical accident that the antitrust status of the reserve clause in baseball was first litigated before the interstate commerce dimensions of the sport had become manifest. What is even more surprising is the tenacity and ostrichlike mentality of baseball management who won the imprimatur of the U.S. Supreme Court. Baseball management had disregarded Ackerman's "Zone of Discretion" opportunity by refusing to consider any policy adaptations unless and until ordered to do so by Congress, and it briefly appeared that this callous strategy had succeeded.

MANAGERIAL IMPLICATIONS

For Curt Flood, the 1972 Supreme Court decision effectively ended both his lawsuit and his career. After sitting out from playing for a year, Flood was traded by Philadelphia to the Washington Senators. Flood started the 1971 season with Washington but, dissatisfied with his performance, he left the club on April 27, 1971, at age 33, and never played professional baseball again.

Major league baseball club owners, however, had little time to savor their victory. The Major League Baseball Players Association (MLBPA) had been formed in the 1960s by a small band of discontented players. Initially it had few members, little support among players, and essentially no power. The injustice and publicity of the *Flood* case, however, galvanized baseball players and gave this fledgling labor organization a fresh breath of life.

In 1970, the same year Curt Flood filed suit challenging the reserve clause, the MLBPA won the right of sole bargaining agent for professional baseball players. In 1972, the year the Supreme Court dismissed Flood's suit, the MLBPA staged a 13-day strike, the first in professional baseball history, causing cancellation of 86 games. By 1973 ball players had won the right to compulsory arbitration of grievances. In 1974 Catfish Hunter won a breach of contract suit and gained free agency from the Oakland Athletics. That same year, Dick Woodson of the Minnesota Twins became the first player to win an Article X arbitration decision. Finally, in 1975, two more players, Andy Messersmith and Dave McNally, won free agency in landmark arbitration proceedings. Only 3 years after Curt Flood's lawsuit had been dismissed, labor arbitrator Peter Seitz cast the deciding vote that effectively nullified the reserve clause in a broad-based ruling that was upheld on appeal. The following year, 22 players gained free agency after refusing to sign contracts. Later that year, a new system of movement, with a modified reserve clause, was adopted as part of a new basic player agreement ushering in a new era in player-management relations. The increased clout of baseball players under the new system (as subsequently revised) was clearly reflected in the rapidly escalating salary and incentive packages successfully negotiated by top players during the 1980s. Today it has become common for such players to negotiate "no trade" clauses in their contracts, something unheard of in the Curt Flood era.

During the twentieth century, collective bargaining has thus become one route to reestablishing some semblance of equality of bargaining power in employment contracts. An employer who persists in taking unfair advantage of its work force may face lawsuits and legislative initiatives. When the legislatures and courts are slow to intervene, however, employees today may have the power to take matters into their own hands through unionization. The result may be to tie the hands of both the employer and the employees with a rigid and inflexible collective bargaining agreement. In many of these cases, a management more sensitive and responsive to the needs of its work force, and aware of the potential for government or union intervention, could have responded in a more creative, flexible, and cost-effective manner to the benefit of both the business and the employees.

CONCLUSION

Many of the key labor relations issues that will have an impact on business in the next century are still located well within a "Zone of Discretion," where managers may exercise considerable leeway in shaping and responding to those labor demands. If management fails to fulfill its social responsibilities to its work force at a time when action is still largely voluntary, it will almost certainly face more costly and burdensome regulation through government or collective bargaining in the future. A better understanding by managers of the dynamic nature of the U.S. legal system, along with a conscious attempt to make sophisticated predictions about the changing environment of labor relations, can lead to an enlightened, proactive management strategy in this area. Early perception of potential labor problems, combined with imaginative and compassionate responses, can, therefore, be good business as well as socially responsible.

REFERENCES

Ackerman, Robert, "How Companies Respond to Social Demands," 51 *Harvard Business Review* 88 (1973).

Auerbach, Carl, "Law and Social Change in the United States," 6 *UCLA L. Rev.* 516 (1959).

Berger, Robert, "After the Strikes: A Reexamination of Professional Baseball's Exemption from the Antitrust Laws," 45 *Univ. of Pitt. L. Rev.* 209 (1983).

Cihon, P. J., and J. O. Castagnera, *Labor and Employment Law*, PWS-Kent, Boston, 1988.

Collins and Friesen, "Looking Back on *Muller v. Oregon*," 69 *American Bar Assoc. Journal* 294–98, 472–77 (1983).

Dicey, A. V., *Law and Public Opinion in England*, Macmillan & Co. Ltd., Toronto, 1905.

Drahozal, Christopher, "The Impact of Free Agency on the Distribution of Playing Talent in Major League Baseball," 38 *Journal of Economics and Business* 113 (1986).

Federal Baseball Club v. National League, 259 U.S. 200, 66 L. Ed. 898 (1922).

Fehr, "The Relationship of the Baseball Player's Association to Management and the League," *Current Issues in Professional Sports*, 1981, p. 166.

Flood v. Kuhn, 407 U.S. 258, 32 L. Ed. 2d 728 (1972).

Friedmann, W., *Law in a Changing Society*, Stevens & Sons Ltd., Great Britain, 2d ed., 1972, pp. 119–161.

Gilbert, "Enforcement of Negative Covenants: Some Old Problems in a Modern Guise," 4 *Calif. L. Rev.* 114 (1915).

Glendon and Lev, "Changes in the Bonding of the Employment Relationship: An Essay on the New Property," 20 *Boston Col. L. Rev.* 457 (1979).

Lee, "A Survey of Professional Team Sport Player-Control Mechanisms under Antitrust and Labor Law Principles: Peace at Last," 11 *Valparaiso Univ. L. Rev.* 373 (1977).

Loftie, W. J., *The Inns of Court and Chancery*, 1893.

Lumley v. Wagner, 1 DeG.M. & G. 604, 42 Eng. Rep. 687 (1852).

Marshall, Ray, "The American Industrial Relations System in a Time of Change," 48 *Univ. of Pitt. L. Rev.* 829 (1987).

Martin, Philip, "The Aftermath of *Flood v. Kuhn*: Professional Baseball's Exemption from Antitrust Regulations," 3 *Western State Univ. L. Rev.* 262 (1976).

McOmber, Robert, "Emerging Issues in Employment Law: The Debate Shifts to the States," 4 *Cooley L. Rev.* 329 (1987).

Mendelson, Wallace, "Law and the Development of Nations," 32 *Journal of Politics* 223 (1970).

National Labor Relations Act of 1935, Public Law No. 74-198, 49 Stat. 449, codified at

29 U.S.C. §§ 151–168 (1982) (employees guaranteed the right to unionize and bargain collectively).

NLRB v. Jones & Laughlin Steel Corp., 301 U.S. 1 (1937) (upholding the constitutionality of the NLRA and recognizing the lack of equal bargaining power in the typical employment contract).

Note, "Entertainment Law—Enforcement of Negative Covenants in Contracts with Performers of Distinction in the Field," 7 *Whittier L. Rev.* 1059 (1985).

Schlossberg, Stephen, and Steven Fetter, "U.S. Labor Law and the Future of Labor—Management Cooperation," 3 *The Labor Lawyer* 11 (1987).

Selznick, P., *Law, Society, and Industrial Justice* (1969).

Shapiro, Daniel, "The Professional Athlete: Liberty or Peonage?" 13 *Alberta L. Rev.* 212 (1975).

Silverstein, David, "Managing Corporate Social Responsibility in a Changing Legal Environment," 25 *Am. Bus. L.J.* 523 (1987).

Steinberg, David, "Application of the Antitrust and Labor Exemptions to Collective Bargaining of the Reserve System in Professional Baseball," 28 *Wayne L. Rev.* 1301 (1982).

Toolson v. New York Yankees, Inc., 346 U.S. 356, 98 L. Ed. 64 (1953).

Williston, Samuel, "Freedom of Contract," 6 *Cornell Law Quarterly* 365 (1921).

Wong, Glenn, "Major League Baseball's Grievance Arbitration System: A Comparison with Nonsport Industry," *Labor Law Journal* 84 (February 1987).

Wood, H., *A Treatise on the Law of Master & Servant* (1877).

Woolley v. Hoffman-La Roche, Inc., 99 N.J. 284, 491 A.2d 1257, *modified*, 101 N.J. 10, 499 A.2d 515 (1985).

DISCUSSION QUESTIONS

1 In the early 1970s, were there any signs or signals that should have alerted baseball management to an impending change in the "reserve" system?

2 If one astute baseball team owner had perceived the need for some kind of adaptation or accommodation to the players, but the rest of the league owners refused to change the standard player contract, what actions could the one owner have taken on his or her own?

3 Is the field of professional baseball just a curious anomaly, or does the lesson of *Flood v. Kuhn* have broad allegorical significance for modern business? Consider the dilemma of a manager or business owner who perceives the need or desirability for improved employee relations, safer working conditions, more job security, and so forth, but who faces the financial constraints of remaining competitive with less socially responsive domestic or foreign competitors.

SUGGESTED ANSWERS

1 Yes. The foremost sign of impending change was the fact that baseball had become an anomaly among professional sports. "Reserve" systems similar to that in baseball had been successfully challenged and declared illegal in every other other sport. The only barrier to change in baseball was the Supreme Court's stubborn adherence to precedent. But precedents can be overruled, and often are, when changed circumstances or new knowledge undermine the foundations of the original decision. The Supreme Court's landmark decision in *Brown v. Board of Education,* overruling the

discredited "separate but equal" doctrine of *Plessy v. Ferguson,* was a dramatic example of such a change. The lesson is that managers cannot rely blindly on the precedential value of a legal decision. Judicial precedents, and laws generally, must constantly be tested against the shifting sands of social change to determine whether the legal foundation is still sound.

2 Because every major league baseball club in the country was bound by the same league contract requiring uniform player contracts containing a "reserve clause," even an enlightened team owner had an extremely limited range of options. First, the owner might establish a club policy of consulting with players in advance about proposed trades and making every reasonable effort to accommodate the players' wishes. Second, the owner might endeavor to reason with other club owners about the urgency of moderating their rigid policies before change was imposed on them by others. But, in the end, the "good" owners might well be swept up in the angry wave of player discontent along with the less astute owners.

3 Contemporary managers often find themselves "between a rock and a hard place." Like the baseball team owner in question 2, the modern manager may have few if any realistic options for addressing a serious emerging labor-management dispute. The fiscal constraints of remaining competitive with less forward-looking firms, especially when management's performance is being judged daily by large institutional stock owners and reflected daily in the price of the company's stock, may be every bit as much of a straitjacket as was the uniform major league contract in baseball. The enlightened manager may have to settle for making relatively minor changes at his or her own company to try to ameliorate the immediate problems while continuing to press his or her counterparts at other firms in the industry to agree on some concerted, long-term industrywide change or self-regulation. Alternatively, in a situation where legal intervention appears inevitable and imminent, instead of fighting a losing battle to prevent government regulation, a firm might actually decide to support legislation in the relevant area rather than risk the unpredictable outcome of a court decision or collective bargaining. One benefit of this approach is that legislation has only prospective effect, whereas a court decision may have retroactive application. Second, a firm or industry, through lobbying efforts and public education programs, can influence the final outcome of the legislative process to ensure the minimum possible damage to business. Third, legislation helps to establish a level playing field by ensuring that at least all domestic competitors in the industry will face a comparable cost structure in which no one can compete unfairly by cutting corners.

17

PROTECTING EMPLOYEES' RIGHT TO COLLECTIVELY BARGAIN:
NLRB v. Gissel Packing Co.

Dennis R. Kuhn
Villanova University

INTRODUCTION

The employer's relationship with its work force is affected by a complex web of government regulation. The government's involvement is attributable not only to organized labor's ability to exercise its muscle in the political arena, but also to a variety of social and economic forces that have arisen over the last 50 years. The result is that managers must follow the lead of government on issues as varied as the minimum wage to be paid to workers, to factors that can and cannot be considered when an employer hires, fires, and promotes, to steps that must be taken to ensure safe working conditions. This chapter will focus on how public policy has created a system designed to ensure that management will permit workers to join organizations designed to promote their interests, and that management will meet with workers' representatives to bargain over issues important to the employment relation.

IMPORTANCE OF A SYSTEM REGULATING THE RELATION OF LABOR AND MANAGEMENT

Critical to the success of western economies has been the development of systems of labor relations that seek to promote stability within a relationship where the parties frequently have diverse and conflicting objectives. The owners and managers of businesses focus on the efficient production of goods and services. Within that framework are pressures to control labor costs and to maximize workers' productivity.

Those who labor for the owners have very different interests. Typically, their concerns center upon their own self-interests. Improved economic benefits, meaningful jobs that avoid repetitive functions, increased time for leisure activities, and improved safety conditions in the workplace are typically the issues workers focus on within this relationship. Obviously these objectives can clearly conflict with the employer's push toward efficiency and improved profitability.

Theoretically, free societies could elect to take no part in resolving the tensions that exist between labor and management. The parties could be left to their own design to resolve conflict with the government simply by making certain that basic legal principles are not violated by their conduct. This environment would likely promote conflict over compromise and would encourage the parties to seek short-term victories over the establishment of a relationship designed to promote long-term stability.

As western societies industrialized, they recognized that allowing the tensions that exist between owners and workers to be resolved within a framework that emphasized economic power and will over compromise and coexistence would risk potentially serious disruptions of the economy and social order. For economies to develop and flourish, there had to be a system designed to reduce and resolve conflicts and to encourage the parties to look at developing a long-term relationship emphasizing their mutual interests and interdependence.

The approaches adopted vary markedly. Some countries have acted to extensively regulate issues relating to workers' interests. For example, some European countries have adopted comprehensive regulations regarding an employer's ability to close facilities or lay off workers that dwarf the modest legislation enacted in the United States. Some countries, such as West Germany and Denmark, have adopted a system in which workers actually participate in making decisions that affect the management of the company. This process, sometimes referred to as codetermination, allows representatives of the workers to serve on the company's board of directors. This approach indicates a clear recognition that business has a duty to address workers' interests and not to focus exclusively on the interests of the owners.

The public policy adopted in the United States concerning labor-management relations has been very different. In the first place, the relationship of the parties has been traditionally viewed as adversarial. Management sees its primary function as promoting the development and profitability of the business. This mentality is in part attributable to the law that imposes on management a fiduciary duty to act in the best interests of the owners of the company—the shareholders. Labor's efforts to wrest from management a larger share of the company's profits or to gain a greater voice within the decision-making process are in conflict with management's fiduciary duty and, thus, resisted.

The tensions created by this conflict required a process that would help dissipate the tensions and promote peaceful resolution of disputes. With the adoption of the Railway Labor Act (1926) and the National Labor Relations

Act (NLRA) (1935), Congress established a national policy aimed at promoting collective bargaining as the means by which labor stability would be assured in the private sector. With collective bargaining, employees are able to select representatives who meet with management representatives to see whether an agreement can be reached on issues that relate to the workers' conditions of employment.

Rather than permitting this system to operate on a voluntary basis, Congress mandated that employers were required to meet and bargain with representatives of the workers. This was critical to the effectiveness of the NLRA. Prior to the adoption of the Norris LaGuardia Act in 1932, the growth and development of the labor movement was retarded in large part because the labor policy that did exist was being established by the judiciary, which had shown itself to be unsympathetic—some would even say antagonistic—to the interests of labor. In the nineteenth century, state courts interfered with efforts to organize workers by finding that attempts to organize in order to increase wages were illegal conspiracies aimed at injuring the public's interest. When that principle was ultimately rejected, courts then turned to the use of injunctions to restrict the union's ability to mount effective pressure on the employer through the use of the strike.

Because of the inhospitable environment generated by the judiciary and the failure of Congress to forge any type of comprehensive vision for labor policy, the position of organized labor in the United States was weak at the start of the Great Depression. Estimates indicated that less than 3 million workers were union members during the worst part of this period.

Congress's inertia had left unchallenged the judiciary's position that the principle of freedom of contract should govern labor-management relations the same way it did commercial relations in the marketplace. State efforts to legislatively regulate the employment relation by protecting workers' interests were unacceptable to many courts in the early part of this century. They found that such regulation infringed "upon natural rights and constitutional grants of liberty,"[1] reflected adversely on the "dignity and independence of the wage earner,"[2] and interfered with "the operation of natural and economic laws."[3]

This freedom of contract concept sought to emphasize the liberty of a worker "to live and work where he will; to earn his livelihood by any lawful calling; to pursue any livelihood or avocation."[4] In choosing to focus on the parties' freedom to contract, the courts elected not to consider the difference in bargaining power between the individual employee and the employer. Although a free-market system may want to promote the right of a party to contract or not contract with another, this notion must be tempered by the realization that in some settings, one party may enjoy considerably more power

---

[1] *State v. Haun*, 61 Kan. 146, 159, 59 P. 340, 345 (1899).
[2] *Id.*
[3] *Street v. Varney Electrical Supply Co.*, 160 Ind. 338, 346, 66 N.E. 895, 898 (1903).
[4] *Allgeyer v. Louisiana*, 165 U.S. 578, 589 (1897).

than another, and society's interest may be served by acting to protect the weaker party.

In the NLRA, Congress explicitly recognized the inequality that existed between the bargaining power of employees and employers. It rejected the notion that employees had actual liberty of contract. Implicitly, it recognized that an employee was dependent on his or her relation with the employer because the employee was not free to move from job to job whenever he or she became disgruntled with working conditions. On the other hand, an employer had little dependence on an employee. Ordinarily the employer could easily replace an unhappy worker. The advantage the employer enjoyed in this relation was further enhanced by the fact that, prior to 1935, the employer generally had the ability to disrupt union efforts to organize workers.

The architects of the New Deal believed that the severity of the Depression was partially attributable to the weak bargaining position of the worker. This inequality permitted employers to pay low wages. Reducing the purchasing power of workers had partially deprived the economy of an important body of would-be consumers whose demand for goods not only could have helped expand the economy prior to 1929, but also could have been a force in helping to stabilize the economy during the downturn.

Thus, in establishing the comprehensive plan to resurrect the economy, the New Dealers concluded that one component of the plan had to ensure that the purchasing power of workers was enhanced. Instead of incorporating a process where government would dictate wage rates and benefits, the decision was to allow market forces and the dynamics of the relation existing between an employer and the workers determine employment conditions. Government's role was to ensure that the process provided sufficient legal protections for workers so that they would be able to overcome some of the advantages employers historically enjoyed in dealing with workers.

To accomplish this change, it was essential that the bargaining power of workers be increased. The recognition within the NLRA that workers possessed a legal right to form or join labor organizations marked an important step. Workers were given assurance that the law would no longer tolerate employer conduct aimed at destroying the workers' ability to organize.

Just as important to workers was the law's recognition that management could not ignore their demands. The NLRA required employers to engage in meaningful collective bargaining with the workers' representative. It also recognized that workers had the right to mount effective economic pressure on employers. By protecting the workers' right to strike, the law ensured that employers would take their duty to bargain seriously.

THE ORGANIZATIONAL CAMPAIGN

Of critical concern to those who supported the NLRA was assurance that the law would make certain that workers were given a fair opportunity to decide whether or not they desired to have a labor organization represent their interests before the employer. To make certain that they were provided this opportunity, the NLRA created the National Labor Relations Board (NLRB) and empowered the NLRB to both scrutinize the conduct of the parties during the campaign and to conduct elections to determine the workers' desire.

Typically, the campaign begins with organizers' asking workers to sign cards indicating that the workers desire to have the union serve as their collective bargaining representative. The organizers will ordinarily wait until they have accumulated cards from a sizable majority of the workers before taking the next step, which usually involves requesting the employer to voluntarily recognize the union as the workers' representative. Most of the time, the employers will not grant the request, and the union usually must then petition the NLRB to hold an election. If a majority of the workers voting support the union, the NLRB will certify it as the bargaining representative for all the workers in the bargaining unit.

Of course, essential to the integrity of the process is assurance that the campaign and election are free of conduct that the NLRA specifies as being unlawful or otherwise interferes with the "laboratory conditions" the NLRB seeks to maintain during this period. Although the NLRA contains unfair labor practices covering both employer and union conduct, it is the employer's behavior that is most often scrutinized by the NLRB. This is attributable to the fact that it is the employer who has the power to create immediate change that will affect the workers. It is the employer who has the power to lay off workers, close the plant, or reduce benefits. The union can promise that it will strive to improve the worker's position, but it's the employer who has the power to improve compensation, job benefits, or working conditions. Because the NLRB believes that the employer's conduct can easily influence the workers' decision to support or not support a union, management must be careful during the organizational campaign not to engage in conduct that can be construed as an interference with the employees' right to form or join a labor organization.

NLRB V. GISSEL PACKING CO.

After the passage of the NLRA, the NLRB took the position that because of the economic power enjoyed by the employer in its relation with the workers, the employer should not be permitted to participate in organizational campaigns. However, as the power of unions grew, the NLRB and the Supreme Court both recognized that management should have the right to present its position to the workers. When the NLRA was amended in 1947, it specifically included a provision recognizing management's right to express its opinion or views as long as there was "no threat of reprisal or force or promise of benefit." It has been left up to the NLRB and the courts to determine whether the employer's conduct involves threats or promises of benefit.

In *NLRB v. Gissel Packing Co.*, 395 U.S. 575 (1969), the Supreme Court was given the opportunity to further define the limits of acceptable employer conduct during a campaign. In this instance, the Supreme Court reviewed four decisions of the NLRB where the employers had been charged with conduct that the NLRB concluded had affected the opportunity to have a fair election.

In one of the cases [*NLRB v. Gissel*, 398 F.2d 336 (4th Cir. 1968)], the employer had engaged in conduct clearly aimed at chilling the workers' interest in union representation. This included telling a new employee that the company was "nonunion" and that if he was caught talking to a union representative he would be terminated. One employee was encouraged to report all workers who signed authorization cards, and another was told that a company representative would be present at a union meeting to report the names of workers who attended. The day after the union meeting, two workers who attended first found their work hours reduced; they were later terminated.

In another case before the court in *Gissel* [*NLRB v. Sinclair*, 397 F.2d 157 (1st Cir. 1968)], the NLRB faced a circumstance where the employer's conduct was not as coercive. Here, the president frequently communicated to his workers his interest in keeping the plant free of the Teamsters. He reminded workers of an earlier strike by a different union that had lasted 13 weeks and had left the company on shaky financial ground from which he claimed it had not yet recovered. He referred to the Teamsters as a "strike-happy outfit" and indicated that another strike could lead the new owners of the plant to close it and transfer the work to other facilities it owned.

In one communication to the workers, the company included a cartoon that showed the names of companies in the region whom the employer claimed had been forced out of business because of union demands. Several times during the campaign, the president indicated to the workers that if the plant did close it would have a considerable impact on them because their ages and lack of education would make it difficult for them to find new employment. The union lost the election by a vote of 7 to 6.

BALANCING THE RIGHTS OF WORKERS AND MANAGEMENT

By recognizing that employers have the right to express their views during a campaign, Congress placed the NLRB in the position of balancing the right of management's expression against the right of workers to freely exercise the right to join a labor organization. In this role, the NLRB realized that it would be impossible to establish precise rules defining what is and is not acceptable employer conduct. Instead, the NLRB decided to look at the "totality of the circumstances" to determine whether the employer's conduct is acceptable. In other words, a communication by an employer in one context may, because of all the circumstances in the case, be viewed by the workers as threatening and could lead the NLRB to conclude that the employer had subverted the workers' right to freely decide. In another instance, that same communication, when viewed with all the other facts, would not be seen as threatening.

Despite this approach, some conduct of management so far exceeds the employer's right of expression that it may be impossible to defend. The employer's conduct in *Gissel* provides an illustration. The employer had not only interrogated workers about their union activities, but he also had threatened them with surveillance to see whether they were participating in union meetings. In such a case, the employer clearly indicated that the worker would be terminated.

In *Sinclair,* the NLRB faced a case where there were no threats of discharge or surveillance and no coercive interrogations. The conduct the union objected to centered around employer communications in which the company expressed concern that the selection of the Teamsters could affect the ability of the plant to stay open. The employer claimed that it was doing no more than exercising its free speech rights guaranteed by the NLRA.

Although the Supreme Court recognized this right, it pointed out that the employer's free speech rights under the NLRA are not as extensive as its right of expression within the legislative or political arenas. Employees have an economic dependence on employers. Because of this, they may be very sensitive to the implications of the employer's communication. An independent listener may be able to objectively evaluate a communication and discount it in a way that may not be possible for a worker who reviews a letter from his or her employer.

The Court stated that an employer is free to communicate "his general views about unionism or any of his specific views about a particular union" provided there is no threat of reprisal or promise of benefit. Predictions must "be carefully phrased on the basis of objective fact to convey an employer's belief as demonstrably probable consequences beyond his control." The employer cannot imply that he or she will act on his or her own initiative without regard to economic necessities. If the employer's conduct gives rise to such an implication, he or she is no longer making prediction based on fact; the employer is threatening retaliation. The Court concluded that predicting selection of the Teamsters may lead the plant to close was not a prediction based on fact unless the employer could prove that this would eventually happen. This was unlikely because the Teamsters had not yet had the opportunity to present the employer with any economic demands.

The NLRB and the Court did not have to depend on one communication in *Sinclair* to support a determination that the employer had interfered with the employees' rights. In looking at the totality of the circumstances, the NLRB concluded that the employer wanted to convey a clear message to the workers that the Teamsters were a strike-happy outfit whose unreasonable economic demands could lead to a strike that could permanently close the plant. Although, in a political forum, a party may freely express a view of the future if a certain event comes to pass, the law cannot give the same license to an employer addressing his or her workers.

THE REMEDY

In the cases before the Supreme Court in *Gissel,* the NLRB had found each employer guilty of engaging in unlawful conduct. In *Sinclair* an election had been held which the union had lost. In *Gissel* the conduct of the employer so disrupted the campaign, that the union concluded that it would be fruitless to request an election and, as a result, simply filed unfair labor practice charges against the employer. In all the cases the unions had obtained the signatures of a majority of the workers on authorization cards which stated that the workers desired representation.

When facing a case where a party charges that an election was lost because the employer or the union engaged in activity that either constituted an unfair labor practice or otherwise destroyed "laboratory conditions," the NLRB will ordinarily order the offending party to stop the unlawful conduct and order that another election be held. If, as occurred in *Gissel,* the employer has unlawfully discharged an employee for union activities, the NLRB has the power to order reinstatement with back pay.

In the cases before the Supreme Court in *Gissel,* the NLRB had imposed a different remedy. Instead of simply ordering the employer to stop the offending conduct and then conducting an election, in the cases where the election had resulted in a union defeat or where no election had yet occurred, the NLRB simply ordered the employers to bargain with the unions. The NLRB viewed the conduct of the employers as so damaging to the election environment that it would be impossible for a fair election to be conducted. The NLRB concluded that proof of the union's majority status was provided by the fact that a majority of the workers in each case had signed union authorization cards.

Before the Supreme Court, the employers argued that authorization cards do not provide adequate proof of a union's majority status. In the first place, the cards were obtained before the employer had the opportunity to express its views to the workers. Implicit in this argument is the belief that the employer could sway at least some of the workers who had originally signed the cards. Second, workers frequently sign the cards because they feel pressure from organizers or fellow workers. These individuals would not necessarily vote for union representation if given the chance in a secret ballot election. Finally, workers are sometimes deceived into signing the cards because of misrepresentations of organizers. For all these reasons, the employers believed that the NLRB should require an election to show majority support instead of relying on authorization cards.

The Court pointed out that the NLRB recognized that elections are the preferred method for determining whether the union has majority support. Where an employer, facing a demand for union recognition based on authorization cards, engages in improper conduct that would seem to have only a minor impact on the election environment, the NLRB's election process will still be used to determine the will of the workers.

However, if the employer's coercive or threatening conduct is serious enough, it may not only undermine the union's support, but also taint the environment to an extent that it will be impossible to hold a fair election. In such a case, the Court determined that the NLRB has the power to enter a bargaining order without requiring an election. The fact that a majority of the workers signed authorization cards presents sufficient evidence that, at least prior to the employer's unlawful conduct, the union had majority support. The Court rejected the employer's arguments that the cards were unreliable indicators of workers' desires. Employees are sophisticated enough to understand the implications of clear language contained on the card. Where there is no indication that threats were used to obtain signatures or that organizers misrepresented the purpose of the card, there is no evidence to consider them unreliable.

The Court realized that allowing the NLRB to base a bargaining order on the cards created the risk that a union may be recognized as a collective bargaining representative for a group of workers the majority of whom oppose the union. However, if the NLRB was confined to simply ordering that an election be held, it would, in a sense, reward an employer for unlawful conduct. If that conduct contributed to the defeat of the union, the employer would have succeeded in delaying the workers' right to be represented until another election could be scheduled. And what would prevent the employer from continuing to engage in unlawful conduct so that it could affect the environment existing in the next election? In some instances, like the cases presented in *Gissel,* the violations may have been so serious that the effect will linger for a long period, making it difficult or impossible to hold a fair election.

The Court also pointed out that permitting the NLRB to enter a bargaining order without an election was not a novel remedy. In earlier cases, the NLRB had been permitted to enter this type of order when the union had not even obtained authorization cards from a majority of the workers. These cases involved circumstances where the employer, from the start of the organizational campaign, had engaged in coercive conduct that was so "outrageous" and "pervasive" as to make it impossible not only for a fair election to be held, but even prevented the union from obtaining signatures on authorization cards. Although the NLRB itself has subsequently retreated from entering nonmajority bargaining orders, the Court in *Gissel* found that there was no reason why the NLRB's right to enter a bargaining order should not be extended to cases where the conduct may not be "outrageous" and "pervasive," although it had the "tendency to undermine majority strength and impede the election processes."

MANAGERIAL IMPLICATIONS

The NLRA recognizes that an employer, facing a campaign to organize the workers, should have a right to present its views and position to the work force. However, this right must be balanced against the recognition that the workers' economic dependence on their relation with their employer allows them to be easily influenced by employer conduct. If the system truly wants to make certain that workers can freely decide to join or not join a labor organization, the law must make certain that the conduct of the employer does not inhibit the exercise of this right.

The problem that management faces is that the line between what is acceptable and what is not is frequently a blurred one. Although management can turn to past decisions of the NLRB and the courts for instruction, this approach does not offer the degree of assurance management would like. In part, this is attributable to the fact that the NLRB is susceptible to changes in the political environment. During his or her term, the president will have the opportunity to replace members of the NLRB with individuals who are aligned to his or her own views on the direction national labor policy should take. As the composition of the NLRB changes, so may the NLRB's position on the conduct that an employer may engage in during an organizational campaign.

An even larger problem employers face in trying to use past NLRB decisions as predictors centers on the fact that the NLRB's resolution of each case focuses on the particular circumstances existing in the case. Frequently it is not one episode that determines whether the employer's conduct falls within permissible bounds. In one context an employer's comment questioning whether the company could survive unionization of the plant could be viewed by the workers as harmless propaganda that the NLRB may conclude had little impact on the vote of the workers. Those same words delivered in a different tone and contained within an environment where workers had been made to feel the employer's hostility toward the union could lead the NLRB to an entirely different result where an unsuccessful union challenges the employer's conduct.

Some types of conduct of management may be so unacceptable as to virtually eliminate the need to look at the "totality of the circumstances." For example, terminating an employee because of union activities is a clear violation of the NLRA. Transferring union supporters to less desirable positions or assigning them positions for which they have no training, also violates the NLRA where the employer's objective is to discourage union membership. As *Gissel* points out, management's threats relating to job security or benefits reductions can also be conduct which so contaminates the environment as to prevent workers from making a free decision.

Neither is the employer allowed to try to undermine the campaign by buying favor with the workers. Creating new benefits for the workers or increasing wages during the campaign can provide clear evidence of the employer's interest in interfering with the employees' right to organize. Just as unacceptable are promises made to individual employees. Promises of promotions or pay raises made to individual employees to gain their support is also improper. Although it may seem that management's conduct in these cases benefits the worker, it must be remembered that, first, not all workers may enjoy the gain. Second, even if the promises are given to all workers, the gain may only be short term. Once management has defeated the union, it may not be so benevolent.

In *Gissel,* the Court recognized that improper management conduct can have a long-lasting impact. In such a case, merely ordering a new election for the workers will not guarantee that it will reflect the free will of the workers. In such an instance, the NLRB has the power to order the employer to bargain with the union even though there may be no clear evidence that the majority of workers desire union representation.

CONCLUSION

From a historical perspective, the relationship that exists between management and labor in the United States can be characterized as adversarial. Management traditionally has viewed union efforts to protect workers' interests as an impediment to increased productivity and profitability. As a result, management feels a responsibility to the company's owners to resist these efforts. This may include hiring outside consultants who are charged with formulating a strategy aimed at defeating the union. It may mean moving operations to another region of the country where the roots of the union movement have not taken hold. It may even mean moving operations out of the country to an economy starving for economic opportunity.

Although the law recognizes that management does have the right to resist efforts to organize, this right is limited. Because the employer is viewed by the workers as having the power to fundamentally affect the terms and conditions existing within the employment relation, workers can be easily influenced by what an employer says or does. If our system truly wants to promote the worker's right to freely decide if he or she wants to be represented, the system must make certain that employers' conduct does not subvert that right.

REFERENCES

Bernstein, Irving, *The New Deal Collective Bargaining Policy,* University of California Press, Berkeley, 1950.

Bok, Derek, "The Regulation of Campaign Tactics in Representation Elections Under the National Labor Relations Act," 78 *Harv. L. Rev.* 38 (1964).

Comment, "Union Authorization Cards: A Reliable Basis for an NLRB Order to Bargain?" 47 *Tex. L. Rev.* 87 (1968).

Cortner, Richard, *The Wagner Act Cases,* Univ. of Tennessee Press, Knoxville, 1964.

Cox, Archibald, "The Duty to Bargain in Good Faith," 71 *Harv. L. Rev.* 1401 (1958).

Cox, Archibald, *Law and the National Labor Policy,* Univ. of California, Los Angeles, 1960.

Cox, Archibald, and John Dunlop, "Regulation of Collective Bargaining by the National Labor Relations Board," 63 *Harv. L. Rev.* 389 (1950).

Cumberland Shoe Corp., 144 N.L.R.B. 1268 (1963).

Derber, Milton, and Edwin Young (eds.), *Labor and the New Deal,* Univ. of Wisconsin Press, Madison, 1957.

Drotning, John, "Employer Free Speech: Two Basic Questions Considered by the NLRB and Country," 16 Labor Law J. 131 (1965).

Franks Bros. Co. v. NLRB, 321 U.S. 702 (1944).

General Steel Products, Inc., 157 N.L.R.B. 636 (1966).

General Steel Products, Inc., v. N.L.R.B., 398 F.2d 339 (4th Cir. 1968).

Gissel Packing Co., 157 N.L.R.B. 1065 (1966).

Golub, Ira, "The Propriety of Issuing Gissel Bargaining Orders Where the Union Has Never Attained a Majority," 29 *Lab. L.J.* 631 (1978).

Heck's Inc., 156 N.L.R.B. 760 (1966).

Lankford, Mary Helen Moses, "Nonmajority Bargaining Orders: A Study in Indecision," 46 *Alb. L. Rev.* 363 (1981).

Miller, Glenn, *American Labor and the Government,* Prentice-Hall, New York, 1948.

NLRB v. Gissel Packing Co., 398 F.2d 336 (4th Cir. 1968).

NLRB v. Gissel Packing Co., 395 U.S. 575 (1969).

NLRB v. Heck's Inc., 398 F.2d 337 (4th Cir. 1968).

NLRB v. Sinclair Co., 397 F.2d 157 (1st Cir. 1968).

Note, "*Gissel* I Bargaining Orders: Employer Deterrence or Employee Protection?" 36 *Baylor L. Rev.* 877 (1984).

Note, "The *Gissel* Bargaining Order: Is Time a Cure-All?" 26 *Duquesne L. Rev.* 447 (1987).

Note, "Labor Law—Bargaining Orders Absent Showing of Majority Support for Union," 47 *Tenn. L. Rev.* 418 (1980).

Note, "Nonmajority Bargaining Orders: The Only Effective Remedy for Pervasive Employer Unfair Labor Practices During Union Organizing Campaigns," 20 *U. Mich. L.J. Ref.* 617 (1987).

Riggs, "The NLRA: Its Restrictions of the Constitutional Rights of Freedom of Speech," 46 *Tex. B.J.* 567 (1983).

Sinclair Co., 164 N.L.R.B. 261 (1967).

Taylor, Benjamin, and Fred Witney, *Labor Relations Law,* Prentice-Hall, Englewood Cliffs, New Jersey, 1987.

Walther, Peter, and Robert Douglas, "NLRB Bargaining Orders: A Problem Solving or Ivory Tower Approach to Labor Law?" 17 *Washburn L.J.* 1 (1977).

Wausau Steel Corp. v. NLRB, 377 F.2d 369 (7th Cir. 1967).

Williams, Robert, *NLRB Regulation of Election Conduct,* Univ. of Pennsylvania, Philadelphia, 1985.

DISCUSSION QUESTIONS

1 The law recognizes that an employer possesses the legal right to express its views during an organizational campaign. Does an employer have a moral responsibility not to exercise this right so that workers can freely decide without any input from the employer?

2 The law recognizes that during an organizational campaign an employer cannot threaten to close the plant if the union prevails in an election. However, what happens in a case where, although no threats were made during the campaign, after the union prevails in the election the employer decides, because of the union victory, to close the plant and go out of business? Is this conduct permissible?

SUGGESTED ANSWERS

1 On the one hand the employer enjoys a position of power within this relationship. Even if the employer's speech or conduct does not involve threats or coercion or promises of benefits, the fact that the employer is addressing the issue at all will probably have an impact on at least some of the workers. That would be particularly

true in an industry where the workers have few marketable skills and low wages. These workers may fear that if they are forced out of work, the next job may be very difficult to find.

On the other hand, management does have a legal responsibility to the owners. Owners expect a return on their investment. They expect management to work to improve productivity and profitability and to work to limit those forces that will inhibit growth. Obviously, facing unionization of a facility creates a risk that owners will find their investment decreasing in value.

There is also the issue of whether management has a duty to educate workers about the downside risk of unionization. The "pie-in-the-sky" approach of unions as they organize needs to be met with a dose of realism. This is especially true as companies are forced to compete in international markets with foreign concerns that benefit from lower labor costs and extensive government aid.

2 In *Textile Workers v. Darlington Mfg. Co.*, 380 U.S. 263 (1965), the Supreme Court concluded that an employer has the right to go out of business even if motivated solely out of a desire to punish a union and its supporters. The Court found that nothing in the law could be construed as requiring a party to stay in business.

The Court pointed out that the NLRB wants to prevent an employer from realizing a gain where it commits an act discriminating against workers because of union activity. Obviously, an employer realizes no gain where it decides to permanently close its doors.

Of course, the result may be different if the employer is only closing a portion of its business. *Darlington* involved circumstances where an employer owned several plants and had elected to liquidate a plant where a union had just prevailed in an election. The Court found that an employer commits an unfair labor practice if the closing was "motivated by a purpose to chill unionism in any of the remaining plants of the single employer and if the employer may reasonably have foreseen...that effect."

The NLRB recognizes that a mere closing of one plant is not enough to substantiate an unfair labor practice charge. For example, there may have been legitimate economic reasons for the decision. For there to be a violation, there must be evidence that the employer's motive was to chill unionism.

18

SEXUAL HARASSMENT:
Meritor Savings Bank v. Vinson

Nancy R. Hauserman
University of Iowa

INTRODUCTION

In 1964, when Congress passed Title VII of the Civil Rights Act, it is doubtful that the legislature could predict the breadth of cases to which that statute would be applied. Among the types of situations that were certainly not actively considered in legislative debate were cases involving sexual harassment. Indeed, it was not until 12 years after the passage of the act that the first court was willing to extend Title VII protection to victims of sexual harassment. Prior to 1976, courts had reasoned that sexual harassment was a "personal matter" and was, therefore, not sufficiently employment-related to constitute a Title VII violation. Furthermore, courts did not see sexual harassment as gender-related and so did not see such harassment as the type of discrimination Title VII sought to curtail. Finally, there was some judicial concern that recognition of sexual harassment as actionable under Title VII would give rise to a flood of litigation.

Although one might argue about the floodgate theory, there have been a fair number of cases brought before the courts since the court first extended Title VII coverage to cases involving sexual harassment. Since the issuance of the Equal Employment Opportunity Commission (EEOC) guidelines in 1980, more than 38,500 cases have been filed just at the federal level. Because sexual harassment may also constitute a violation under some states' laws, the number of cases filed under Title VII alone does not begin to reflect the magnitude of the problem or the potential for litigation in this area. Many surveys have found that sexual harassment is a problem common in most businesses and many areas of government, including federal government workplaces. Some surveys have attempted to find out whether such complaints are, in fact, valid or simply lodged by disgruntled or "overly sensitive" employees. The findings seem to be consistent: Most complaints are valid. Certainly the issue of sexual harassment is relevant for employers and employees, and ignoring the issue is, at least, bad business.

In 1980, four years after the court in *Williams v. Saxbe* [431 F. Supp. 665 (D.D.C. 1976), *reviewed and remanded* on other grounds *sub. nom. Williams v. Bell,* 587 F.2d 1240 (D.C. Cir. 1978), *on remand sub. nom. Williams v. Civiletti,* 487 F. Supp. 1387 (D.D. C. 1980)] ruled that sexual harassment could constitute sexual discrimination until Title VII, the EEOC, issued guidelines that defined sexual harassment as a Title VII violation. Although the courts are not technically bound to follow the EEOC guidelines, they tend to give the guidelines great deference. The EEOC's definition effectively creates two types of sexual harassment cases: those based on a *quid pro quo* concept, and cases that involve the creation or maintenance of a hostile work environment. According to the EEOC, unwelcome sexual advances, requests for sexual favors, and other verbal or physical conduct constitutes sexual harassment when (1) submission to the conduct is either explicitly or implicitly a term or condition of an individual's employment, (2) submission to or rejection of such conduct by the employee is used as the basis for employment decisions affecting that employee, or (3) such conduct has the purpose or effect of unreasonably interfering with an individual's work performance or creating an intimidating, hostile, or offensive working environment. The first two definitions constitute the *quid pro quo* concept of sexual harassment; the notion of hostile environment is reflected in the third definition. The scope of behaviors included in the concept of sexual harassment certainly extend beyond the physical act of sex. Sexual harassment can include jokes, touching, and innuendoes.

MERITOR SAVINGS BANK V. VINSON

In 1986 the U.S. Supreme Court for the first time affirmed the notion that sexual harassment was covered by Title VII. Although lower courts had recognized such suits since 1976 and had relied on the EEOC guidelines on sexual harassment since 1980, *Meritor Savings Bank v. Vinson,* 106 S. Ct. 2399 (1986), marked the first time that the Supreme Court had ruled on such a case. The case involved a bank employee, Mechelle Vinson, who claimed that she had constantly been subjected to sexual harassment by her supervisor. According to Ms. Vinson, the harassment had begun some time after she had completed her probationary training period as a teller. The supervisor, Mr. Taylor, had then begun to harass her and demand sexual favors. Ms. Vinson suggested that although she initially resisted Mr. Taylor's demands, she eventually gave in for fear of losing her job. Her testimony revealed that over the next several years she had sexual intercourse with the supervisor on numerous occasions, that he fondled her in front of other employees, exposed himself to her in the bank, and had forced sex on her on several occasions. Ms. Vinson alleged that she did not report these incidents for fear of reprisal. The supervisor denied the allegations and suggested instead that Ms. Vinson was merely a disgruntled employee who made up the stories in response to a work dispute.

The district court which first heard the case ruled for the defendants, finding that Ms. Vinson was not a victim of sexual harassment. To the extent that a sexual relationship had existed between Ms. Vinson and Mr. Taylor, the court said, it was a voluntary relationship and not related to her continued employment. Furthermore, the court ruled, the employer, Meritor Savings Bank, would not have been liable for Mr. Taylor's behavior in any event, because it had no notice of the same. The district court took note of the fact that the bank did have a policy against discrimination and a procedure by which employees of the bank could file a grievance. Ms. Vinson, the court noted, had declined to use that procedure.

When the case was heard on appeal, the court of appeals reversed the decision of the district court. The appellate court held that whether or not the relationship was voluntary was irrelevant to the question of sexual harassment as a condition of employment. Moreover, the court held that an employer was absolutely liable for sexual harassment committed by a supervisor; the issue of actual or constructive notice to an employer is irrelevant.

The U.S. Supreme Court agreed to review the case. In essence, the Court focused on three questions, all of which raised important issues for employment law: (1) Do unwelcome sexual advances that create a hostile or offensive working environment constitute discrimination based on sex and, therefore, give rise to a Title VII violation? (2) Does the "voluntariness" of a sexual relationship obviate any finding of sexual harassment? (3) Is an employer strictly or absolutely liable for sexual harassment by its supervisory personnel even if the employer has no knowledge, and could not reasonably have known, of such actions? These three questions go to the nature of sexual harassment and to the liability of employers for sexual harassment. The Court answered these questions with varying degrees of clarity.

The first two issues were clearly resolved by the Court. The Court unanimously held that sexual harassment is covered by Title VII. Furthermore, the Court agreed that a plaintiff need not show any economic or tangible injury to bring such an action. Instead, the Court held, Title VI gives employees the right to work in an environment free from the kind of hostility or abuse created by insults, jokes, or other forms of degradation based on race, sex, national origin, or religion. The Court found that when such abuse is so severe and continual as to change the victim's working environment, it will constitute a Title VII violation.

The Supreme Court went on to find that the "voluntary" aspect of a sexual relationship would not necessarily preclude a finding of sexual harassment. Instead, the Court determined that the central question should be whether or not the conduct was *welcomed*. Obviously, such a determination is not an easy one, and how a plaintiff acted may suggest whether or not the conduct was welcome. Nonetheless, it is important to note that simply because an employee participates in the requested sexual activity will not work as an automatic defense to allegations of sexual harassment. To the extent that victims of sexual harassment perceive that their only "choice" is to submit or to suffer some employment-related retaliation, the notion of "voluntary" is complicated.

Finally, the Court considered the issue of employer liability. It was on this final issue that the Court was less definitive. Accepting neither the absolute liability standard proposed by the court of appeals, nor the "no liability without notice" standard of the district court, the Supreme Court suggested that it would use the principles of agency law for such determination. In the *Vinson* case, the Court noted that the issue of employer liability should not have been considered initially by the district court. Because the trial court found no sexual harassment, the Supreme Court reasoned, the issue of employer liability was moot. Similarly, the court of appeals had no need to consider the liability issue because the existence of sexual harassment had not yet been determined. Declining to decide the issue of liability on such an "abstract" basis, the Supreme Court clearly rejected the absolute liability notion and further noted that absence of notice was not an automatic preclusion of liability.

It should be noted that in its discussion about employer's liability, the majority opinion specifically notes that an employer will not avoid liability simply by asserting that it had a grievance procedure and an antidiscrimination policy in effect at the time of the alleged harassment and that the plaintiff-employee failed to utilize this procedure. At a minimum, such a policy must clearly and specifically address sexual harassment as prohibited behavior. Furthermore, the employer must demonstrate a sincere commitment to eradicating such offensive behavior. The Court also noted that a grievance policy which provides that employees must initially report grievances to their supervisors would hardly have helped Ms. Vinson. Finally, the Court suggests that employers would be wise to develop policies and practices that not only prohibit discriminatory behavior, but encourage victims of such discrimination to seek a remedy for the same.

Meritor Savings Bank v. Vinson clearly establishes sexual harassment as a Title VII violation. Both the *quid pro quo* and hostile environment theories developed in the 1980 EEOC guidelines are viable methods of establishing the existence of sexual harassment. Again, in a *quid pro quo* situation, a victim has been or thinks he or she has been threatened with a decision that will negatively affect his or her job status. Because the person making the threat is presumed to have the power to carry it out, *quid pro quo* situations will almost invariably involve someone in a position superior to the victim. It is certainly conceivable that the *quid pro quo* theory could be applied after one incident, depending, of course, on the severity of the threat.

It is less likely that a finding of hostile environment will be found upon proof of an isolated incident (but certainly possible), particularly if the one incident involved physical conduct such as touching. Based on the Court's language in *Vinson,* hostile environment seems to imply a pattern of incidents sufficient to interfere with an individual's work performance. To the extent that one of the major purposes of Title VII was to ensure that employees not be denied an equal opportunity to succeed in the workplace because of race, sex, national origin, or religion, it stands to reason that behavior by the employee's coworkers or supervisors which creates an abusive environment will not allow the employee to perform at the same level as other employees who are not subject to such abuse. The intent of Congress was to prohibit the consideration of certain factors in employment situations, and presumably they meant to do this whether the consideration was explicit or implicit.

The EEOC has suggested a number of factors that may affect a finding of hostile environment including (1) whether the conduct was verbal or physical or both, (2) how often the conduct occurred, (3) whether the conduct was hostile or obviously offensive, (4) the employment relationship or status of the alleged harasser and the purported victim, (5) whether more than one person took part in the harassing conduct, and (6) whether more than one employee was harassed. Conduct that is trivial or merely annoying is not likely to result in a finding of a hostile environment. In general, the EEOC and the courts will apply the objective or reasonable person standard to determine whether or not the conduct should be considered offensive or hostile enough to affect the work environment of a reasonable person.

Moreover, the Court has made it clear that a defendant in a sexual harassment suit cannot defend by claiming that any relationship between the defendant and plaintiff was "voluntary." Instead, the Court has determined that the gravamen of a sexual harassment complaint is whether or not the behavior was "welcomed." Again, because sexual harassment cases so often involve questions or perceptions of power, at least when the alleged harasser is the victim's supervisor, the burden is not upon the employee to show resistance. Although the Court in *Vinson* did not elaborate on what would constitute proof of unwelcome advances, it did suggest that the complaining employee's behavior would be relevant to the extent it suggested whether or not he or she "welcomed" the alleged harassment. For instance, in the *Vinson* case, the defendant, Mr. Taylor, had introduced evidence about Ms. Vinson's style of dress ("provocative") and the notations in her diary about her sexual fantasies. The Supreme Court cautiously acknowledged that such evidence could be relevant to establish whether or not sexual advances were "welcomed." Obviously, evidence about whether or not an employee solicited or incited challenged conduct will be relevant to show that the conduct was regarded as undesirable or offensive. Like most law cases, a determination of welcomeness would be based on the totality of the evidence and would be specific to the facts of a given case. Obviously, the more that the alleged victim had explicitly and clearly complained about the alleged behavior, the more likely a finding that the conduct was unwelcome.

MANAGERIAL IMPLICATIONS

Although it is less clear what the extent of employer's liability for sexual harassment will be in a given situation, certainly some rules and guidelines are available. First, it is imperative to note that the facts of *Vinson* suggest that the employer had no direct knowledge of the harassment and may not have had indirect or constructive notice of the behavior. In other cases, where the employer clearly had or should have knowledge of sexual harassment by one or more of its supervisory personnel, relying on agency principles suggests that the absolute standard suggested by the court of appeals in *Vinson* is the likely rule. Furthermore, to the extent that the Court's decision in *Vinson* was based on the hostile environment theory where the plaintiff did not claim to have suffered tangible economic injury as a result of the harassment, a case involving *quid pro quo* theory will result in employer's absolute liability if agency principles are followed. The reason for the distinction is that in a *quid pro quo* case, the ability of harassers to threaten employment-related retaliation flows directly from their power or authority delegated to the harassers by the employer.

Although there are fewer cases in which the harasser and the victim are co-workers, employers are still likely to be liable if the employer knew or should have known about the harassment and took no action to eliminate the behavior. Particularly in coworker cases where the victim-employee complains about the behavior to the employer and where the harassment was pervasive, a finding of employer liability is likely.

Finally, because the Court in *Vinson* did not conclusively resolve the issue about the employer's liability, it is not altogether clear what an employer may or must do to avoid or at least minimize its liability for sexual harassment. Certainly the issue of employer liability is important and potentially costly: Under Title VII, employers could be liable for back pay and reinstatement as well as injunctive relief. Moreover, in many states, plaintiffs might be able to bring suit in tort under a variety of theories including intentional infliction of emotion distress, willful interference with a contractual relationship, invasion of privacy, and assault and battery. The monetary damages available in a tort action may not be limited to actual damages; punitive damages may be available as well.

Based on the *Vinson* decision and a host of lower court decisions, the prudent employer will not rely on a generalized antidiscrimination policy, but will, instead, generate a written policy directed specifically at the prohibition of sexual harassment. Such a policy should be widely distributed in the workplace and discussed with supervisory personnel who, in turn, should be responsible for informing their subordinates. The employer should affirmatively raise the subject of sexual harassment with employees and should at all times express strong disapproval for such behavior. Appropriate sanctions should be developed and announced and imposed as necessary. Furthermore, because the *Vinson* Court noted that an employee who is the victim of harassment might be unwilling to utilize a grievance procedure in which he or she has to report to the very person who is harassing him or her, employers should develop a grievance procedure under which an employee may grieve to a senior officer or to an ombudsperson. Ideally, the system will allow the complaining employee to remain anonymous so that he or she does not fear retaliation. Obviously, all complaints of sexual harassment should be investigated, and sanctions should imposed as appropriate. Employees should be informed of their right to raise the issue of sexual harassment under Title VII. In addition, the EEOC recommends that employers have codes of conduct and develop methods for making sure that employees are not only aware of but also are sensitive to the required conduct and reasons for the same. Furthermore, because in *Vinson* the Supreme Court allowed for the possibility of an employer being held liable even if it had no knowledge of the harassment, employers might be wise to survey their workplace to determine the extent of any problem with sexual harassment that may currently exist.

CONCLUSION

The Court's decision in *Meritor Saving Bank v. Vinson* evidences the Court's clear recognition that sexual harassment is discrimination based on gender. As such, it represents the kind of stumbling block that Congress intended to remove when it passed Title VII of the Civil Rights Act of 1964. Sexual harassment is expensive: It produces lawsuits and employees who are not working as well as they might in a supportive environment. Eliminating sexual harassment is legally correct, economically sound, and ethically desirable.

REFERENCES

Attanasio, "Equal Justice Under Chaos: The Developing Law of Sexual Harassment," 51 *Cinn. L. Rev.* 1 (1982).

Baxter, R. H., *Sexual Harassment in the Workplace: A Guide to the Law*, Executive Enterprises Publications, New York, 1985.

Biles, George E., "A Program Guide for Preventing Sexual Harassment in the Workplace," *Personnel Administrator*, June 1981, pp. 49–56.

Boyce, Michael T., "Sexual Harassment: Understanding the Guidelines." *Management World*, June 1983, p. 17.

Breslin, Catherine, and Michele Morris, "Please Leave Me Alone," *Working Woman*, December 1988, p. 74.

Bundy v. Jackson, 651 F. 2d 934 (1981).

Collins, Eliza G. C., and Timothy B. Blodgett, "Sexual Harassment...Some See It Some Won't," *Harvard Business Review*, March–April 1981, pp. 77–95.

Comment, "Sexual Harassment in the Work Place: New Rules for an Old and Dirty Game," 14 *U. Cal, Davis* 711, 725–729 (1981).

Cooper, Kenneth C., Ph.D., *Stop It Now! How Targets and Management Can End Sexual Harassment*, Total Communication Press, Ballwin, Mo., 1984, p. 29.

Corne v. Bausch & Lomb, Inc., 390 F. Supp. 161 (D. Ariz. 1975), *vacated*, 362 F. 2d 55 (9th Cir. 1977).

"Damages for Sexual Harassment Title VII and State Tort Law." *Cap. U. L. Rev.* 663–666 (1981).

Faley, R. H., "Sexual Harassment: Critical Review of Legal Cases with General Principles and Preventive Measures." 35 *Personnel Psychology* 583–599 (1982).

Faucher, M. D., and K. McCulloch, "Sexual Harassment in the Workplace: What Should the Employer Do?" *E.E.O. Today*, vol. 5, 1978, p. 38.

Greenlaw, P. S., and J. P. Kohl, "Sexual Harassment: Homosexuality, Bisexuality and Blackmail." 26 *Personnel Administrator* 59–62 (June 1981).

Gutek, B. A., "A Psychological Examination of Sexual Harassment," in B. A. Gutek, (ed.), *Sex Role Stereotyping and Affirmative Action Policy,* University of California, Institute of Industrial Relations, Los Angeles, pp. 131–163.

Henson v. City of Dundee, 682 F.2d 897 (11th Cir. 1982).

James, Jennifer, "Sexual Harassment," *Public Personnel Management Journal,* Winter 1981.

Licata, B. J., and P. M. Popovich, "Preventing Sexual Harassment: A Practice Approach, 4 (5) *Training and Development Journal* 34–38 (1987).

Linenberger, Patricia, and Timothy J. Keaveny, "Sexual Harassment in Employment," *Human Resource Management* 11–17 (Spring 1981).

Livingston, J. A., "Responses to Sexual Harassment on the Job: Legal, Organizational and Individual Actions," 38 *Journal of Social Issues* 5–22 (1982).

MacKinnon, Catherine, *Sexual Harassment of Working Women.* Yale University Press, New Haven, Conn., 1979, pp. 165–166.

McClain, Lynn, "The E.E.O.C. Sexual Harassment Guidelines Welcome Advances Under Title VII," 10 *Univ. Of Baltimore L. Rev.* 323–324 (1981).

McQueen, Iris, *The Management View: Sexual Harassment.* McQueen & Son Publishing Co., Citrus Heights, Calif., 1982, p. 43.

Meyer, Mary Coeli; Jeanenne Oestriech; J. Frederick; and Inge Berchtold, *Sexual Harassment,* Petrocelli Books, Inc., New York, 1981, p. xiii.

Note, "Sexual Harassment and Title VII: The Foundation for the Elimination of Sexual Cooperation as an Employment Condition," 76 *Mich. L. Rev.* 1007, 1032 (1978).

Note, "Sexual Harassment in the Workplace: A Practitioner's Guide to Tort Actions," 10 *Golden Gate U. L. Rev.* 879 (1980).

Petersen, Donald J., and Douglass Massengill, "Sexual Harassment—A Growing Problem in the Workplace," *Personnel Administrator,* October 1978, pp. 79–89.

Polanski, E., "Sexual Harassment in the Workplace," *Human Rights,* 1980.

Popovich, Paula, "Sexual Harassment in Organizations," *Employee Responsibilities and Rights Journal,* vol. 1, no. 4, December 1988, pp. 273–282.

Popovich, P. M., and B. J. Licata, "A Role Model Approach to Sexual Harassment." 13 (1) *Journal of Management* 149–161 (1987).

Powell, Gary N., "Sexual Harassment, Confronting the Issue of Definition," *Business Horizons* 24–28 (July–August 1983).

Rogers v. EEOC, 454 F.2d 234, 238 (5th Cir. 1971).

Samples of corporate policies on sexual harassment can be found in 107 *Lab. Rel. Rep.* (BNA) 75, App. G. (1981).

Sandroff, Ronni, "Sexual Harassment in the Fortune 500." *Working Women,* 69 (December 1988).

Saunders, Jolene, "Sexual Harassment." *Working Women* 40 (February 1984).

Sculnick, Michael V., "A Policy and Procedure for Handling Harassment Complaints," *Employment Relations Forum* 161–175 (Summer 1983).

"Sexual Harassment Claims of Abusive Work Environment Under Title VII," 97 *Harv. L. Rev.* 1456–1460 (April 1984).

Seymour, William C., "Sexual Harassment: Finding a Cause of Action under Title VII," *Labor Law Journal* 143 (March 1979).

Simison and Trost, "Sexual Harassment at Work Is a Cause for Growing Concern," *The Wall Street Journal,* June 24, 1986, p. 1, col. 6.

Somer, "Sexual Harassment in the Office," *Management World* 10–11 (November 1980).

Tompkins v. Public Serv. Elec. & Gas Co., 422 F. Supp. 553 (D. N.J. 1976).

Tong, Rosemarie, *Women, Sex, and the Law*. Rowman & Allanheld, New Jersey, 1984, p. 71, 78.

U.S. Merit Systems Protection Board, *Sexual Harassment in the Federal Workplace: Is It a Problem?* U.S. Government Printing Office, 1981.

Wesman, Elizabeth, C., "Shortage of Research Abets Sexual Harassment Confusion." *Personnel Administrator* 63 (November 1983).

DISCUSSION QUESTIONS

1 According to the EEOC when do unwelcome sexual advances, requests for sexual favors and other verbal or physical conduct constitute sexual harassment?
2 In *Meritor Savings Bank v. Vinson* did the U.S. Supreme Court find that a hostile working environment violates Title VII of the 1964 Civil Rights Act?

SUGGESTED ANSWERS

1 This conduct amounts to sexual harassment when submission to the conduct is explicitly or implicitly a term or condition of an individual's employment, or when submission to or rejection of such conduct by the employee is used as the basis for employment decisions affecting that employee (both *quid pro quo* theories of liability), or such conduct has the purpose or effect of unreasonably interfering with an individual's work performance or creates an intimidating, hostile or offensive working environment (the hostile environment theory of liability).
2 Yes. Unwelcome sexual advances that create a hostile or offensive working environment constitute discrimination based on sex and give rise to a Title VII violation.

   The mere fact that an employee participates in the requested sexual activity is not an automatic defense to allegations of sexual harassment. The central question is whether or not the conduct was welcomed.

   The mere fact that an employer has a grievance procedure and an antidiscrimination policy in effect and that the employee did not use this procedure does not mean an employer will automatically avoid liability.

19

THE CRUCIAL, YET DIFFICULT, PARTNERSHIP BETWEEN SCIENCE AND LAW IN LITIGATION AND REGULATION RELATED TO TOXIC SUBSTANCES

Paulette L. Stenzel
Michigan State University

I. INTRODUCTION

Over the past 20 years, the public has become increasingly aware of toxic substances in our environment. Hardly a day goes by without a reference on the front pages of our newspapers to a toxic spill, the hazards of pesticides in our foods, the risks presented by the chemicals to which workers are exposed at their jobs, and similar concerns. As they have become more aware of toxic substances in our environment and of their exposure to those substances, individuals and groups have turned to our legal system to "do something." They try to gain compensation for damages suffered by individuals or seek protection from risks related to toxic substances in our environment. Thus, we have seen an increase in "toxic tort" litigation—litigation using causes of action from tort law (for example, negligence and nuisance) to gain compensation for damages resulting from exposure to toxic substances or to seek an abatement of hazardous conditions. In addition, extensive regulatory systems on both a state and federal level have been established in efforts to monitor, limit, and clean up toxic hazards. For example, on a federal level, we have assigned responsibility for "managing" risks to agencies such as the Environmental Protection Agency (EPA), the Occupational Safety and Health Administration (OSHA), the Consumer Product Safety Commission (CPSC), the Food and Drug Administration (FDA), and the Nuclear Regulatory Commission (NRC).

In lawsuits seeking compensation for injury resulting from exposure to toxic substances and in regulatory proceedings, judges, juries, and regulators rely on scientists to give them the "facts" on which to base their decisions. However, scientists are often unable to provide the "facts" and "answers" sought by lawmakers. Frequently, the questions asked by lawmakers cannot be answered, or, at best, can only be answered tentatively with educated guesses by scientists. Yet, lawyers in court and within regulatory agencies want answers *now*. Thus, the working relationship between law and science is an uncomfortable one. In fact, many legal scholars and regulators have referred to the relationship between the law and science in toxic substance–related litigation and regulation as resulting from a "shotgun wedding." That is an appropriate description, because the relationship between the two disciplines is and will continue to be unavoidable, yet difficult. Decision makers in courts and within regulatory agencies may use policy to supplement the "facts" or data before them, but the data supplied by scientists are always the bases for decisions concerning toxic substances.

In this chapter, I provide examples of how decision makers in courts and regulatory agencies use scientific data in their decisions concerning toxic substances. Then, I will discuss the sources of the uncertainties inherent in that data and why those uncertainties cannot be eliminated. Included will be some examples of how courts and regulators use policy to supplement the data (or educated guesses) provided by scientists. I will conclude with a brief discussion of the ramifications of the relationship between law and science for citizens and for business managers. Throughout this chapter, as I discuss the "law," the reader needs to remember that the law is relevant to business managers because they must work with parties charged with enforcing the law and they must ultimately comply with it.

II. TOXIC TORT LITIGATION

The Woburn, Massachusetts (*Anne Anderson et al. v. W. R. Grace & Co. et al.*, Civ. A. No. 82-1672-S, U.S. Dist. Ct., D. Mass., Jan. 3, 1986, amended Feb. 21, 1986) case provides a good example of the use of science in toxic tort litigation. Between 1969 and 1983, nineteen cases of leukemia (all victims but one were children) were reported within a six-block area in the city of Woburn, Massachusetts, a small community north of Boston. Families of the victims discovered that they all had obtained their drinking water over a number of years from two wells. After extensive studies, the families became convinced that the leukemia was caused by industrial solvents in the water supply. Families of 14 of the victims sued two companies, W. R. Grace & Co. and Beatrice Foods Co., alleging that they contaminated the wells by knowingly dumping industrial cleaning solvents including trichloroethylene (TCE) and tetrachloroethylene (also called perchloroethylene—PCE) onto soil and alleging that those chemical wastes leached into an underground aquifer. Because the facts of the case were extremely complicated, the judge took the unusual step of dividing the trial into three separate phases, each of which would be separated in time by several months. In a first phase of the trial, a jury cleared Beatrice of the allegations but found that Grace had contaminated the well water with TCE and PCE. That phase of trial alone was long and costly; Grace estimated that it spent $2.5 million in defense and investigation costs.

At the next phase of trial, the jury would have been asked to determine (1) whether TCE or PCE is capable of causing leukemia, and (2) whether one or both of those chemicals caused the plaintiffs' leukemia. In other words, that phase of the trial would have determined whether or not Grace's failure to exercise due care (by dumping the chemicals) was the proximate cause of the plaintiffs' leukemia. If the jury had found that the dumping was the proximate cause of the leukemia, a third phase of trial would have been conducted.

Before the second phase of trial took place, however, the lawsuit was settled with nine of the victims (or their surviving family members), who received a reported total of $9 million and additional amounts going to the remaining five. In announcing the settlement, Grace denied any blame but cited the enormous costs of continuing to litigate the case as its reason for the settlement. Plaintiffs, on the other hand, claimed a victory and pointed out that by settling the case, Grace avoided the possibility of setting a precedent which might be harmful to future corporate defendants.

It is easy to see why it would be extremely expensive to litigate the second phase of trial. Various scientists would have to be hired by each side to testify as to whether TCE, PCE, or both are capable of causing leukemia. The testimony of these scientists would be based primarily on "quantitative risk assessments" obtained through laboratory studies of the chemicals involved. However, such risk assessments, at best, provide only educated estimates as to the carcinogenicity (cancer-causing characteristics) of an individual chemical. Also involved would be epidemiologists who would testify as to studies, if any are available, of people exposed to those chemicals. (A description of the risk assessment process and a brief discussion of epidemiology are in section IV of this chapter.)

Assuming that a jury could be convinced that TCE, PCE, or both are capable of causing cancer, the jury would have to be convinced that one or both of those chemicals caused the leukemia in each person alleged to be a victim in this case. Thus, there would be testimony from various other scientists as to the flow of water from the defendants' property into the aquifer and ultimately into the wells from which the leukemia victims drank. If TCE and PCE were present in the two wells, did they come from Grace and not from some other business not named as a defendant? Scientists and medical doctors would have to answer many questions related to exposure of the individuals who developed leukemia. Did each victim drink from the two wells? When? How much water? What were the concentrations of TCE and PCE in that water? Was each victim exposed to other agents that might have caused the leukemia such as X rays before or after birth or other cancer-causing chemicals in the air, water, or food consumed by the victim? These are just a sampling of the questions that would be addressed by expert witnesses (scientists) at the trial. Few or none of the questions can be answered with any degree of certainty.

III. THE REGULATORY APPROACH

We have created a variety of regulatory agencies that are charged with protecting us from harm from toxic substances in our environment. Within those agencies, as in the courtroom, decision makers rely substantially on information supplied by scientists. On a federal level, the OSHA is charged with protecting workers' health and safety. In doing so, it makes regulations-setting limits on the amount of a specific substance to which a person can be exposed in the workplace. For example, OSHA has studied the harmful effects of substances including benzene, cotton dust, and formaldehyde. Risk assessments are compiled by OSHA's scientists *and* by scientists from industry and labor groups who may support or contest OSHA's proposals for action. Based on these risk assessments, OSHA makes a decision setting exposure limits for each substance. For example, 10 ppm (parts per million) in the workplace air is the limit for a worker's exposure to benzene over an 8-hour work day.

Similarly, the EPA sets limits for substances to which the general public is exposed. Thus, pursuant to its powers under the Clean Air Act, the EPA has set emission standards regulating the amounts of benzene, mercury, asbestos, vinyl chloride, and other hazardous substances released into our outdoor air. As another example, under the Safe Drinking Water Act, the EPA has set standards for maximum levels of toxic chemicals such as benzene and lead in our drinking water. All these limits and standards are set based on studies conducted by scientists.

IV. WHY THE "ANSWERS" PROVIDED BY SCIENCE ARE UNCERTAIN

When a scientist testifies in court or in a regulatory proceeding as to the toxicity of a substance in question, he or she provides a "quantitative risk assessment" of the substance in question. *Quantitative risk assessment* is the use of available facts to quantify numerically the effects of exposure to a potentially hazardous material or situation. For example, a scientist might estimate that exposure to a given chemical in the air for 20 years, for 24 hours per day, in a given quantity will result in an increase of 5:100,000 (5 out of 100,000 people) chance of developing lung cancer over the number of cancer cases otherwise to be expected in 100,000 people over that period of time. However, the process through which such quantitative risk assessments are compiled is riddled with uncertainties. "The proceedings are characterized by very few 'hard facts,' many assumptions and inferences, large uncertainties, and the unavoidable exercise of policy judgment."[1]

The biology of cancer is a major example of a topic about which scientific

---

[1] McGarity, "Judicial Review of Scientific Rulemaking," 9 *Sci., Tech., & Human Values* 98 (1984).

knowledge is limited. Scientists rely substantially on animal bioassays to evaluate the carcinogenicity of a substance. An *animal bioassay* is a procedure in which scientists administer the substance being studied to one group of animals and compare their response to that of a "control" group of animals that have not been exposed to that substance. The results of such bioassays are full of uncertainties because finances limit both the number of animals used in the test and the duration of the test period.

In order to quantify the risks that chemicals pose to humans, scientists have developed a wide variety of dose-response models. Such models are used to predict risks to humans by extrapolating from data gathered from animal bioassays. But such extrapolation involves numerous assumptions and "guesses." It is assumed that the effects shown in animals are the same as those which will occur in humans even though the species tested such as rats or mice may be more or less sensitive than humans to the substance being studied. Also, scientists extrapolate from high doses administered over a short period of time (months or, at best, a few years) to predict responses to low doses received over long periods of time, such as a 70-year lifetime. They also extrapolate from tests on hundreds of animals to predict effects in millions of humans. Further, such testing involves the study of only one substance at a time. It totally ignores potential "synergistic" effects. (*Synergistic effects* are those effects resulting from exposure to a combinations of two or more different substances in the environment, which is what actually happens to human beings in daily life.)

Further, there are wide variations in individual susceptibility. For example, an infant or elderly person may be far more susceptible to harm from a chemical than are most adults, or one adult may be far more susceptible to harm than another because of his or her genetic background.

Beyond these extrapolations, risk assessors must make assumptions as to exposure. In the workplace, there can be some knowledge of exposure in terms of number of hours per day and weeks per year. Also, years until retirement (such as 20 or 30) can be predicted with some degree of certainty. However, even in the workplace there are wide variations in individuals' exposure. For risks in the environment in general, possible variations from assumptions made in predicting exposure are even greater. For example, in calculating risks to humans exposed to airborne toxins, the EPA has assumed that a person lives within a half mile of the pollution source and is outdoors 24 hours per day for a 70-year lifetime. Yet, what of the person who lives 2 miles away? Or lives there for only 2 years before moving? Or spends an average of only 1 hour per day outdoors? This shows how a set of assumptions for a hypothetical person may be inaccurate for nearly all persons actually exposed to the hazard.

Epidemiology is another important method used for assessing risks. It involves the retrospective or prospective study of correlations between rates of disease in a designated group of human beings and specific environmental factors. (The study of people who smoke and their rates of lung cancer is a good example of the use of epidemiology.) However, epidemiology is an extremely limited tool, because scientists cannot deliberately expose a group of humans to a chemical such as benzene and then study that group for 20 years to determine the chemical's effects. Because retrospective epidemiology studies look at people exposed in the past, they lack critical data such as the dose each person received and the length of time of exposure. Prospective studies can look at groups of people who may be exposed at some future time, but such exposure will only be by chance. Such prospective studies are further limited because they take many years to complete, and it is difficult to keep track of each person in a group over such long periods of time.

V. EXAMPLES OF HOW SCIENTISTS AND REGULATORY AGENCIES HAVE DEALT WITH UNCERTAINTIES INHERENT IN RISK ASSESSMENTS

To deal with uncertainties inherent in the risk assessment process, a variety of devices based on public policy are used. Scientists often use an arbitrary multiplication factor, usually 100, called a "safety factor" when extrapolating from animal studies to humans. The policy there, of course, is to build in a factor to allow error, if it occurs, to be on the side of safety for humans.

Legislators and regulators also make policy decisions as they decide how to use risk assessments in the regulatory process. For example, in 1957 Congress passed the Delaney amendment to the Federal Food, Drug and Cosmetics Act. The Delaney amendment prohibits the use of any food additive that has been found to induce cancer in animals or humans in any amount. This amendment promotes a public policy of "no risk." However, such legislation creates a public policy dilemma by forcing regulators to categorize a food, drug, or technology as either safe or unsafe instead of recognizing that safety is a continuous variable. The defects in such a "no risk" policy can be easily illustrated. First, scientists cannot tell us with certainty whether a substance is or is not carcinogenic; they can only make educated guesses. Second, many foods which we consume each day contain toxic chemicals that can be harmful in large quantities. For example, aflatoxins, which are present in peanut butter and sometimes in milk, can cause liver cancer. In spite of the appeal of a promise of "no risk" in food, the public has rejected it as being undesirable on some occasions. Owing to public demand for artificial sweeteners, Congress made a statutory exemption to the Delaney amendment for saccharin, which has been shown to produce cancer when large doses are administered to laboratory animals. (Many people reasoned, "I'm not going to drink 1000 cans of diet soda everyday!")

Other approaches have been less "absolute" in nature. At the opposite extreme of the specific language of the Delaney amendment, Congress gave vague instructions to OSHA under the Occupational Safety and Health Act; OSHA was instructed to do what is necessary to protect worker health and safety "to the extent feasible."[2] That vague "feasibility" requirement left a great deal to OSHA's discretion in regulating worker exposure to harmful substances in the workplace. The term *feasible* is vague because it does not define the type of "feasibility" involved. Does it mean financially feasible? Technologically feasible? Politically feasible? The vague standard was a costly one in terms of legal proceedings. Decisions made by OSHA setting limits for exposure to benzene and to cotton dust were contested for over 10 years in regulatory proceedings and in our federal courts. Regulatory limits for both substances were reviewed by the U.S. Supreme Court in *Industrial Union Department, AFL-CIO v. American Petroleum Institute,* 448 U.S. 607 (1980) (the benzene case), and in *American Textile Manufacturers Institute, Inc. v. Donovan,* 452 U.S. 490 (1981) (the cotton dust case). In the *Cotton Dust* case, a plurality (not even a majority) of the U.S. Supreme Court ultimately accepted the Secretary of Labor's interpretation of the "feasibility" language as being authorization for OSHA to do what is technologically and economically feasible to protect workers' health and safety. That interpretation was a rejection of the idea that regulation made by OSHA pursuant to those provisions should be subject to a cost-benefit analysis.

As another example, in 1988 the EPA adopted a "negligible risk" standard which it is using as it enforces the Federal Insecticide, Fungicide and Rodenticide Act (FIFRA). Under the "negligible risk" standard, the EPA allows chemical residues on our foods as long as, according to risk assessments on which the EPA is relying, the residues present a risk of less than one case of cancer per million people exposed. Again, this presents an example of a policy judgment on the part of the agency. The EPA is rejecting a "no risk" approach. Notice, also, the problems caused by an attempt to use a number, such as one in a million, as a basis for the decision. (See section IV, which discusses the uncertainties and assumptions built into the quantitative risk assessment process.) Scientists cannot tell us with any degree of certainty whether a chemical poses a risk of cancer of 1 to 1 million. Reputable scientists often reach different estimates using the same data obtained from animal bioassays.

Lacking conclusive factual findings to direct them, agencies and courts reviewing agency decisions must rely on policy to serve as a guideline for filling in the gaps left by scientific analysis. The U.S. Court of Appeals, District of Columbia Circuit, summarized this situation saying,

> Some of the questions involved in the promulgation of these standards are on the frontiers of scientific knowledge, and consequently as to them insufficient data is presently available to make a fully informed factual determination. Decision making must in that circumstance depend to a greater extent upon policy judgments and less upon purely factual analysis.[3]

---

[2] The Secretary of Labor (OSHA is under his or her direction) is instructed to set "the standard which most adequately assures, to the extent feasible, on the basis of the best available evidence, that no employee will suffer material impairment of health or functional capacity." Occupational Safety and Health Act of 1970, §6 (b) (5), 29 U.S.C. §655 (b) (5).

[3] *Industrial Union Department, AFL-CIO v. Hodgson,* 499 F.2d 467 (D.C. Cir. 1974).

VI. RAMIFICATIONS FOR ALL CITIZENS WHO PARTICIPATE IN OUR POLITICAL AND LEGAL SYSTEMS

Ramifications of the uneasy partnership between science and the law extend beyond courts, regulators, lawyers, and legislators. Uncertainty in the risk-assessment process forces scientists doing the assessments as well as decision makers within the legal system to formulate and implement public policy to supplement the limited factual base available to them. Because public policy decisions are being made, it is crucial that individual citizens understand what is going on and provide input into the formulation of that public policy. That is because when a decision is made whether to adopt a no-risk policy, a "negligible risk" standard, or some other "level" of "acceptable" risk, value choices are being made. For another example, a decision whether or not to require a cost-benefit analysis before promulgating a regulation designed to protect the health of workers or the general public also involves value choices.

VII. MANAGERIAL IMPLICATIONS

Business managers are included among my comments regarding the participation of *all* citizens in our political and legal systems when risk-management decisions are being made. In order to participate in regulatory proceedings before agencies such as the EPA, OSHA, CPSC, and NRC, business managers need to understand the nature of the "factual" base being used to make decisions regarding toxic substances. Understanding that the factual base is limited and that, therefore, agencies rely substantially on public policy to supplement that information as they make risk-management decisions, business managers will understand the importance of their own involvement in the regulatory decision-making process. Such participation can be direct, by sending representatives to regulatory hearings and by submitting written comments to agencies. Or, it can be through trade associations representing groups of similar businesses.

Beyond participation in the lawmaking process, business managers should be aware that our lack of "hard" data regarding the effects of toxic substances on human beings means that it is especially important that businesses do everything possible to avoid tort litigation resulting from improper disposal of toxic substances. Such lawsuits are extremely costly to litigate no matter which party ultimately prevails. The business manager may avert future costly lawsuits by taking a thorough inventory of all work sites to be sure that toxic substances are being properly stored, and that they are not being improperly stored, dumped onto business properties, flushed down drains, or otherwise handled in a manner that might allow them to seep into the environment surrounding the business site. An "environmental audit" by a firm qualified to do such audits is usually well worth the money it costs. Business managers should remember that compliance with environmental regulatory laws now is not necessarily protection in a tort suit later brought because someone becomes ill or dies owing to chemicals that the company negligently allowed to seep onto surrounding land, into the air, or into the aquifer (underground water).

VIII. CONCLUSION

In closing, it is crucial to remember that through the risk-assessment process, scientists usually provide us only with educated guesses, not "hard data." Therefore, decision makers formulate and implement public policy to "fill in the gaps" left by science. Setting policy involves the selection of goals and guiding principles from among various available alternatives.

Therefore, it is particularly inappropriate and even harmful to abandon policy decisions to "experts" such as scientists, regulators, judges, and lawyers. No "expert" can tell another person whether it is better to risk a higher level of exposure to asbestos in order to save a hundred jobs or to bear the "costs" of the loss of 10 lives. All individual citizens including, but not limited to, those representing business may have equally valid and valuable opinions and preferences as to the value choices being made. But the first step toward active participation in the making of public policy related to toxic substances must be an understanding of the processes involved. As citizens study and begin to understand the uncertainties inherent in the risk-assessment process and in risk-management decisions, they will become prepared to make informed input into the decision-making process.

REFERENCES

Bazelon, David L., "Science and Uncertainty: A Jurist's View," 5 *Harv. Envtl. L. Rev.* 209 (1981).

Davis, Devra Lee, "The 'Shotgun Wedding' of Science and Law: Risk Assessment and Judicial Review," 10 *Colum. J. Envtl. L.* 67 (1985).

Kamrin, Michael, *Toxicology—A Primer on Toxicology Principles and Applications.* Lewis Publishers, Chelsea, Mich., 1988.

Leape, James P., "Quantitative Risk Assessment in Regulation of Environmental Carcinogens," 4 *Harv. Envtl. L. Rev.* 86 (1980).

Ottoboni, M. Alice, *The Dose Makes the Poison—A Plain Language Guide to Toxicology,* Vincente Books, Berkeley, Calif., 1984.

Stenzel, Paulette L., "The Need for a National Risk Assessment Communication Policy," 11 *Harv. Envtl. L. Rev.* 381 (1987).

——, "A Proposal for a National Risk Assessment Clearinghouse, 14 *Colum. J. Envtl. L.* 549 (1989).

Wald, Matthew L., "W. R. Grace Guilty of Polluting Wells," *Detroit Free Press*, July 29, 1986, p. 5A. col. 4.

Wong, Jan, "Grace Settles Suits Charging it Polluted Wells Near Boston, But It Denies Blame," *The Wall Street Journal,* September 23, 1986, p. 5 col. 1.

DISCUSSION QUESTIONS

1 Why is quantitative risk assessment generally a more useable tool than epidemiology for assessing the toxicity of a substance? In what kinds of instances does epidemiology provide information that toxicology cannot provide?

2 What are some practical suggestions for business managers who wish to avoid being the defendant in a "toxic tort" lawsuit?

3 What should a business's goals be as it participates in regulatory decision making regarding a toxic substance? Should a company always advocate a cost-benefit analysis approach? Should a company be allowed to subject workers or neighbors to potential illness or death as a result of a toxic substance as long as the company's profits from use of that substance are worth more than the value measure in dollars and cents of the potential victims' lives?

SUGGESTED ANSWERS

1 Quantitative risk assessment involves the study of animals that are exposed to a toxic substance. Their response is compared to that of a "control" group which have not been exposed to the substance. Such testing is useful because scientists can control the dose given to the animal, shield the animal from exposure to other potentially toxic substances, and closely observe the animal's reactions.

Epidemiology is useful to observe the reaction of human beings to a suspected toxic substance. In our society, we refuse to purposefully subject humans to such substances for testing purposes. However, if humans are exposed voluntarily (such as by smoking cigarettes) or exposed before steps are taken to protect them (such as workers exposed to asbestos on the job before OSHA began to regulate for "acceptable" asbestos levels), we can at least study the results "after the fact."

2 This is an open-ended discussion question. Some suggestions include:

a Hire an outside firm to conduct an environmental audit for each of the employer's work sites in order to identify potentially hazardous practices or conditions.

b Institute an employee suggestion program and reward system asking employees to look out for and report potentially hazardous conditions.

c Institute some kind of program for communication with the surrounding community. Accept, listen to, and respond to (in a meaningful way) the concerns of the community, especially the concerns of those who live in the neighborhood of one of your company's work sites.

3 There is no one right answer to this question. However, as a law professor who has studied this area and as a private citizen, I am extremely troubled by our extensive reliance on cost-benefit analysis in such decision making. Such analysis wrongly presumes that one can place a dollar value on a human life. Further, such analysis ignores important values other than money, such as quality of life, freedom from daily worry about the risks of exposure to toxic chemicals, the pain and suffering of families of victims of toxic pollution, and so on. Part of my purpose in writing this chapter is to illustrate that all this should be of concern to you as individual citizens, not just as business managers.